Hiding in Plain Sight:
Steganography and the Art of Covert Communication

Eric Cole

Ronald D. Krutz, Consulting Editor

WILEY

Wiley Publishing, Inc.

Publisher: Bob Ipsen
Editor: Carol Long
Developmental Editor: Nancy Stevenson
Editorial Manager: Kathryn Malm
Managing Editor: Angela Smith
Media Development Specialist: Greg Stafford
Text Composition: John Wiley Composition Services

This book is printed on acid-free paper. ∞

Published by Wiley Publishing, Inc., Indianapolis, Indiana
Published simultaneously in Canada

For general information on our other products and services please contact our Customer Care Department within the United States at (800) 762-2974, outside the United States at (317) 572-3993 or fax (317) 572-4002.

Wiley also publishes its books in a variety of electronic formats. Some content that appears in print may not be available in electronic books.

Library of Congress Cataloging-in-Publication Data:

ISBN: 0-471-44449-9

Printed in the United States of America

10 9 8 7 6 5 4 3 2 1

This book is dedicated to Kenneth Marino, the members of Rescue 1, and all New York City Fire Fighters who lost their lives on and after September 11, 2001. They made the ultimate sacrifice by giving up their lives so others could live.

I still remember getting the phone call that Kenny was missing, and it upset me more than words could describe. Kenny was probably one of the nicest people I had the privilege of knowing, and he would do anything to help someone else out. That is probably why being a fire fighter was one of his dreams.

Contents

Acknowledgments

Sometimes you meet people in the strangest places and build interesting friendships with them. Ron Krutz is one of those people whom I met awhile back in a training class, and we continue to stay in touch and communicate. It is Ron who introduced me to the wonderful people at John Wiley who have been very helpful and supportive through the process of writing a book. Carol Long is an insightful and energetic executive editor who was open to publishing a book on such a cutting-edge technology. Nancy Stevenson provided constant guidance and expertise, and without all of her help and hard work, this book would not be where it is today.

One of the rules I live by is to take good care of your friends because if you get into trouble they are going to be the ones who help you out. Jim Conley is one of those friends. When deadlines started getting tight and the code for this book needed to get finished/written, Jim eagerly agreed and took the bull by the horns. Jim is an amazing person to know, an amazing friend, and an amazing coder.

I also want to thank all of my friends at Sytex who give continuous support and encouragement on a daily basis: Brad, Scott, John, Bryan, Nick, Jon, Matt, Marty, Dan, Fred, Evan, and Mike. Continuous thanks to Sid Martin and Ralph Palmieri for understanding the importance of research and for allowing creative minds to think of solutions to complex technical problems.

There are also my friends like Gary Jackson, Marc Maloof, and the great people at SANS who give constant insight and advice.

In terms of continuing this research and creating an environment for creative learning, I thank Fred Grossman and all of the wonderful people at Pace University for creating a great doctorate program that really focuses on learning.

Most of all, I want to thank God for blessing me with a great life and a wonderful family: Kerry Magee Cole, a loving and supportive wife without whom none of this would be possible, and my wonderful son Jackson and my princess Anna, who bring joy and happiness everyday to me. Ron and Caroline Cole and Mike and Ronnie Magee have been great parents to me, offering tons of love and support. And thanks to my wonderful sister, brother-in-law, and nieces and nephews: Cathy, Tim, Allison, Timmy, and Brianna.

For anyone that I forgot or did not mention by name, I thank all of my friends, family, and coworkers who have supported me in a variety of ways through this entire process.

About the Author

Eric Cole is the best-selling author of *Hackers Beware* and one of the highest-rated speaker on the SANS training circuit. Eric has earned rave reviews for his ability to educate and train network security professionals worldwide. He has appeared on CNN and has been interviewed on various TV programs including CBS News and 60 Minutes.

An information security expert for more than 10 years, Eric holds several professional certificates and helped develop several of the SANS GIAC certifications and corresponding courses. Eric, who obtained his M.S. in Computer Science at the New York Institute of Technology, is finishing up his doctorate degree in network steganography from Pace University.

Eric has created and directed corporate security programs for several large organizations, built numerous security consulting practices, and worked for more than five years at the Central Intelligence Agency. Eric is currently Chief Scientist for The Sytex Group's Information Warfare Center, where he heads up cutting-edge research in steganography and various other areas of network security. He was an adjunct professor at both New York Institute of Technology and Georgetown University. Eric has provided expert testimony in many legal cases, including his work as an expert witness for the FTC in their case against Microsoft. Eric is a sought-after speaker on the topic of steganography and other areas of network security.

Introduction

I have always been fascinated by steganography (stego for short), so much so that I am completing my Ph.D. in that area of study. It is amazing to me to sit back and reflect about how the field of secret communications and steganography has developed and changed over the past 10 years. From a technology standpoint, this is an exciting time to be alive.

Why I Wrote This Book

I decided to write this book because of a deep frustration I felt after September 11, 2001. In all areas of security, including steganography, the bad guys always seem to have an upper hand and do a better job at breaking into assets than we do protecting them.

After September 11, based on briefings and interviews, I became very aware that a large percent of the population, including many law enforcement agencies, do not even know what steganography is. I wanted to write a book that would help people understand the threat so that we can take action to minimize the damage going forward.

As you will learn in this book, stego is not a new field. Stego has played a critical part in secret communication throughout history.

NOTE If you are ever in Washington, D.C., stop by the newly opened Spy Museum. I was amazed as I walked through and saw example after example of stego in action.

What's Covered in This Book

Combining the art of steganography with the powers of computers, networks, and the Internet has brought this method of hiding information to a whole new level.

This book is meant to give you a crash introduction to the exciting world of secret communication. Here's what's covered:

- In Part One, you learn what steganography is and how it has evolved over time. You'll also learn about cryptography and digital water-marking because those two companion technologies are often used in concert with steganography.

- In Part Two, you discover who is using steganography and explore some of the ethical and legal challenges we face when detecting and cracking secret communication. Then you study the nuts and bolts of using steganography tools and transmitting hidden data over networks.

- Part Three is where you learn about methods you can use to crack steganography and cryptography, ideas for keeping your own communications secure, and the future direction of steganography.

To add even more value to the book, source code for the techniques that are discussed in Chapters 6 and 8 has been included in Appendix A and on the accompanying CD so that you can try these techniques out and build your own stego.

Special Features

In this book there are three special features to look for:

- Notes provide additional or background information for the topic at hand.

- Stego in Action Stories are interspersed throughout the book. They represent fictionalized versions of the kind of secret communication scenarios I've observed in my years working for the CIA and as a security consultant.

- The CD includes not only source code for steganography techniques discussed in the book, but also some popular steganography tools and color versions of images so you can see clearly how images with and without hidden data appear. You can read all about the contents of the CD in Appendix B.

In addition, I've set up a companion Web site where you can learn more about the fascinating world of steganography: www.securityhaven.com/stego.

Exploring the World of
Covert Communication

Covert Communication: It's All Around You

"Uncrackable encryption is allowing terrorists—Hamas, Hezbollah, al Qaeda and others—to communicate about their criminal intentions without fear of outside intrusion. They are thwarting the efforts of law enforcement to detect, prevent and investigate illegal activities."

—Louis Freeh, former FBI Director

"Hidden in the X-rated pictures on several pornographic Web sites and the posted comments on sports chat rooms may lie the encrypted blueprints of the next terrorist attack against the United States or its allies."

—Jack Kelley, reporting for *USA Today*, February 6, 2001

"Civilization is the progress toward a society of privacy. The savage's whole existence is public, ruled by the laws of his tribe. Civilization is the process of setting man free from men."

—Ayn Rand, *The Fountainhead*

Though security is nothing new, the way that security has become a part of our daily lives today is unprecedented. From pass codes that we use to enter our own highly secure homes, to retina-scanning technology that identifies us as we enter our office buildings, to scanners in airports, we have made security technology as much a part of our daily lives as the telephone or automobile.

We are also surrounded by a world of secret communication, where people of all types are transmitting information as innocent as an encrypted credit card number to an online store and as insidious as a terrorist plot to hijackers.

The schemes that make secret communication possible are not new. Julius Caesar used cryptography to encode political directives. Steganography (commonly referred to as stego), the art of hidden writing, has also been used for generations. But the intersection of these schemes with the pervasive use of the Internet, high-speed computer and transmission technology, and our current world political climate makes this a unique moment in history for covert communication.

BUSINESS AS USUAL?

Franklin glances at his watch as he listens to the boarding announcement for his flight to Hong Kong. He drops his empty coffee cup in a trash container, picks up his laptop, and strides through the corridors of Dulles Airport, heading toward Terminal C.

Though his cell phone is safely tucked in his jacket pocket, he scans the gate areas for a pay phone. He has to make one more call before he leaves the country—a very important call. He finds a phone and dials the number. The answering machine on the other end picks up, and he begins his well-planned message. "Sandy, I was hoping to catch you to ask a quick question. I wondered how you like your IBM ThinkPad A22p laptop? Anyway, I hope all is well. I'll talk to you when I get back." He hangs up and heads to Gate C-23.

As he boards the plane, he contemplates how closely he'll be watched when he arrives in Hong Kong. You don't do a multimillion dollar business deal these days without anxious competitors looking over your shoulder, trying to pick up whatever crumb of information they can to give them an edge in the negotiations.

He knows that the most important numbers for these negotiations won't be ready for another day or so. And he's confident that when the information is sent to him, nobody will be able to intercept it. Let them watch, he thinks.

After a few days of meetings Franklin makes sure everybody in the conference room notices he's having problems with his laptop. He comments that he'll have to pick up another computer for a backup. That night in his hotel room overlooking Hong Kong harbor, he connects to the Internet and logs onto eBay. To anyone observing his online activities he's just checking out the latest prices and specs of various laptop computer models.

After looking around for a while he pulls up information on four current auctions featuring the IBM ThinkPad A22p and downloads a couple of auction pages. He surfs around a while longer, then disconnects from the hotel's high-speed Internet connection. No longer online, he confidently pulls out a CD and runs a steganography program called S-Tools. Because he doesn't know which of the four auction pictures were posted by his colleague Sandy, he proceeds to drop each one into the program and enter his password.

The third file is a match. The program pops up a message confirming that a file has been extracted and displays the name of a Word document. He opens the file and scans all the bidding information and final numbers for the buy-out negotiations.

Franklin pours himself a scotch from the hotel mini-bar, sits back, and contemplates how much his competitor would give to get his hands on those numbers. And even though he knows his competitor has probably eavesdropped on every phone call and read every email he's sent and received since he arrived, he smiles to think that he retrieved the valuable data from inside a graphic image posted on a public auction site.

What Is Steganography?

Steganography derives from the Greek word *steganos*, meaning covered or secret, and *graphy* (writing or drawing). On the simplest level, steganography is hidden writing, whether it consists of invisible ink on paper or copyright information hidden in an audio file.

TIP   **You'll also hear this field referred to as data hiding or information hiding.**

Today, steganography is most often associated with the high-tech variety, where data is hidden within other data in an electronic file. For example, a Word document might be hidden inside an image file, as in the preceding story. This is usually done by replacing the least important or most redundant bits of data in the original file—bits that are hardly missed by the human eye or ear—with hidden data bits.

Where *cryptography* scrambles a message into a code to obscure its meaning, steganography hides the message entirely. These two secret communication technologies can be used separately or together—for example, by first encrypting a message, then hiding it in another file for transmission.

As the world becomes more anxious about the use of any secret communication, and as regulations are created by governments to limit uses of encryption, steganography's role is gaining prominence.

Where Hidden Data Hides

Unlike a word-processed file where you're likely to notice letters missing here and there, it's possible to alter graphic and sound files slightly without losing their overall viability for the viewer and listener. With audio, you can use bits of the file that contain sound not audible to the human ear. With graphic images, you can remove redundant bits of color from the image and still produce a picture that looks intact to the human eye and is difficult to discern from the original.

It is in those little bits that stego hides its data. A stego program uses an algorithm, to embed data in an image or sound file, and a password scheme, to allow you to retrieve the information. Some of these programs include both encryption and steganography tools for extra security if the hidden information is discovered.

The higher the image or sound quality, the more redundant data there will be, which is why 16-bit sound and 24-bit images are popular hiding spots. If the person snooping on you doesn't have the original image or sound file with which to compare a stego file, he or she will usually never be able to tell that what you transmit isn't a straightforward sound or image file and that data is hiding in it.

To understand how steganography techniques can be used to thoroughly hide data, look at the two images shown in Figures 1.1 and 1.2.

One of these images has a nine-page document embedded in it using steganography. Just by looking at the images, you cannot tell the difference between them. (Figure 1.2 has data embedded in the image).

Where Did It Come From?

One of the earliest examples of steganography involved a Greek fellow named Histiaeus. As a prisoner of a rival king, he needed a way to get a secret message to his own army. His solution? Shave the head of a willing slave and tattoo his message. When the slave's hair grew back, off he went to deliver the hidden writing in person.

In 1499 Trithemius published *Steganographia*, one of the first books about steganography. Techniques such as writing between the lines of a document with invisible ink created from juice or milk, which show only when heated, were used as far back as ancient Rome. In World War II, Germany used microdots to hide large amounts of data on printed documents, masquerading as dots of punctuation.

Figure 1.1   Graphics file containing the picture of a landscape.

Figure 1.2 Another version of the same image.

Today steganography has come into its own on the Internet. Used for transmitting data as well as for hiding trademarks in images and music (called *digital watermarking*), electronic steganography may ironically be one of the last bastions of information privacy in our world today.

Where Is It Going?

Today software programs used for data hiding are available for free across the Internet. In fact, there are more than 100 different programs available for various operating systems with easy point-and-click interfaces that allow anybody to hide data in a variety of file formats. In addition, several commercial stego software packages are available. In fact, a recent shift from freeware to commercial software products shows that there is indeed a market for this technology—and a market that's willing to pay to use it.

Steganography has traditionally been used by the military and criminal classes. One trend that is intriguing today is the increase in use of steganography by the commercial sector. In the past, when I talked about steganography at conferences, attendees came largely from research organizations, government entities, or universities. In the last year, the tide has turned: Now the biggest interest is definitely from the business sector.

When Steganography Inspires Terror

Today terrorist groups are on the cutting edge of technology. They use computers, the Internet, encryption, and steganography to conduct business. If their cryptography is good, it can take decades to crack. If they use steganography, their transmission of data may go completely undetected.

Cryptography, which has been around for centuries, allows these groups to encrypt their communications. *Encryption* involves garbling a message in such a way that only the intended recipient, who has a key to decode the encrypted data, can read the message. Anyone else intercepting the message would not be able to read it.

In essence, using an encryption key is like using a lock. If you have a metal box and you want to allow only two people to gain access to the box, you would put a lock on it. You could then give a key to the people you want to have access. If the lock is strong, only the people who have the key will be able to see what is inside the box. Other people could see the lock and know that something is inside (probably something of value, given that it is locked up), but they would not be able to see the contents. Encryption works just like a cyber lock. And just like a physical lock, encryption keys can be strong or weak.

When encryption is very strong, it can't be broken (or at least not for years and years). Government agencies unable to read secret messages have developed various methods of tracking online transmissions to uncover underground activity. One method is called *inference tracking*. Though the messages they observe being sent among known terrorists may not be decipherable, the existence of the messages provides some clues as to what's afoot. When law enforcement sees a great many messages being sent, many containing encrypted content, they infer that something important is about to happen. By correlating this increase in encrypted messages with world events, they can begin to draw some conclusions.

But is inference of such activity enough?

NOTICING PATTERNS

It's late 1997. Two terrorists known only as F1 and F2 sit together in the corner of a small pub in a town somewhere in central Germany. They seldom meet in person, and now that they are under surveillance by the CIA, they know this will be their last in-person contact. They must come up with a plan for safely exchanging information going forward.

Because both men have an interest in architecture, they decide on a pattern of communication that will misdirect those observing them. Every week they will send unencrypted messages to each other containing pictures of various buildings and notes about architecture. Every three to five weeks they will download random text from the Internet, encrypt it, and send it back and forth in a series of messages. The encrypted messages will contain nothing of value, but the large number of encrypted messages will catch the CIA's attention. Law enforcement will spend a great deal of time trying to unencrypt these messages and, with any luck, will ignore the hidden writing contained in the images sent routinely by email every week.

The terrorists will use encryption to draw attention away from their true covert communication, data hidden in images by means of steganography.

NOTE Want evidence that stego is being used all over the Internet today? I have developed techniques for detecting stego, one of which will detect data hidden in JPEG images. I randomly downloaded 500 images from eBay, and over 150 had data hidden in them. Somebody out there is very busy.

Who Is Using Stego?

People ask me all the time whether I think stego was used by the September 11 terrorists. I have no definitive answer to that question, but I do have an educated opinion.

I believe the terrorists did use stego because they had the technical savvy, the money, the access to technology, and the images to hide data in. Perhaps most important, they had not only the means, but the motive for hiding information.

The reality is that secret communication is used for a variety of reasons and by a variety of people, from businesspeople protecting company trade secrets while traveling to criminals transmitting child pornography. Governments hide information from other governments, and technophiles amuse themselves by sending secret messages to each other just for fun. The only tie that binds all these people is a desire to hide something from someone else.

Sadly, in a world on security alert, the methods available to anybody who wants to hide information are bound to become more sophisticated to match the times and will be misused.

Ironically, you may not read about steganography and those who use it in the front-page news, even though it is a tool used by groups that appear in the headlines every day. That's because of the unusual nature of information crime. Often, victims don't even know that their information has been tampered with. In other cases, a company or government might know that it has been deceived, but advertising that fact just isn't good for business.

NOTE Think hidden communication is happening only between spies? I have performed forensic analyses of computer networks for some very large companies, and the results almost invariably show that steganography tools are being used to hide various activities or disguise the fact that people are trying to extract data from the system.

Protecting Your Rights

The flip side of a desire to be able to monitor the use of secret communication for violent or unethical purposes is a justifiable concern about your own civil rights. In response to the heightened need for security against terrorism, legislation has been proposed in more than one country that would allow governments legally to look at any online communication. Some countries can send you to jail if you refuse to give up your key to encrypted data. Law enforcement works with ISPs all the time—possibly your own ISP—to get information about their subscribers' online activities.

All of this begs the question: If you cannot encrypt data and send it over the Internet without your government being able to decrypt it as it wishes, could stego become one of your only options for truly keeping your personal information private?

This is the concern of groups such as Hacktivisimo, a hacker group that is dedicated to circumventing state-sponsored invasion of online privacy and censorship of the Internet. The Electronic Frontier Foundation is a more mainstream group at the forefront of protecting individuals' rights to privacy and information online. The EFF supports legislation that requires companies to alert customers buying CDs and other media when copyright protection is built in—for example, in the form of digital watermarks that may make the products unusable in certain circumstances.

Keeping Your Business Secure

Businesses, too, have a stake in protecting their data. Still, most businesses lag behind terrorists when it comes to having aggressive security strategies. Many companies today believe that they can use a single technology, such as Secure Sockets Layer (SSL) for online transactions, or network software with a firewall or VPN, and they will be protected. Some companies protect their data in their offices and then forget about protecting it in transit as it flies over the Internet. What's required today to both protect a business from information theft and detect encryption and hidden data used on a company network is an all-encompassing security strategy.

One problem is that, though practicing security has become second nature in our daily lives with our magnetic ID badges at work and checks at airport security points, security online is still a new concept. Employees send confidential information in an email, a completely unprotected form of communication, without a second thought. People provide their corporate credit card number to rental car agencies over their cell phones, where anybody roaming the wireless ether for information can pick up the conversation.

NOTE One problem businesses have in trying to prevent attacks is that they don't share information when they are attacked. On the other hand, attackers share information all the time, picking up on each other's ideas and techniques. They constantly get smarter, while companies are constantly retrenching.

Vendors would like companies to believe that if you use their security products you will be safe. But, in reality, only a combination of products and approaches, called *defense in depth*, will work. You have to be alert to vulnerabilities of information not only in transit over the Internet, but as it sits on your network and when it is downloaded by your VP sitting in a customer's conference room. If your network has a wide open back door, or if that VP saves the confidential file in plaintext on a floppy disk, all the security technology in the world won't help you.

Some security measures are preventive, meant to stop an attack before it starts. Others are reactive, used to detect an attack that is either completed or in progress. Because you cannot prevent every attack, you must also set up reactive security measures. Prevention is ideal, but detection is a must.

To create a comprehensive security program you will make trade-offs. You can't have so many security procedures in place that people can't get their work done. You have to evaluate levels of risk and act accordingly. In the final analysis, security is all about mitigating and minimizing risk.

SECURITY BY INTIMIDATION

I was presenting at a conference recently and talking about the problem of users being alert to the dangers of opening unexpected email attachments. I was suggesting some solutions, and the attendees were poking holes in them because there is no perfect solution. Then one man raised his hand and said he worked in Colombia, South America. At his company they give users two warnings about violating security procedures. If they continue to have problems, they pull them into an alley and teach them about security with baseball bats.

(continued)

SECURITY BY INTIMIDATION *(continued)*

Everybody laughed, and the discussion went on. After the session the man came up to me and told me he was offended that I solicited ideas and then laughed at them. Incredulously, I asked if he had been serious about beating up security violators, and he said yes. Then he expressed disbelief when I told him we weren't allowed to do that in America.

In your business you must, needless to say, find other ways to make good security practices second nature for your employees. But driving home the importance of security at your company is something you neglect at your own peril.

Looking Ahead

Secret communication is everywhere around us today. Cryptography is being used to encrypt messages so that they can be read only by someone who has the key. Steganography hides messages so that their very existence is undetectable. Both forms of secret communication are being used in business, in government, and in war—both overt and covert.

Because these technologies are often used in concert, in the next chapter you'll learn about the world of cryptography, its history, and how it's being used today by a wide variety of groups and individuals.

CHAPTER 2

Cryptography Explained

When it comes to network security, there is no single solution, but there is one technology that comes close. That technology is cryptography, often referred to as simply "crypto." Ironically, few companies use crypto in their security strategy because they don't really understand it or its potential.

Cryptography encodes information in such a way that nobody can read it, except the person who holds the key. Just think about that for a second. If all of your information was encoded in this way, how much better would your security be? With cryptography in place, if someone intercepted your communication or accessed your server, he or she would not be able to read any of the information contained there. If an attacker can't read the information, he or she has struck out.

So if cryptography is that effective, why don't people use it all the time? The answer isn't obvious because cryptography is a very complex and broad topic, one on which several books have been written. In this chapter I will cover some of the key concepts and principles that you need to know to understand how cryptography might—or might not—apply to your own need for secure communication.

CRIME DOESN'T PAY

The bar, not far from the Air Force base, wasn't busy on a Sunday afternoon. The Texas sun found its way through the single window at the front of the room, but the bar at the back was in dim shadow. A man sat at one end of the bar, nursing a scotch and soda. He was a large man with an air of authority about him. The bartender, who had worked at this place for years, was used to the large number of military customers. He could tell that though his customer wore jeans today, he was a man more at home in uniform.

A couple of locals nursed their beers while they played a game of pool in a haze of smoke on the other side of the bar. The only other customer sat a few stools down from the first man. After a while they struck up a conversation. It seemed the second man was there to get away from his wife, who hounded him about chores every weekend. He went on about the miseries of his marriage in great detail. After a few more drinks, the first man began to talk about his own wife. But he didn't talk about petty arguments or domestic chores. As the bartender eavesdropped, this guy bragged to the other man that his wife was dead and that he was the one who'd had her killed.

Lieutenant Sam Masters sat at his desk sipping cold coffee, waiting for his partner to arrive. He was thinking about what the bartender had told him a few days earlier, thinking about a colonel who bragged in a bar that he'd paid a guy to off his wife. Had this guy been drunk, was he just stupid, or did he have reason to be confident that he'd never get caught?

Sam fingered the document in his hand. It gave him the right under military law to search the colonel's house for evidence. He knew they'd have to get the goods on the first run, before the colonel was alerted to their suspicions and had time to get rid of the evidence. That's why Sam's partner, Al, had called this computer expert from D.C. to help out. Al had heard him at a lecture in Dallas a few weeks ago, talking about ways that people can hide information in computer files. Knowing their colonel was a computer nut, they figured maybe he stashed something incriminating on his home computer.

When Al, the computer guy, and his assistant arrived, they all headed over to the colonel's quarters.

One of the best parts of Sam's job was being able to tell a ranking officer to sit down and shut up. Of course, he was more polite than that, but that's what it came to. The colonel sat in a chair on the front porch, definitely not happy having to sit still under the wary eye of Al, who watched him in case he decided to bolt.

Sam was hunting around the colonel's desk, while the computer guy and his partner worked on the two computers in the house. After a while he wandered over to see what the computer expert was up to.

"I'm looking in the lower bits for patterns," the guy explained. "That's like the last six pixels in an electronic image. If there are no peaks and valleys in the data, it suggests there might be hidden images in there." It was all Greek to Sam, but the news that the guy might be on to something was welcome. Sam himself had drawn a blank looking through the colonel's papers. The computer guy started explaining what he was doing. "I'm using this program called S-Tools, and a few other programs I'm writing on the fly, to extract hidden data. And there's definitely stuff here. But what I've found so far is encrypted—that means it's kind of in code and we need a key to break it." Sam could hear the frustration in the guy's voice: They were so near, but without a key, the hidden information would stay hidden.

They were just discussing whether the existence of hidden data could be used in court to show some kind of covert activity, when they heard the other computer guy give out a whoop from the next room. They both rushed in to see what was up. The guy was holding up a floppy disk. "I found it," he said, excitedly. "The guy left the encryption keys in this document on his hard drive, plain as day. What a jerk!" They ran back to the other computer and used the key he had copied onto the floppy to read the hidden data.

An hour later the colonel was in custody, the unencrypted emails between him and a contract killer name Leon, including a payment schedule for his deadly services, safely in hand.

Cryptography Defined

According to www.dictionary.com, cryptography is "the process or skill of communicating in or deciphering secret writings or ciphers." In practice, crypto is used to keep secrets secret. It transforms information in such a way that no one other than the intended recipients can read what was actually written. More advanced crypto techniques ensure that the information being transmitted has not been modified in transit.

Cryptography is a complex subject, so it is important that you take a brief look at the basics of this technology and understand where it fits in the world of secret communication.

Crypto 101

Cryptography has been around for thousands of years. In fact, many of us have used it, perhaps without knowing it, when we played with a decoder ring or cracked a secret code on a cereal box. Whenever information is placed into any form of code, that's cryptography.

It's worth noting that, throughout history, crypto has been used for a variety of purposes, both ethical and not so ethical. As with any technology, cryptography can be used both legitimately and by those who have illegal or immoral secrets to hide. Of course, though prey to its users' scruples or lack thereof, cryptography itself is neither good nor bad.

Cryptography has been used to protect the following:

- Launch codes of nuclear weapons
- The location of military troops

- Names of suspected criminals
- The formula for a new product
- A new research idea

But it has also been used to do the following:

- Convey stolen industrial secrets
- Send directives to terrorists
- Plan criminal activities

Crypto Lingo

An understanding of cryptography begins with a basic understanding of some essential terminology:

- *Plaintext* refers to any type of information in its original, readable, unencrypted form. A word-processed document, an image file, and an executable file are all considered plaintext documents.
- *Ciphertext* refers to a message in its encrypted form, what some people refer to as *garbled* information. The meaning of the information in ciphertext is obscured.
- *Encryption* is the process of taking a plaintext message and converting it into ciphertext.

NOTE You will often hear people use the words "encryption" and "cryptography" interchangeably, but they actually have slightly different meanings. Cryptography or crypto refers to the art of using various encryption and decryption methods to protect information.

- *Decryption* is the opposite of encryption. Decryption takes a ciphertext message and converts it to plaintext. It's important to remember that there is a relationship between the encryption and decryption processes. If I encrypt a message using one scheme and try to decrypt the message using a different scheme, the decryption process will not yield the original plaintext message; it will yield garbage text.
- A *cryptanalyst* is a person who tries to find weaknesses in encryption schemes. These people often work for those hush-hush agencies that we are not allowed to talk about, such as NSA (which is rumored to stand for No Such Agency). A cryptanalyst will often figure out how to break a crypto scheme, and then the developer of the scheme will use that information to make it stronger.

■ A *key* is what actually protects data; a key is required to unscramble an encrypted message. Many people may use the same encryption algorithm, but as long as they use different keys, information is protected. For crypto to be secure it is critical that the key be protected and that nobody can guess its value.

Now that you understand the basics of cryptography, it's time to take a quick look at where cryptography came from and how it's being used today.

Early Cryptography

Cryptography was in use long before computers ever arrived on the scene. In fact, one of the earliest uses of crypto dates all the way back to Julius Caesar.

Julius Caesar utilized a basic level of encryption, often referred to as a *Caesar cipher*, to communicate his political and military secrets. The Caesar cipher is also referred to as an *ROT* or *rotation scheme*.

Caesar or ROT ciphers simply rotate a character a certain number of places in the alphabet. Say that you are using an ROT 3 scheme with the English language; in that case, each letter would be rotated three spaces in the alphabet. The word "cat" would become "fdw" by rotating the letters three places forward—letter "c" rotated three places to the letter "f", and so on.

This table shows an ROT 1 scheme where each letter moves one letter to the right:

a	b	c	d	e	f	g	h	i	j	k	l	m	n	o	p	q	r	s	t	u	v	w	x	y	z
b	c	d	e	f	g	h	i	j	k	l	m	n	o	p	q	r	s	t	u	v	w	x	y	z	a

To encrypt a message with an ROT 1 scheme you find the letter on the top row and replace it with the letter on the bottom row. In this case "cat" would become "dbu". To translate "dbu" back into the original message, you find the letter in the bottom row and replace it with the letter in the top row.

Here's an ROT 2 table, which works the same way with a two-letter shift:

a	b	c	d	e	f	g	h	i	j	k	l	m	n	o	p	q	r	s	t	u	v	w	x	y	z
c	d	e	f	g	h	i	j	k	l	m	n	o	p	q	r	s	t	u	v	w	x	y	z	a	b

Even though ROT is a very basic scheme, it illustrates at a fundamental level how cryptography works. The following table shows how a couple of different words are translated into unreadable text using the two rotation schemes outlined here. Try taking each scrambled message and using the preceding tables to translate it back to the original message.

ROTATION NUMBER	TEXT 1	TEXT 2	TEXT 3	TEXT 4
	Cat	Hello	this is a test	Hello
ROT 1	dbu	ifmmp	N/A	N/A
ROT 2	ecv	jgnnq	N/A	N/A

Notice that the last two rows in the table, "This is a test" and "Hello," could not be translated precisely, because this scheme does not account for spaces or uppercase letters. It is important even in basic cryptography schemes to account for all characters that may appear in your input text.

The cryptography that was used by Julius Caesar is similar to what is used today to illustrate basic cryptography. It is the scheme that is used on cereal boxes where a "secret decoder" is presented as a game for children playing spies. Often you see this scheme used in a simple cardboard device that contains two circles, one smaller than the other and both connected in the center by a pin. Each circle may have the alphabet or words written on it; when you line them up a certain way, the information matches up correctly.

Compared to modern cryptography with high-speed computers, this kind of simple scheme is considered very weak. In fact, this inevitable obsolescence is a characteristic of cryptography: Techniques that are considered secure today will probably not be secure 10 years from now.

How We Got to Modern Cryptography

Cryptography played a major role during World War II. Both sides spent a lot of time and money trying to crack the cryptography schemes of the other. In fact, throughout most of the major (and minor) wars of history, cryptography has played a critical role.

AN ENIGMA

During World War II the Germans used a cipher machine called Enigma. This machine offered more than 712 million possible keys, and it seemed unbreakable. In fact, rumor had it that even if you captured one of these machines you couldn't break the cipher scheme because the key was rotated on a regular basis. In Bletchley Park in England, a center was set up to break Enigma. Machines called turing bombes were constructed to break the cipher. In the end, the Allies were able to intercept and decrypt Enigma transmissions, and great effort was expended to ensure that the Germans were unaware that their messages were being read—and more importantly—understood.

More recently, in the last 10 years, a lot of public attention has focused on cryptography. Several critical events elicited this attention, but two are particularly worth noting.

The United States government launched a big effort in the 1990s to require the escrow of all encryption keys. This would essentially lead to a country where there was no way to protect secure information. Law enforcement would have to go through a legal process, but in the end these agencies could essentially read any messages they wanted to. This resulted in such a public uproar that the proposal was quickly put on the back burner, and the government stopped pursuing it. During this time there was heightened interest in steganography because people realized that the only way to keep information secure might be by keeping it hidden. My guess is that with renewed interest in security and the homeland defense initiative, something similar to key escrow will resurface relatively soon.

Another development in recent years that has had an impact on cryptography is the fact that Data Encryption Standard (DES) is no longer considered secure. DES was the standard symmetric-based encryption scheme developed in the late 1980s and early 1990s. Because computers are now much faster than they were 10 years ago, DES was no longer considered secure, and a replacement was needed. Triple-DES became the de facto standard; however, the National Institute of Standards and Technology (NIST) began to spearhead an effort to find a replacement for DES. This effort was called the Advanced Encryption Standard (AES). AES resulted in a scheme called Rijndeal (pronounced "rain doll") being selected as the new standard. Because crypto takes a long time to test, it is still too early to estimate the impact that Rijndeal will have, but it's definitely worth watching.

Cryptography and Network Security

Whenever I examine security technologies to determine their strengths and weaknesses I like to map my analysis back to the three core standards of network security: confidentiality, integrity, and availability. There is a reason that these standards have stood the test of time: They represent the most critical concepts of network/computer security and emphasize what is most important when trying to protect a network.

Confidentiality

Confidentiality deals with protecting, detecting, and deterring the unauthorized disclosure of information. Confidentiality is what most people think about when you say "security." A desire for confidentiality is what causes you to keep your financial records in a password-protected file, for example.

The main goal of cryptography is to take a plaintext message and garble it in such a way that only the intended recipient can read it and no one else. This is precisely the goal of confidentiality.

Because most people think of confidentiality when they think of security, it is no surprise that this was one of the first security problems addressed when the Internet, and more significantly the World Wide Web, took off. One of the first protection mechanisms put into Web browsers and servers was Secure Sockets Layer (SSL). SSL provides point-to-point encryption of critical information and directly addresses the need for confidentiality.

NOTE SSL is an application built into Web browsers that utilizes encryption to protect information in transit. SSL is only a partial solution for online confidentiality because information is still unprotected before it is sent and after it arrives.

Integrity

Integrity deals with preventing, detecting, and deterring the unauthorized modification of information. It is a common misconception that if your data is protected and someone cannot read it, then they cannot modify it. Unfortunately, that is not true. Even if an attacker cannot read information, there is nothing stopping him or her from modifying it.

An integrity attack is potentially more dangerous than a confidentiality attack. With a confidentiality attack someone reads your secrets, but if the attacker does nothing with that information there may be no impact on your company. With an integrity attack, someone might, for example, tamper with your data to change the value of a key field to a false value, which creates an immediate threat. Your information is now invalid, which could have a serious impact on your company.

Imagine the spreadsheet that your HR department maintains to track people's salaries across the company. The fields that contain the employee names and titles are in plaintext because that information is not considered secure; however, the salary field has been encrypted because that is secure information. Although I can't read the salaries field to learn what other people are making, I can assume that the VP of Engineering makes more money than I do. Even though I can't read the value in that field I can copy the encrypted content from the VP's salary field and paste it into my salary field. By making some logical guesses, I can perform an integrity attack, even though I am unable to perform a confidentiality attack.

HIGH-TECH INTEGRITY ATTACKS

A similar attack was popular on UNIX systems a while back. Originally the etc/passwd file contained both the user IDs and associated encrypted passwords. If attackers wanted to gain root access (which is essentially God access on the computer) they needed to find out the root password. One way to accomplish this was to go in and create a new user account for which attackers created the password. They would then go into etc/passwd and take the encrypted value for the password for the account just created and copy it over the current value for root. (Usually attackers would save the original value of root so that they could put the system back to the way it was to cover their tracks). Essentially, attackers could change the password for the root without knowing what the original value was. Bottom line: There is no need to breach confidentiality in order to breach integrity.

Cryptography addresses integrity by performing verification and validation of data. In essence, it performs a digital signature check across information; if any bit of data changes, the signature will be different. This use of crypto allows companies to perform integrity checks against their information to make sure that nothing has changed in transit.

NOTE A program called Tripwire has such an integrity-checking feature. Tripwire performs cryptographic hashes or digital signatures of all key files and lets you know if any of these files has been modified. More information can be found at www.tripwire.com/.

You can use methods of cryptography that use straight encryption to protect against integrity attacks but provide no confidentiality protection. That means that someone cannot read the information, but he or she can modify it. As you will see later, you can use other methods of cryptography such as digital signatures to provide both integrity and confidentiality for information.

Availability

Availability relates to preventing, detecting, or deterring the denial of access to critical information. Availability (or *denial of service*) attacks can be broken down into two general categories: *incorrect data* and *resource exhaustion*.

Incorrect data denial of service attacks involve sending data that a service or process is not expecting, which causes the system to crash. This type of attack can usually be fixed by applying a vendor patch or reconfiguring the system, and it can usually be prevented.

Resource exhaustion attacks are the most popular form of availability attack and are extremely difficult to prevent. Essentially, a resource exhaustion attacker will try to send more data than your network, router, or server can handle. This will cause your network to be overloaded, and it will not be able to respond to legitimate requests. Preventing these types of attacks is very difficult and usually involves acquiring additional resources.

Though cryptography can play a key role in preventing confidentiality and integrity attacks, it does little to protect a company from availability attacks. This should not be surprising: As stated in the introduction to this chapter, cryptography is close to a total security solution, but it is, in the end, not a silver bullet. There is no silver bullet when it comes to network security. Cryptography must be combined with other defense measures to create a robust solution for your site, one that provides defense in depth.

Authentication and Non-Repudiation

In addition to the three core areas of security, two other security goals are critical relative to cryptography: authentication and non-repudiation.

Authentication

In most transactions you need to be able to authenticate or validate that the people you're dealing with are who they say they are. If I buy a computer on the Internet, the company selling me the computer wants to be able to authenticate who I am and verify that I can pay for the purchase. I want to be sure that I am giving my credit card number to a company I can trust, and not to an online con man.

Not only do online merchants want to validate who a customer is, they also want to make sure that what they agreed to sell and the amount they agreed to sell it for do not get modified during the transaction. In this sense, they are authenticating the validity and accuracy of the information.

With integrity checks, the goal is to make sure that the information has not changed. With authentication, it is okay if the information has changed, so long as the information is accurate. This becomes very critical in Web transactions where, at the end of a shopping transaction, the server presents a customer with final order information. The customer can then add or remove items, change the quantities, and select the shipping method he or she would like to use; then the customer sends those changes back to the server. The server needs to be able to authenticate the accuracy of the information. Without a human in the loop, authentication is a much bigger challenge.

I was recently hired to perform a penetration testing or ethical hacking exercise against an e-commerce site. Essentially, I was playing the role of an attacker to see if I could break in or compromise the site. One of the tests that I performed involved going to the site and ordering several items. I then clicked the checkout button, and the server returned a page that listed all of the items in my order. The list looked something like this:

ITEM	UNIT PRICE	QUANTITY	TOTAL PRICE
Widget 1	$5.00	3	$15.00
Widget 2	$20.00	5	$100.00
Widget 3	$35.00	1	$35.00
Widget 4	$40.00	2	$80.00
		Total Price	$230.00

I decided at this point that I was going to examine how well the company authenticated the information they receive back from the client, so I saved the page locally to my system. Then I went in and changed the values to the following: This kind of change is extremely easy to do with a simple text editor. I submitted the page back to the system and placed my order. Instead of paying $230, I paid a bargain price of $24. Needless to say, this was a major problem.

The creators of the site had assumed that customers would follow instructions to adjust their order and not make changes manually that would invalidate the data. Because they did not authenticate the information received back from the client, the server was wide open to attack.

When confronted with the vulnerability, the developers were not very happy with me. Their initial response was, "Who would do this?" I replied that it only takes a handful of people doing this to cause major problems for your company and potentially put it out of business. I also pointed out that cryptography can play a key role in authenticating individuals and the validity of information received online.

Non-repudiation

One of the last things that President Clinton did before leaving office was to sign a bill that made digital signatures binding for contracts with the federal government. If a digital signature is going to be binding, you must be able to prove that a specific person actually sent it and make sure that no one else can spoof his or her signature.

ITEM	UNIT PRICE	QUANTITY	TOTAL PRICE
Widget 1	$1.00	3	$3.00
Widget 2	$2.00	5	$10.00
Widget 3	$3.00	1	$3.00
Widget 4	$4.00	2	$8.00
		Total Price	$24.00

This is exactly the goal of non-repudiation. Non-repudiation deals with the ability to prove in a court of law that someone sent something or signed something digitally. By signing your name on a written contract you are obligating yourself to fulfill your side of the contract; if you do not, you can be taken to court and either forced to perform or pay a penalty. Without a parallel form of non-repudiation, digital signatures and contracts would be useless.

If I could send a company an order for 400 widgets at $100 a piece and 10 days later, when the price of widgets drops to $40 each, deny that I ever sent the order, it would make e-commerce unworkable. In order for e-commerce to go to the next level there has to be some way to implement non-repudiation across digital transactions, just as there is with written contracts.

One of the big strengths of cryptography is that it can be used to provide non-repudiation for any type of digital information, including digital contracts.

Principles of Cryptography

By now you have a basic understanding of how crypto works and how it may have uses in securing transactions and communications. To understand the nature of cryptography better, take a look at what I call the key principles of cryptography.

You Cannot Prove Crypto Is Secure

Ideally, you would like to feel safe in the knowledge that the technique you are using to protect information is secure and that there is no weakness that can be exploited. Unfortunately, with crypto, there is no definitive way to prove that an algorithm is secure. In fact, the only way to determine that a crypto algorithm is *probably* secure is to have a bunch of really smart people try to break it. If, after five or more years, they cannot break it, you can assume that it is probably secure. There could still be a vulnerability that they missed, but the chances are slim. That is why new algorithms are not considered to be secure for at least five to eight years.

In doing an analysis of an algorithm there is no mathematical principle that guarantees that you tested for every possible vulnerability. You can test for known vulnerabilities and for vulnerabilities that were found in other algorithms, but there is no way to determine that the algorithm is not susceptible to some new vulnerability that has not been discovered.

DES PROPHETS?

DES was originally created back in the 1970s by brilliant people from IBM and NSA. As they were creating the algorithm they had cryptanalysts constantly trying to break the algorithm and make it stronger. The real value of their work did not really become evident until 20 years later.

With NSA working on DES, there were always rumors floating around that the agency planted back doors into the system. No one was able to prove it, but if you examined the code you noticed that certain things looked suspicious, such as how the agency broke up the data before it was encrypted. Something called an S-box was used to group pieces of the data together. The way NSA handled this data grouping was unusual, and people thought that might have been the back door; however, nobody could ever prove it.

In the mid 1990s a technique to break encryption came out called *differential crypt analysis*. When this technique appeared it looked as if it could be used to break some implementations of DES. It turned out, though, that the version of DES created by IBM and NSA was not vulnerable to this attack because of how they had used S-boxes. Now everyone could see the value of the way they broke up the groups of data. This brought up a very interesting question: How were IBM and NSA able to design DES in such a way that it was protected against a vulnerability that came out 20 years later? Either they were very lucky, which I doubt, or their cryptanalysts were so good that they knew about a vulnerability that would take more than 20 years for the rest of the world to figure out. I guess we should just be glad that they are on our side!

New ways to break crypto are discovered all the time, and there is actually a low survivability ratio for new crypto algorithms. Most algorithms that are released are broken very quickly. In many cases, fixing the problem would defeat the reason for inventing the algorithm in the first place. For example, if a new algorithm is invented to be extremely fast and a major flaw is found in it, after the flaw is fixed the algorithm might function very slowly.

The bottom line is that you can never be absolutely sure that a crypto scheme is secure, but it is possible to prove that some crypto schemes are insecure.

Algorithm versus Implementation

When talking about the strength of various encryption schemes it is important to remember the difference between an algorithm and the implementation of that algorithm. An algorithm is the blueprint or design for the encryption process to follow. An implementation occurs when someone takes that design and creates a working piece of software.

The problem when you take an algorithm and implement it in a piece of software is that the designer has to interpret or make choices about certain properties. An implementation is really one person's interpretation of how he or she thinks the algorithm should work because the algorithm does not specify every single detail. For example, the algorithm may pick a large prime number. Depending on what number is used, you may end up with a solid encryption scheme or one that can easily be broken.

This is an important distinction to keep in mind when you hear about encryption being broken. The media doesn't differentiate between a weakness found in the algorithm and a weakness in implementation. When you hear about a popular scheme being broken, the implementation is usually at fault. If a weakness is found in the algorithm, though, that means that all implementations are also breakable, which is a much bigger problem. Weak implementation is not critical, but a weak algorithm is.

Never Trust Proprietary

If you can never prove that crypto is secure, how can you ever use an algorithm and have any sense that it is secure? The way the security community does this is to release the algorithm to the public and have really smart cryptanalysts beat on it for many, many years. If they cannot find a way to break it, then it is considered secure. Therefore, using an algorithm when it is in its infancy is not a smart choice because it has not had a chance to be tested. There are always problems—minor or major problems—when an algorithm is first released. In fact, all of the algorithms that we use today, such as Triple-DES and RSA, were not perfect when they were first released.

Based on this fact, why would you ever trust proprietary algorithms? With these algorithms all of the information and details of the implementation are concealed. No one else would have looked at the algorithm or validated it. Vendors often make the claim that proprietary algorithms are actually more secure because no one knows how they work and therefore it is harder for someone to break them. That is essentially a *security-through-obscurity* argument. Security through obscurity says that if you hide the inner workings of your system you will be secure. This philosophy doesn't work when it comes to security, and it doesn't work when it comes to cryptography.

BUYER BEWARE

Be very careful when you buy security products that implement encryption, such as programs used to encrypt your hard drive. If you ask a salesperson what type of encryption the company uses in a product, that person might tell you the company uses Triple-DES-like encryption. Some customers would walk away thinking that's great—they are using Triple-DES and Triple-DES is considered secure. Think about it. The Triple-DES algorithm is considered secure, and some implementations are robust, but that doesn't mean that all implementations are secure. In most cases, the design decisions made during implementation will be the wrong ones, and the resulting implementation will be weak. Also, notice something tell-tale about the statement "We are using Triple-DES-*like* encryption." That means that the company did its own interpretation of the algorithm. Because crypto is very hard to do and only a small group of people is very good at building it, think twice when buying security products with proprietary implementation.

Good crypto is designed in such a way that, even if you share the inner workings of the algorithm, it is still secure because of the key. Think about padlocks. Lock companies have a patent on their locks. This means that you can get a copy of the patent and see exactly how their locks work. Yet even if you know how their locks work, their locks are still secure. Knowing the design of the locks does not help you to open the locks, if they are designed correctly, because the keys are unique. The same holds true for good cryptography.

GOING HOLLYWOOD

What happened when Hollywood needed to come up with an encryption scheme to protect DVD? This is not some run-of-the-mill company we're talking about—this is Hollywood. These are the people who make it possible for Tom Cruise to infiltrate CIA headquarters, suspended from the ceiling as he breaks into highly secure computers. This is the fantasy mill where the rugged individual who bucks the system is always the hero.

So when Hollywood leaders came up with DVD to distribute movies, like a typical Western hero they went their own way. They decided that encryption was the way to go, and, rather than using a proven crypto scheme, they hired a company to develop a proprietary crypto scheme. They released DVD with this proprietary crypto built in. In fact, Hollywood and the movie industry made a huge investment in this crypto algorithm because it was used on all DVDs and was built into all DVD players.

A month or so after it was released, in a scenario worthy of a blockbuster movie, two pimple-faced teenagers broke the algorithm. How do you tell the public that you are changing the DVD standard and that all of the disks and players they bought will no longer work?

(continued)

GOING HOLLYWOOD *(continued)*

I once gave a presentation at a conference and mentioned the DVD scenario. One attendee began to get very agitated as I was speaking. It turns out that he worked for the company that developed the crypto algorithm for DVD. He was upset, he told me after the talk, because his company knew that proprietary encryption was not that secure. The technical staff figured that was okay because they wanted something that would only stop the casual attacker, not something that would be bullet proof. They knew it could be broken with some effort, but they *did not care*. I pointed out that there are good crypto algorithms out there that they could have used—why in the world would they purposely develop a new crypto algorithm that they knew would be broken?

The Strength of an Algorithm Is in the Key

In the previous section you discovered that the strength of crypto is never based on the secrecy of the algorithm; in fact, keeping the algorithm private can actually result in less secure communication. In fact, letting people know what specific crypto algorithm you are using, such as Triple-DES or RSA, is considered good practice. That's because the strength of crypto is based not on the secrecy of the algorithm, but on the secrecy of the key.

It's very important that you take due care to protect your crypto key. To drive home this point, consider this example of how a key is misused.

Wireless technology has a lot of security issues associated with trying to protect information as it flies through the air. The Wired Equivalent Privacy (WEP) algorithm was developed to provide encryption of the information that flows over a wireless network. The problem is that the key that is used to encrypt the information is embedded in the message; therefore, anyone who intercepts the encrypted message can also extract the key and read the information. This is like taping your house key to your locked front door.

Cryptography Stays in Place

SSL allows for point-to-point encryption between a client's browser and a server. SSL is often used to protect credit card numbers or any information in transit, but it offers protection only while in transit. The information is unprotected before it leaves the client system and unprotected once it gets to the server. SSL has nothing to do with end-point encryption, yet end-point encryption is critical to the overall security of the information. Cryptography provides protection not only during transmission, but up to the point where a recipient decrypts it.

Cryptography Must Be Designed In

Secure communication involves more than just building a functional site and adding crypto or SSL at the end. Security must address all points of vulnerability. Remembering that an attacker is always going to try to break the weakest link, all security measures must be designed into a site from the beginning.

You can understand this concept better by looking at the process of building a house. You would think a builder was crazy if he finished building a whole house and left out the electrical wiring. To fix this the builder would have to rip out all the walls, install the wiring, fix all of the sheet rock, and repaint all the walls. Not only would this be much more expensive, but the end product would be inferior.

Just as it makes more sense to include the electrical wiring in the original blueprints of a house, security must be designed in from the beginning, or the end product will be more expensive and not as effective. Building in protection for the data after the fact usually requires rebuilding and potentially redesigning the database and resulting interfaces for a Web site.

All Cryptography Is Crackable, in Time

Anyone who claims that he has a crypto scheme that is not crackable is lying to you. Crypto is based on a key; by trying every possible combination you will eventually obtain the plaintext. This is called a *brute-force* attack because it involves the unsophisticated technique of laboriously trying all possible combinations until you successfully crack the code. Although there are easier ways to crack crypto, because brute force is guaranteed always to find the key, it is usually used as a baseline.

Take a look at how brute force actually works. If you were using a binary alphabet and had a two-character key, here are all the possible combinations.

00

01

10

11

This would take about five seconds to crack. To make this harder there are two things I could do. First, I could increase the number of possibilities; instead of binary I could use the letters of the alphabet, which would give me 26 possible keys. The problem with this approach is that computers represent everything in binary. The second option would be to increase the size of the key, so that, instead of two characters, we use a four-character key, like this:

0000

0001

0010

0011

0100

0101

0110

0110

1000

1001

1010

1011

1100

1101

1110

1111

Just by making the key 2 characters longer, you increase the number of possible combinations from 4 to 16.

The 4-key example would probably take about 60 seconds to crack. The longer the key, the longer a brute force attack will take. That's why key length is usually associated with crypto strength.

Although all crypto is crackable, you'll sometimes hear people refer to non-crackable crypto. With non-crackable crypto the theory is that if, by the time you crack the encryption the information is useless, the crypto is as good as uncrackable. The trick with using encryption is to make sure that the time during which the information is useful is less than the time it takes to break the encryption with brute force.

For example, let's say a spy has to leave the country tonight; if his enemy finds out his plans, he'll never make it out of the country alive. In this case, the usefulness of the information is less than 12 hours. Our spy doesn't really care if someone cracks the encryption tomorrow because by then he will have already left the country. In this case, a lower-grade of encryption could be used.

What if you are building a state-of-the-art fighter plane that is going to take 10 years to complete? If a competitor cracks your encryption in a year, that company could find out your plans and build the plane before you. This scenario calls for some very high-grade encryption.

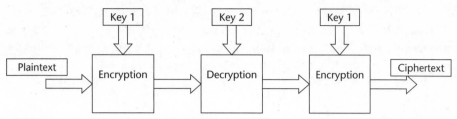

Figure 2.1 Triple-DES using two keys.

Security Becomes Obsolete

Computers are constantly getting quicker, and the programs they run are getting smarter. A crypto algorithm that could be cracked with a brute-force attack in 40 years in the past might only take 10 years to break with today's technology. In other words, if you need to protect something for 25 years you may have to use crypto that would take 500 years to crack, just to account for future changes in technology.

DES is a good example of the way a secure algorithm can become insecure. DES has an effective key length of 56 bits. DES is no longer considered secure, not because the algorithm has been cracked, but because of the key length.

Triple-DES has become the de facto standard today because it has an effective key length of either 112 or 168 bits, depending on whether it uses two or three keys. This will become clear by looking at an example. Figure 2.1 shows Triple-DES using two keys, which gives an effective key length of 112 bits.

Triple-DES is structured in this way so that the algorithm is downwardly compatible with DES. If I set Key 1 and Key 2 to the same value, this is, in effect, a single DES operation. The first encryption and decryption would cancel out, and only the last encryption would be performed. If Key 1 and Key 2 are different, then you get an effective key length of 112 bits.

Figure 2.2 shows Triple-DES using three keys. This gives an effective key length of 168 bits.

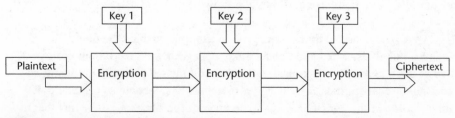

Figure 2.2 Triple-DES using three keys.

Triple-DES is typically used with three keys, which is obviously much more secure than DES with its single key. Yet even though Triple-DES is considered secure today, there will come a time in the near future when it is no longer secure. This is a problem inherent in fixed-length keys. (That is why Triple-DES is likely to be replaced with AES, which has a variable key length.)

Types of Cryptography

There are three general types of encryption schemes: symmetric, asymmetric, and hash. Each one has its own pros and cons. To understand the strengths and weaknesses of each, you need to understand a bit about how each one works.

Symmetric

Symmetric key encryption is single-key encryption. You use one key to encrypt the plaintext and the same key to decrypt the ciphertext. Symmetric encryption is fairly straightforward and very fast. The drawback to symmetric encryption is that if the key that you use to encrypt and decrypt the message is not sent over a secure channel, the encryption can be broken. But the irony is this: If you have a secure channel to send information between two parties, why bother to use encryption at all?

Another drawback to symmetric encryption is that you cannot use it to achieve non-repudiation. (Remember, non-repudiation allows you to prove in a court of law that someone was, in fact, the sender of a specific piece of information.) If both parties have access to the same key, it is impossible to prove which party was the sender.

Diffie-Hellman Key Exchange

One way to get around the need for a secure channel solution in symmetric encryption is to use Diffie-Hellman key exchange. Diffie-Hellman's algorithm is used solely to be able to exchange a key over a nonsecure channel; it is not used to encrypt data to be communicated between two parties. Crypto packages usually have some form of key exchange such as Diffie-Hellman built in.

NOTE You may notice that when I give an example such as the one that follows, I often use Alice and Bob as the people who want to communicate and Eve as the attacker. This is considered standard practice across the industry, so I continue in that spirit. In fact, using these names has become so popular that John Gordon at the Zurich Seminar came up with the Alice and Bob story that you can find at www.conceptlabs.co.uk/alicebob.html.

Take a look at a couple of algorithms to gain an appreciation for how powerful crypto can be. Alice and Bob want to use symmetric encryption, but they do not have a secure channel to exchange the key. Therefore, they decide to use Diffie-Hellman key exchange. To start off, Alice and Bob both decide on two very large prime numbers, "n" and "g", and share them over an open, nonsecure channel. Alice then generates a private key called "xa" and does not share it with anyone. Bob does the same and generates his own private key called "xb".

The n, g, xa, and xb in this example are simply numbers that Alice and Bob pick to use with the algorithm. In most cases these would be large prime numbers, but they are essentially variables to which you assign a value. For example:

n = 5

g = 7

xa = 11

xb = 17

Only Alice knows xa, and only Bob knows xb. Alice computes the following: ya = g^{xa} mod n. Bob computes yb = g^{xb} mod n.

In this case yb = g^{xb} mod n means to take the value of g and raise it to the power of xb. For example, if g is 2 and xb is 3, you would raise 2 to the power of 3, which means 2×2×2, which equals 8. You then take that value and mod it by n. This means to divide the first value by n and take the remainder. If g is 2, xb is 3, and n is 3, you would take 2 to the power of 3, which is 8, and divide it by n, which is 3, and take the remainder. In this case the remainder is 2.

Alice and Bob share ya and yb with each other over the open, nonsecure channel. Alice computes k = yb^{xa} mod n and Bob computes k' = ya^{xb} mod n. The magical thing about Diffie-Hellman is k = k' because k = k' = $g^{(xa)(xb)}$ mod n. Even though the attacker knows the values for n, g, ya, and yb because he or she does not know the value for either xa or xb, the attacker cannot compute the key. You need to know one of those values for the equation to work. Bob and Alice just exchanged a key over an open, nonsecure channel. Welcome to the wonderful world of crypto.

Take a look at another example. Alice and Bob assign values to g and n (g = 2 and n = 3) and send them over the Internet where Eve can also intercept them.

In the following table you can see what information is needed for this algorithm to work. The table shows what information Alice knows, what Bob knows, and what Eve knows at each of the four steps in this process.

Step 1: Alice picks a value of 2 for xa, and Bob picks a value of 3 for xb; they do not share these values with anyone.

Step 2: Alice computes ya = 2^2 mod 3, which gives a value of 1. In this case, you take 2×2, which equals 4, and divide it by 3; the mod says to take the remainder, which in this example is 1.

Step 3: Bob computes yb = 2^3 mod 3, which yields a remainder of 2. Bob and Alice exchange ya and yb with each other.

Step 4: Alice now computes k = 2^2 mod 3, which yields 1. Bob computes k'=1^3 mod 3, which also yields 1. Both Bob and Alice were able to compute the same key, and poor Eve has no idea what the value is. For this example I used very small values, but in real life the values you pick for n and g could be 40 or 50 numbers long, making this scenario much more complex and secure.

Common Implementations of Symmetric Encryption

Common implementations of symmetric encryption include DES, which is no longer considered secure; Triple-DES, which is the de facto standard for symmetric encryption; and Rijndeal. Rijndeal is still being tested, but because it allows for variable key length, it will most likely replace Triple-DES.

Three common schemes are used as the basis of symmetric algorithms:

- Substitution
- Permutation
- XOR

Substitution

Substitution involves taking one letter and replacing it with another letter. In order for this scheme to work, there must be a one-to-one mapping between the letters. For example, if the letter A is replaced with the letter W, for this scheme to work no other letter can be replaced with the letter W. If you ignored the one-to-one mapping requirement and set it up so that both A and B were replaced by W, the encryption stage would work fine. The letter A would be replaced with W, and the letter B would be replaced with W. During decryption, it would not be possible to determine accurately which letter you would use to replace W.

STEP	ALICE	BOB	EVE
1	g = 2,n = 3	g = 2,n = 3	g = 2,n = 3
2	xa = 2	xb = 3	
3	ya = 1	ya = 1	ya = 1
4	yb = 2	yb = 2	yb = 2

Given this requirement for one-to-one mapping, take a look at a detailed example of substitution. For this example I'll use the following for a key:

A B C D E F G H I J K L M N O P Q R S T U V W X Y Z

H S N U W B J M T A V Y F Q L X D Z G P E R C O I K

The plaintext message for this example is HELLOWORLD. The encryption process converts this plaintext message to ciphertext by finding the letter on the top row and replacing it with the letter in the bottom row. H becomes M, E becomes W, and so on, so that HELLOWORLD becomes MWYYLCLZYU. To decrypt the information you would find the letter in the bottom row of the key and replace it with the top letter to retrieve the original plaintext message. Now M becomes H, W becomes E, and so on, so that MWYYLCLZYU becomes HELLOWORLD.

This is considered fairly weak encryption exactly because each letter is always encrypted to the same value. In the English language certain letters appear more often than others, so frequently appearing letters are likely to map to one of those. Also, look at the encrypted value MWYYLCLZYU very closely. Notice that there are two Y's next to each other; this indicates that there are two instances of the same letter appearing together. There are only a certain number of words that have the same letter repeated in sequence; this provides another clue to the cryptanalyst. Also notice that the letter Y appears three times and the letter L appears twice. All of this information can help in performing an analysis to crack the encryption.

Permutation

With substitution, one letter is replaced with another letter based on a mapping dictated by the key. With permutation, all of the letters in the plaintext message stay the same, they are just moved into different positions. Permutation is like taking five pieces from a game of Scrabble and spelling out the word HELLO. Imagine if you mixed up all of the pieces and put them back together in random order, say LEOHL. In effect you permutated the plaintext HELLO into the ciphertext LEOHL. In order to accurately decrypt the ciphertext, this permutation can't be random: You need to use a key to dictate the movement of letters.

For example, assume that the plaintext message is my name, ERICCOLE. E is in the first position, R is in the second position, I is in the third position, and so on. Also assume that the key is 47153826. This key shows where each letter in the plaintext message appears in the ciphertext. The encryption process uses the key to take the letter that is in the fourth position and place it in the first position. The seventh letter moves to the second position and so on, following the key. In this case the plaintext message ERICCOLE would be encrypted to CLECIERO.

The reverse process can be followed to decrypt the message. During decryption you would lay the key over the ciphertext, matching C to the fourth position, L to the seventh position, and so on, until you return the plaintext message.

Both substitution and permutation are fairly easy and straightforward to understand, which is a feature of symmetric encryption. In fact, most symmetric encryption is based on high-school-level mathematics.

> **NOTE** Although both substitution and permutation are relatively simple operations and easy to crack, when you combine these techniques and segment the input data into blocks it becomes increasingly more difficult to crack.

XOR

XOR is more robust than either permutation or substitution. XOR is a mathematical operation that has a unique property: It is performed at the binary level so that it requires converting a message into its binary equivalent. If you take a plaintext message and you XOR it with a key, you would get the ciphertext. If you XOR the ciphertext with the same key, you will get back the original plaintext message.

> **NOTE** XOR is a mathematical operation that takes two binary numbers as input and produces an output. If the two numbers are the same, the output is 0. If the two numbers are different, the output is 1.

To encrypt the word ERIC, you first translate it into binary using ASCII mapping. (An ASCII table can be found at www.asciitable.com/.) According to the ASCII table:

E–01000101

R–01010010

I–01001001

C–01000011

The key can be any value I want. The key I am going to use in this example is 11101101. Even though someone knows I am using XOR, if that person does not know the key, he or she cannot retrieve the original plaintext message.

INPUT VALUE 1	INPUT VALUE 2	RESULTS OR OUTPUT
0	0	0
0	1	1
1	0	1
1	1	0

Here's how XOR works: If the two values you are XORing are the same, the value is 0; if the two values are different, the value is 1. The following table is a cheat sheet for performing XOR.

Using the previous table, I can encrypt the information by performing XOR against each letter and the key.

The next chart shows each letter in binary form, followed by a space. In this example each letter is encrypted with the same key. The first line contains the plaintext, the second line contains the key, and the third line contains the ciphertext or the output of the XOR operation.

```
0 1 0 0 0 1 0 1 0 1 0 1 0 0 1 0 0 1 0 0 1 0 0 1   0 1 0 0 0 0 1 1
1 1 1 0 1 1 0 1 1 1 1 0 1 1 0 1 1 1 1 0 1 1 0 1   1 1 1 0 1 1 0 1
1 0 1 0 1 0 0 0 1 0 1 1 1 1 1 1 0 1 0 0 1 0 0 0   1 0 1 0 1 1 1 0
```

To see how XOR works, try decrypting the message. In the following chart the first line contains the ciphertext, the second line contains the key, and the third line shows the results of performing XOR on the first two lines, which produces the plaintext message. Notice that the last line in this table matches the first line in the previous table, showing that you successfully retrieved the binary representation of the message. You would then have to take that value, look it up in an ASCII table, and match it with the corresponding letters to get the original message.

```
1 0 1 0 1 0 0 0 1 0 1 1 1 1 1 1 0 1 0 0 1 0 0 1 0 1 0 1 1 1 0
1 1 1 0 1 1 0 1 1 1 1 0 1 1 0 1 1 1 1 0 1 1 0 1 1 1 1 0 1 1 0 1
0 1 0 0 0 1 0 1 0 1 0 1 0 0 1 0 0 1 0 0 1 0 0 1 0 1 0 0 0 0 1 1
```

XOR is a fairly powerful method of performing symmetric encryption. The trick with XOR, as with all symmetric encryption, is making sure that the key is long and that you keep it secure.

Asymmetric

Asymmetric encryption uses two keys: a public key and a private key. Whatever is encrypted with one key can be decrypted only with the other key. In this scenario, I give my public key out to the world so anyone can retrieve it. Then I keep my private key secure. When someone wants to send me an encrypted message that person encrypts it with my public key. Once it is encrypted with my public key it can be decrypted only with my private key.

This solves both the key exchange problem and the non-repudiation problem. Asymmetric encryption, though, is very slow.

The important thing to remember with asymmetric encryption is that the key does not have to be sent over a secure channel, but it does have to be sent over a trusted channel. A secure channel is one on which no one can read any information in transit. A trusted channel is one on which you can read information, but you are assured that the information comes from a trusted source and therefore has not been modified in transit. Asymmetric encryption requires a trusted channel because anyone can generate a key pair and spoof someone's public key. To minimize or reduce the chance of spoofing you have to have some level of confidence that the key came from the expected recipient.

How does asymmetric encryption solve the non-repudiation problem? Remember that with asymmetric encryption, anything encrypted with one key can be decrypted only with the second key. If I want to prove that I sent something I would encrypt it with my private key. By doing this, although anyone could read the message, only I could have sent it because the public key will work only on a message encrypted with my private key.

As you will see shortly, you can encrypt with your private key to achieve non-repudiation and also encrypt with the recipient's public key to achieve confidentiality.

NOTE Common implementations of asymmetric encryption used today are RSA and El Gamal. RSA, the most common implementation, works essentially like the Diffie-Hellman key exchange.

Hash

A hash algorithm is a one-way transformation of the plaintext message that cannot be reversed. A hash takes plaintext in any size and produces a smaller fixed-length output that is irreversible. Given the ciphertext, there is no way to produce the original plaintext message. Hash is useful for storing passwords and for digital signatures because there is no key.

At this point you may be asking, what good is ciphertext that you can't decrypt? Here's how it works. You run a customer password through the hash algorithm. The next time the user goes to log on, the system prompts for a password. The user enters it, and then the password is run through the hash algorithm and compared to the encrypted text. If they match, the user is granted access. If they don't match, the user is denied access.

Another use for hash is with digital signatures. A digital signature is added to a document with the sender's private key, so the recipient can use it for non-repudiation. Signing the entire message with the sender's private key will work, but is very inefficient because asymmetric encryption is very slow. Instead, because hash takes a message and produces a smaller, fixed-length output, it would make sense to run the message through a hash first, then encrypt the smaller output with the sender's private key. The less information that has to be encrypted, the quicker the process will go.

NOTE The following are the common implementations of hash in use today: MD5, MD4, HMAC, SHA.

Putting the Pieces Together

Now that you understand all of the different pieces of crypto, it's time to take a look at how these pieces might work together. For that we'll call on Bob and Alice again.

Assume that Alice wants to send Bob an order. Alice wants to make sure that no one can read the order and that it arrives unaltered; Bob wants to be able to prove in a court of law that Alice sent the message.

First, Alice takes the message and runs it through a hash to produce a smaller signature for the file. Alice signs the output of the hash with her private key. She then attaches the private key to the original message. Alice generates a session key (a unique symmetric key generated on the fly during encryption) and uses symmetric encryption to encrypt the message and digital signature. Alice then takes the session key, encrypts it with Bob's public key, attaches it to the encrypted message, and sends it to Bob.

CRYPTO SUBMERGED

Sometimes you don't even have to decrypt crypto to take advantage of its sender. During World War II the Germans used submarines called U-boats to sink Allied troop and supply ships. The Germans would bring the U-boats to the surface periodically to look for American ships. If they spotted a commercial vessel they would send out a flood of encrypted messages to all of the other U-boats in the area with the coordinates of the ship so they could converge and attack. The Americans quickly figured out that, even though they could not read the encrypted messages, the messages themselves would allow them to locate the source. They could then close in on the U-boats and attack.

Bob receives the message, finds the first portion, and decrypts it with his private key to obtain the session key. He then uses the session key to decrypt the message and digital signature. Next, Bob takes Alice's public key and uses it to decrypt the hash value that was encrypted with Alice's private key. (Remember that, to make sure no one modified the key, Alice encrypted the hash with her private key; Bob uses Alice's public key to retrieve the original hash value to be sure that no one modified it in transit.) Bob would then run the message he decrypted through the same hash and compare the two hashes. If the hashes match, not only can Bob prove that Alice sent the message, but he also knows the message was unaltered in transit.

This example shows how you would typically use all three types of crypto—symmetric, asymmetric, and hash—to achieve all of the goals of secure communication.

Using Cryptography Tools

To see crypto in action, take a look at two applications being used today. The first application is PGP, which allows you to use public and private keys to encrypt files and email. The second is SSH Secure Shell, which allows you to set up a secure encrypted link with a remote host. SSH is essentially a secure alternative to telnet.

Working with PGP

PGP, which stands for Pretty Good Privacy, is an application that allows you to encrypt files or email. PGP also has plug-ins for most email clients so that users can instantly encrypt email as it is sent out.

Generating a Privacy Key with PGP

To use PGP you have to create a new key pair. When you first open PGP it automatically starts the Key Creation wizard, which presents you with a screen describing key generations. Click Next to begin the wizard.

The screen that follows, shown in Figure 2.3, asks for your full name and the email address associated with the key you are creating. It's important to note that no validity check is done on this information. You can put in any name or email address you like, which makes it very easy to spoof keys.

After you've entered your name and email address, the next screen that appears is where you designate which type of encryption you want to use. You are given two options: Diffie-Hellman/DSS and RSA. Diffie-Hellman is the newer scheme, and the recommended choice, but either will do. Select one of the options, and proceed to the next step.

Now you need to pick the size of the key on the screen shown in Figure 2.4. Some people pick the largest key size possible because the longer the key, the harder it is to crack. The problem is that large keys are also harder to compute, which slows the process down. Based on the speeds of computers today and where technology is going, 2048 is a reasonable size to pick for a key.

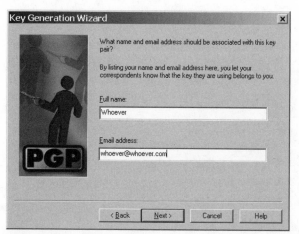

Figure 2.3 The first step in the process of generating a key is associating it with an email address.

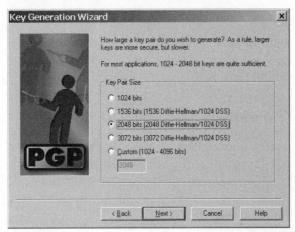

Figure 2.4   Note that you can also create a custom key size from this screen.

The next step in generating a key is to decide whether you want your key pair to never expire or to expire on a given date (see Figure 2.5). Keep in mind that what is considered secure today will not be secure tomorrow; therefore, your key pair should be changed at some time. Setting an expiration date that is a year or two from now can cause problems. If you forget about the date you entered and find that your key pair expires while you are in a foreign country, that might make it impossible to function securely. I prefer to have a key pair never expire; then every year I check my key and determine whether it is still valid. Check the option you prefer, and continue to the next step of the wizard.

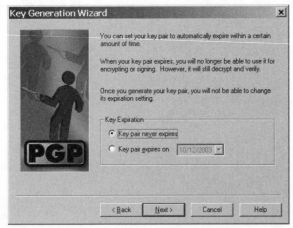

Figure 2.5   If you choose to set an expiration date, choose the date from the calendar field.

The next step involves keeping your private key secure. One way of doing this is to have a pass phrase or password that you must enter to unlock your private key. PGP uses a pass phrase because passwords are considered weak and pass phrases provide a higher level of protection. The pass phrase you enter here should be hard to guess and follow all the typical rules for hard-to-break passwords. PGP offers a pass phrase quality bar (see Figure 2.6); theoretically, when the bar indicates full strength you have a strong password. All that the bar measures, though, is the number of characters, not the overall strength.

When you have chosen your pass phrase click Next.

The system takes a couple of seconds or minutes (depending on the speed of your system) to calculate the key pair, and then it asks whether you want your key sent to an Internet server that stores PGP public keys. It is usually recommended that you send your public key to the server. This will allow others to be able to obtain your public key and communicate with you. (The more paranoid among you will be glad to know that the system will still function if you skip this step.)

When you make that choice and continue, the final wizard screen appears. Click Finish, and you're done.

You now have a key pair. You should send your public key to everyone who would want to communicate with you securely; however, make sure that you send it over a trusted channel and that you keep your private key private.

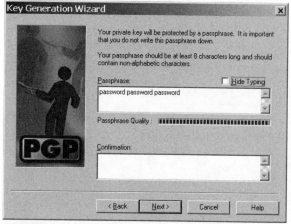

Figure 2.6 Here you can see that a fairly weak password came back with a full-strength password quality.

GEEK HEAVEN

There's an interesting story behind my preference for Diffie-Hellman mentioned in the previous example. I was presenting at a conference in California. When I finished my presentation about key generation and PGP we took a break. A woman came up to me at the break and started asking more detailed questions about Diffie-Hellman. Her badge was turned backward so that I could not see her name. After we chatted a while I asked her why she was so interested in Diffie-Hellman. She flipped over her badge, and I saw that her last name was Hellman. I just stared for a second, then asked if she were related to Martin Hellman (the Hellman in Diffie-Hellman). She responded that Martin Hellman was her father.

Being the geek that I am I asked if I could get his autograph. She agreed and took down my address, and I forgot all about it. Several months later I received an envelope and inside was an autographed picture of Martin Hellman that I keep up on my geek wall of fame. That's why I recommend Diffie-Hellman. If RSA (that is, Rivest, Shamir, and Adelman, the developers of RSA) want me to recommend their algorithm, they will have to send me an equally valuable autographed picture.

How PGP Works with Email

If you are using a supporting mail client such as Outlook, after you have created a private key, when you create a new mail message you will notice that new options are available, as shown in Figure 2.7. You now have additional tool buttons to use to encrypt and/or sign a message.

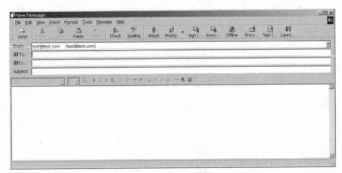

Figure 2.7 PGP automatically modifies Outlook to include encryption options for your email.

To give you a feel for the overhead involved in generating an encrypted message, take a look at a plaintext message and the resulting ciphertext message. The plaintext message is as follows:

Hello, how are you?

I hope all is well.

Take care.

Remember this is a test.
Encrypted with PGP this becomes the following:

```
-----BEGIN PGP MESSAGE-----
Version: PGPfreeware 6.5.8 for non-commercial use <http://www.pgp.com>

qANQR1DBwU4DTXSPVNDXY20QCACvoxAwIxg4mrwwvVE56cRkEhMes1sjJ1m+2nly
es+cmm4S51gUe/u6F5LhT15oxNCL3MKq85QThfoA6nkcw/rrOhD1rbNjYi2M3Q1P
Ej1ke5FfrvQeZYiCWE1rdA0KcqbQ+wMVjzFPwE7mJr64WGIC03u58MEJRxV5WxIj
KGxFf8DRtfMtTRfykoBr3c/X+7zPzTpx39Y7PVR6H1ar5ndMQ6phnLnkH7iHOSqm
7Kc8FSK6p66ohIpz3OOTGC8dcMvjPPjLYG0rZdqvJ8SZpRWkEdtzDO16C7MHfUzE
o/umS43G2XUZ+3TeI/kGp6g7Sm8+m1wsPeqKZT8b4tuV9Ee9B/9YYaw5tHIqTkc7
L14yORdjOJSRgiKwKQIYZbIAp/0rQK6vT4cfGOhdny6Mvdf3UF64164CCzQRu1sd
qcFoo7m/+8P/3pzg1fQh+97CG/CyM6Z6gA/AcfVv1s/M3Oh9w19nkhGVApH25984
G1ZXR4aPzCm+N3BxTQsUojD+i4rdWxZ1oKH6rK1QYRLSUNx1zPbouLzfFu2X+V4+
DdOmUtjCTFWfZkCq5vOffcIANy0ebgTYbwQA15ipNfYz8pzYunsNOm4drBnaNAxn
Kzk0bDJ6xwBCT/TtO1xkoi4Hy2ysHKF95preAIS6xIAST4fjxG5/Nn1p+d3Vxbj1
uH/IDouSyWHQpq0Kfw9qnzXQ6meI7x3stIPEnJWCPxTeeDwUBCK+mF6O3dNhvjE+
/1MsIKVq1qUCWg+TFBJfXdIkBkHBnb0iI6S21gP1MLLEKVQ3QW8fvfDvJVJW2J1D
vixiWtSKHSjx
=5B/s
-----END PGP MESSAGE-----
```

This message is encrypted with one key. Encrypting with additional keys increases the length.

Using SSH

SSH Secure Shell uses crypto to connect to a remote system and transfer information. Many people use a client program such as telnet to connect to a remote system. The problem with telnet is that all information is transferred in the clear, including the user ID and password. If anyone is sniffing the line (reading all of the traffic going over a network segment), not only can that person see everything you are doing, but he or she can acquire your user ID and password.

For remote access or access to critical devices such as firewalls or routers, having your user ID and password transferred in the clear is very dangerous and should be avoided at all costs. To understand this vulnerability, look at the sniffer output of a telnet session in which you can see the password being sent over the wire in plaintext. To save space, instead of showing the entire session, I am going to show the remote telnet server asking for the password and the user typing in the password. The letters in the password are in bold so you can spot them easily.

In the first packet you can see the system asking for the password. Then the user types in the password (which in this case is the word "password"). One letter is sent in each packet.

> **NOTE** Sending one character per packet is typical of Windows-based telnet programs. UNIX telnet programs usually send multiple characters per packet.

> **NOTE** I used Snort to generate the sniffer output for this example. Additional information on Snort can be found at www.snort.org.

```
=+=+=+=+=+=+=+=+=+=+=+=+=+=+=+=+=+=+=+=+=+=+=+=+=+=+=+=+=+=


10/01-13:13:52.552476 10.10.1.1:23 -> 10.10.200.200:2335
TCP TTL:52 TOS:0x0 ID:209 IpLen:20 DgmLen:66
***AP*** Seq: 0xA82D73AB Ack: 0x52B6695C Win: 0x400 TcpLen: 20
0x0000: 00 03 47 8C 73 0A 00 90 92 F8 80 00 08 00 45 00  ..G.s.........E.
0x0010: 00 42 00 D1 00 00 34 06 A6 B2 CD E8 6F 66 80 96  .B....4.....of..
0x0020: 21 4E 00 17 09 1F A8 2D 73 AB 52 B6 69 5C 50 18  !N.....-s.R.i\P.
0x0030: 04 00 77 DA 00 00 FF F9 FF FB 01 44 61 74 61 2D  ..w........Data-
0x0040: 4C 69 6E 6B 0D 0A 50 61 73 73 77 6F 72 64 3A 20  Link..Password:

=+=+=+=+=+=+=+=+=+=+=+=+=+=+=+=+=+=+=+=+=+=+=+=+=+=+=+=+=+=


10/01-13:14:00.614837 10.10.200.200:2335 -> 10.10.1.1:23
TCP TTL:128 TOS:0x0 ID:15707 IpLen:20 DgmLen:41 DF
***AP*** Seq: 0x52B6695F Ack: 0xA82D73C8 Win: 0x3FEB TcpLen: 20
0x0000: 00 90 92 F8 80 00 00 03 47 8C 73 0A 08 00 45 00  ........G.s...E.
0x0010: 00 29 3D 5B 40 00 80 06 00 00 80 96 21 4E CD E8  .)=[@.......!N..
0x0020: 6F 66 09 1F 00 17 52 B6 69 5F A8 2D 73 C8 50 18  of....R.i_.-s.P.
0x0030: 3F EB DF 4E 00 00 70         ?..N..p

=+=+=+=+=+=+=+=+=+=+=+=+=+=+=+=+=+=+=+=+=+=+=+=+=+=+=+=+=+=


10/01-13:14:01.080644 10.10.200.200:2335 -> 10.10.1.1:23
TCP TTL:128 TOS:0x0 ID:15709 IpLen:20 DgmLen:41 DF
***AP*** Seq: 0x52B66960 Ack: 0xA82D73C8 Win: 0x3FEB TcpLen: 20
0x0000: 00 90 92 F8 80 00 00 03 47 8C 73 0A 08 00 45 00  ........G.s...E.
0x0010: 00 29 3D 5D 40 00 80 06 00 00 80 96 21 4E CD E8  .)=]@.......!N..
0x0020: 6F 66 09 1F 00 17 52 B6 69 60 A8 2D 73 C8 50 18  of....R.i`.-s.P.
```

```
0x0030: 3F EB DF 4E 00 00 61         ?..N..a
```

=+=

```
10/01-13:14:01.367385 10.10.200.200:2335 -> 10.10.1.1:23
TCP TTL:128 TOS:0x0 ID:15710 IpLen:20 DgmLen:41 DF
***AP*** Seq: 0x52B66961 Ack: 0xA82D73C8 Win: 0x3FEB TcpLen: 20
0x0000: 00 90 92 F8 80 00 00 03 47 8C 73 0A 08 00 45 00  ........G.s...E.
0x0010: 00 29 3D 5E 40 00 80 06 00 00 80 96 21 4E CD E8  .)=^@.......!N..
0x0020: 6F 66 09 1F 00 17 52 B6 69 61 A8 2D 73 C8 50 18  of....R.ia.-s.P.
0x0030: 3F EB DF 4E 00 00 73         ?..N..s
```

=+=

```
10/01-13:14:01.606404 10.10.200.200:2335 -> 10.10.1.1:23
TCP TTL:128 TOS:0x0 ID:15711 IpLen:20 DgmLen:41 DF
***AP*** Seq: 0x52B66962 Ack: 0xA82D73C8 Win: 0x3FEB TcpLen: 20
0x0000: 00 90 92 F8 80 00 00 03 47 8C 73 0A 08 00 45 00  ........G.s...E.
0x0010: 00 29 3D 5F 40 00 80 06 00 00 80 96 21 4E CD E8  .)=_@.......!N..
0x0020: 6F 66 09 1F 00 17 52 B6 69 62 A8 2D 73 C8 50 18  of....R.ib.-s.P.
0x0030: 3F EB DF 4E 00 00 73         ?..N.. s
```

=+=

```
10/01-13:14:01.825372 10.10.200.200:2335 -> 10.10.1.1:23
TCP TTL:128 TOS:0x0 ID:15712 IpLen:20 DgmLen:41 DF
***AP*** Seq: 0x52B66963 Ack: 0xA82D73C8 Win: 0x3FEB TcpLen: 20
0x0000: 00 90 92 F8 80 00 00 03 47 8C 73 0A 08 00 45 00  ........G.s...E.
0x0010: 00 29 3D 60 40 00 80 06 00 00 80 96 21 4E CD E8  .)=`@.......!N..
0x0020: 6F 66 09 1F 00 17 52 B6 69 63 A8 2D 73 C8 50 18  of....R.ic.-s.P.
0x0030: 3F EB DF 4E 00 00 77         ?..N..w
```

=+=

```
10/01-13:14:02.060036 10.10.200.200:2335 -> 10.10.1.1:23
TCP TTL:128 TOS:0x0 ID:15714 IpLen:20 DgmLen:41 DF
***AP*** Seq: 0x52B66964 Ack: 0xA82D73C8 Win: 0x3FEB TcpLen: 20
0x0000: 00 90 92 F8 80 00 00 03 47 8C 73 0A 08 00 45 00  ........G.s...E.
0x0010: 00 29 3D 62 40 00 80 06 00 00 80 96 21 4E CD E8  .)=b@.......!N..
0x0020: 6F 66 09 1F 00 17 52 B6 69 64 A8 2D 73 C8 50 18  of....R.id.-s.P.
0x0030: 3F EB DF 4E 00 00 6F         ?..N..o
```

=+=

```
10/01-13:14:02.264669 10.10.200.200:2335 -> 10.10.1.1:23
TCP TTL:128 TOS:0x0 ID:15716 IpLen:20 DgmLen:41 DF
***AP*** Seq: 0x52B66965 Ack: 0xA82D73C8 Win: 0x3FEB TcpLen: 20
0x0000: 00 90 92 F8 80 00 00 03 47 8C 73 0A 08 00 45 00  ........G.s...E.
0x0010: 00 29 3D 64 40 00 80 06 00 00 80 96 21 4E CD E8  .)=d@.......!N..
0x0020: 6F 66 09 1F 00 17 52 B6 69 65 A8 2D 73 C8 50 18  of....R.ie.-s.P.
0x0030: 3F EB DF 4E 00 00 72         ?..N..r
```

=+=

```
10/01-13:14:02.486194 10.10.200.200:2335 -> 10.10.1.1:23
TCP TTL:128 TOS:0x0 ID:15717 IpLen:20 DgmLen:41 DF
***AP*** Seq: 0x52B66966 Ack: 0xA82D73C8 Win: 0x3FEB TcpLen: 20
0x0000: 00 90 92 F8 80 00 00 03 47 8C 73 0A 08 00 45 00 .......G.s...E.
0x0010: 00 29 3D 65 40 00 80 06 00 00 80 96 21 4E CD E8 .)=e@.......!N..
0x0020: 6F 66 09 1F 00 17 52 B6 69 66 A8 2D 73 C8 50 18 of....R.if.-s.P.
0x0030: 3F EB DF 4E 00 00 64         ?..N..d
```

=+=

If you took the same example but connected to a remote system using SSH, the information is all encrypted, and you cannot read the password or any other information being sent. To conserve space I will show only a couple of packets, but you can see that the password is no longer visible.

```
=+=+=+=+=+=+=+=+=+=+=+=+=+=+=+=+=+=+=+=+=+=+=+=+=+=+=+=+=+=+
10/12-12:13:27.988999 10.10.1.1:22 -> 10.10.200.200:2012
TCP TTL:48 TOS:0x0 ID:10234 IpLen:20 DgmLen:72 DF
***AP*** Seq: 0x4F7DC3C7 Ack: 0x8D8BC9FA Win: 0x1D50 TcpLen: 20
0x0000: 00 A0 F8 2E A1 11 00 D0 B7 13 CB E5 08 00 45 00 ..............E.
0x0010: 00 48 27 FA 40 00 30 06 34 88 CE EF 0B 19 AC 11 .H'.@.0.4.......
0x0020: 68 14 00 16 07 DC 4F 7D C3 C7 8D 8B C9 FA 50 18 h.....O}......P.
0x0030: 1D 50 D7 F5 00 00 BF 18 B0 BC 01 97 4E C4 F2 D0 .P..........N...
0x0040: AB DF D2 77 B7 81 57 30 3E ED 3D 25 8E 65 42 D4 ...w..W0>.=%.eB.
0x0050: F3 17 40 1E 98 ED         ..@...

=+=+=+=+=+=+=+=+=+=+=+=+=+=+=+=+=+=+=+=+=+=+=+=+=+=+=+=+=+=+
10/12-12:13:28.024458 10.10.1.1:22 -> 10.10.200.200:2012
TCP TTL:48 TOS:0x0 ID:10235 IpLen:20 DgmLen:88 DF
***AP*** Seq: 0x4F7DC3E7 Ack: 0x8D8BCA3A Win: 0x1D50 TcpLen: 20
0x0000: 00 A0 F8 2E A1 11 00 D0 B7 13 CB E5 08 00 45 00 ..............E.
0x0010: 00 58 27 FB 40 00 30 06 34 77 CE EF 0B 19 AC 11 .X'.@.0.4w......
0x0020: 68 14 00 16 07 DC 4F 7D C3 E7 8D 8B CA 3A 50 18 h.....O}.....:P.
0x0030: 1D 50 CF 8A 00 00 23 CB 7F FD 75 8E 3B 50 F8 D4 .P....#...u.;P..
0x0040: 29 3F 0B BF E4 7B C1 BE C1 9B CC 2A 87 96 6F 20 )?...{.....*..o
0x0050: B3 EB 77 C7 C7 96 6A ED 9E E4 F4 FE 4E ED 93 08 ..w...j.....N...
0x0060: CA F0 AB 53 69 EE         ...Si.

=+=+=+=+=+=+=+=+=+=+=+=+=+=+=+=+=+=+=+=+=+=+=+=+=+=+=+=+=+=+
10/12-12:13:28.063778 10.10.1.1:22 -> 10.10.200.200:2012
TCP TTL:48 TOS:0x0 ID:10236 IpLen:20 DgmLen:72 DF
***AP*** Seq: 0x4F7DC417 Ack: 0x8D8BCA7A Win: 0x1D50 TcpLen: 20
0x0000: 00 A0 F8 2E A1 11 00 D0 B7 13 CB E5 08 00 45 00 ..............E.
0x0010: 00 48 27 FC 40 00 30 06 34 86 CE EF 0B 19 AC 11 .H'.@.0.4.......
```

```
0x0020: 68 14 00 16 07 DC 4F 7D C4 17 8D 8B CA 7A 50 18  h.....O}.....zP.
0x0030: 1D 50 5A CC 00 00 82 DF 30 AC 95 FF 21 9C 7E 35  .PZ.....0...!.~5
0x0040: 9B 29 0D 7C A8 06 C0 33 3A C7 84 8F 8A 2B 7C B6  .).|...3:....+|.
0x0050: 0C 79 30 9B D8 4A         .y0..J
```

=+=

Essentially, you set up an SSH session with a remote system. The SSH session is like an encrypted tunnel within the remote system. Over that encrypted tunnel you can send email (SMTP), Web (HTTP), or any other traffic you wish. This is done at the protocol level.

There are many programs you can use to set up an SSH session with a remote system. The program that I like to use is called Secure CRT. To set up an encrypted channel within a remote system using Secure CRT you would choose the option to set up a new session on the opening screen. The screen shown in Figure 2.8 then appears.

For a general session you put in a hostname (for example, securityhaven.com) or an IP address (such as 10.10.10.5), plus a username. When you connect to the system you will be prompted for a password. Once you enter it, you will be connected to the remote system via an encrypted channel. As you can see in Figure 2.8, there are a lot of categories of options you can configure for SSH, but for most connections, the defaults are acceptable.

Because setting up an SSH session is so easy, there is really no reason for you to use telnet again.

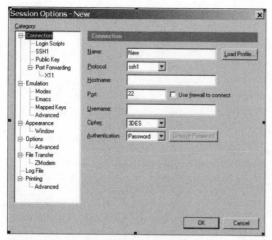

Figure 2.8 Default choices here work for most people.

Looking Ahead

Cryptography is a fairly complex subject. This chapter was included to give you a sort of Cliffs Notes version of an important topic that will help you to view steganography in the context of the broader universe of secret communication. This information also provides a foundation for understanding the examples of crypto and stego used in concert cited throughout this book.

In Chapter 3, you'll learn more about the history of steganography, how it works, and how it's being used in the world today.

Hiding the Goods with Steganography

You have to send a message with extremely sensitive content to a colleague. How can you guarantee that no one else can read the message as it's being transmitted? How can you be sure that no one has modified the message as it is being sent? How can your colleague know that the message is really from you? These are some of the questions at the heart of the use of secret and secure communications.

There are two ways to address these questions. One method is to encipher the message in such a way that no one else can read it. In this case, people may be able to tell that a secret message is being transmitted; they just can't read the message. The second method is to hide the very fact that a message is being transmitted. This can be done with invisible ink or by placing the true message in a nonsuspicious message. The first method relies on cryptography, and the second method relies on steganography. Both techniques are useful in covert communication, but each serves a different purpose. Cryptography provides the means for secure communications; steganography provides the means for secret communication.

In the previous chapter, you learned the basics of cryptography and its benefits. In this chapter, you'll take a detailed look at steganography and compare how the two technologies sometimes became strange bedfellows in the world of covert communication.

HIDDEN FELONY

Margaret is the CEO of a successful company. Occasionally over martinis after a long day she and a couple of colleagues who run their own thriving companies compare notes about future business strategies. Sometimes they buy each other's stock based on this information. That's called insider trading, and it's against the law.

Eventually the activity escalates along with their greed. Wary of being caught, a handful of them work out a scheme for more safely communicating about potential windfalls or losses in their companies before this news is announced to the public. There is a picture of each CEO on their respective Web sites. Each is located on a page of the site that is seldom changed by their Webmasters. The executives recruit a hacker with no relationship to any of them to go into their sites periodically and switch their pictures: A picture with a green background will contain a financial report embedded in the image that can be downloaded and extracted using steganography software. A picture with a brown background has no secret communication. The pictures look similar enough to anyone not in on the scheme that their Webmasters never notice the change. Now the parties have a covert way to communicate, with minimal traceability between them. And, at least for a while, their illegal activities will go unnoticed and unpunished.

Overview of Steganography

This story involved the use of steganography, which you learned in Chapter 1 is data hiding, the technique of hiding a secret message in often publicly available data. With steganography, the sender of a message would hide it in a *host file*. The host file, or *overt message*, is the file that anyone can see.

When people use steganography, they often hide the true intent for communicating in a more commonplace communication scenario. For example, two people might be fans of classic cars. They could exchange pictures of classic cars and not look suspicious, when in reality they are passing their plans to take over a company, hidden in the images of the cars. The key to the success of this plan is that the two parties must have a reason for communicating so that nobody monitoring their communication suspects them. If somebody knew the two and knew that they had no interest in classic cars, that person might become suspicious about their motives.

It should be noted that if the open exchange either becomes significantly more frequent or correlates closely with other events, this could tip someone off to what's going on. For example, two coworkers normally exchange 2 or so emails per week, but during one week they exchange 20 emails. The next week there is a shortfall in the company books. If this pattern continues, someone could start to tie the two parties together and infer that they are embezzling from the company.

Just as with encryption, two people using steganography must agree on the algorithm they are going to use and exchange this algorithm prior to communicating. The steganography algorithm is a mathematical formula used to place bits of data in another file, and then used again to extract those bits back into their original order. It is often not a particularly complex formula.

Imagine an algorithm as being like a piece of cardboard that has certain squares cut out. When you place this template over a text message, the characters of the message that appear in the cut-out squares reveal the secret message. In one sense, this cardboard template serves the function of a computer algorithm: It offers a guide to placing and extracting hidden data. In steganography running such an algorithm would take a *covert* message and embed it in an *overt* file to hide the data.

For example, look at a simple algorithm. This algorithm embeds data in a text document. The algorithm takes the covert message (in binary form) one bit and a time, and starting at the beginning of the overt text document, it finds the end of the first sentence. If the binary bit from the covert file is a 1, the algorithm places a period at the end of the sentence. If the binary bit from the covert file is a 0, the end of the sentence would then have an exclamation mark. The algorithm then moves on to the next sentence in the overt file to continue the process. To extract the hidden message the algorithm goes to each sentence. If there is a period it inserts a 1 into the file, and if there is an exclamation mark it inserts a 0, thereby recreating the covert file.

The Growth of Steganography

Steganography is a technology where modern data compression, information theory, spread spectrum, and cryptography technologies are brought together to satisfy the need for privacy on the Internet.

Although some electronic (computer-based) steganography references can be found before 1995, most of the interest and action in the field has occurred since 2000. Research reporting in the literature, news reports and press releases, start-up stego software companies, and entry into the field by large, established technology firms have all been recent trends. Steganography methods themselves are rapidly evolving and becoming increasingly sophisticated.

Steganography has become a hot topic on the Internet in the context of electronic privacy and copyright protection. The Deja News search engine allows you to query the Internet's large number of newsgroups for specific keywords.

Newsgroup postings related to steganography started at fewer than 10 per month in early 1995, grew to more than 40 per month in late 1996, and and reached more than 100 per month in 1998. As I write this book, there are well over a thousand queries per month. The fact is that interest in steganography has exploded over the past few years.

This trend is even more pronounced on the World Wide Web. In 1995, a search using steganography as a keyword produced fewer than a dozen responses. In 1996, the same query produced about 500 hits. In 1998, such a search produced well over a thousand hits. Today, the results are closer to 10,000 hits.

Several researchers are experimenting with different steganography methods and seem driven by the perception that there is the potential to make money. Even though there are early entrepreneurial digital watermarking service offerings, the field is also attracting the attention of several large corporations (for example, IBM, NEC, and Kodak). The field seems poised for rapid growth.

Steganography in Use

Most companies are more concerned with security of information than they are with secrecy. Therefore, they have explored the benefits of encryption, but less so those of steganography. In fact, when communication about highly confidential topics is needed, steganography combined with cryptography would be the most secure way to go. Because the mere existence of an encrypted communication draws attention to it, hiding it in another file ups your security level substantially.

> **NOTE** There are several foreign countries where the use of cryptography is actually illegal. Add to that the debate occurring over export controls on encryption, and steganography may be a logical recourse for hiding transmission of encrypted data in certain parts of the world.

Stego is a very powerful tool if two people can be tied together by a communication path. For example, if an American businessman is in France on a business trip and he communicates with his home office, that wouldn't look suspicious or draw attention. If, however, the businessman sends frequent communications to somebody at a competing company with whom he shouldn't be communicating, suspicion would be raised and somebody might start looking for messages hidden within messages.

Look at another example. Let's say someone is working for the CIA and is a spy for the Russians; the mere fact that this person is communicating with the Russian Embassy on a regular basis is extremely suspicious. Does that mean he can't use stego? He can, but he'll have to get a little more creative. In this case he could post his message to one of numerous newsgroups, bulletin boards, or FTP sites that exist across the Internet. He would hide his message in an innocent-looking file and post that to a public location. His contact at the Russian Embassy would go to that site, download the message, extract the hidden message, and read it.

This concept is referred to as a *digital dead drop,* and it might take the form of a phony email address or public location online. Dead drops have long been used in criminal or espionage activity where two parties cannot meet in person. Instead, they arrange a time and place where one party drops off a message or package, and the other party picks it up. For example, if you were an organized crime hit man and I needed to provide the name and location of a target to you, I might go to a particular restaurant and tape a message on the bottom of a specific table. No one else would be able to see it, but when you arrived at the restaurant you would quietly reach under the table and remove the message.

In situations where parties cannot be seen communicating, combining stego with digital dead drops provides an elegant solution.

Flaws of Steganography

Of course, steganography is not perfect—no security technology is. Even though a message is hidden by stego, if someone knows it is there and knows the algorithm that was used to hide it, and if the message is not encrypted, he or she can read it. Even if the message is encrypted, in some cases just knowing that data has been hidden in a file is enough to raise suspicions.

Another problem with stego is that, if someone thinks you are using stego, he or she could easily destroy any hidden message without destroying the host file. Here's how. In most cases, when you hide data in an image you insert your message into the least significant bits. An easy way to destroy that information is to convert it to another format and either leave it in that format or convert it back to the original format. If the bit composition changes even slightly, your message will be destroyed. So, if you have embedded a message in a JPEG image and you convert it to TIFF, then back to JPEG, even though the image looks exactly the same to the human eye, the actual bit composition of the image is different.

DETECTING TERROR

Jenna Davidson, a special agent with the FBI, was uneasy about bringing the young cryptanalyst named Steve Biggs into the case because what was at stake was so hush-hush. Even in early 1999, everybody was getting really sensitive about anything to do with terrorism.

But Jenna had an instinct about all the images she'd downloaded from the suspect Web site. She figured if this guy from the computer analysis group could just help her figure out if some kind of data was hidden in them, she could contact the NSA to actually decrypt it.

Jenna and her partner had spent days monitoring the Web site, rumored to be maintained by a terrorist group known to be responsible for the bombing of a U.S. consulate the year before. Every hour for days on end they had pulled down the opening image on the Web site and saved it. Now she called Steve in to look over the 350 or so images and tell her if there was any variation among them.

The next day her phone rang, and it was Steve with the results. What he told her gave Jenna the chills. Almost every image was slightly different from the one before. The differences were usually in the most insignificant bits in the files, and when he pulled the data out of one it was encrypted. That meant that as often as every hour somebody somewhere was transmitting hidden data to members of the terrorist group who could access it from anywhere in the world.

Jenna thanked Steve for his work and told him to destroy his copy of the files then and there. Then she dialed her contact at the NSA to arrange for somebody in that super-secretive group to take the images and figure out exactly what the terrorists were saying to each other.

Variations on Stego

There is sometimes confusion about how steganography differs from some other technologies, such as Trojan horses or Easter eggs. Pure steganography includes the motive of hiding data for the purpose of communicating it to somebody. In that sense, Trojan horses and Easter eggs are subsets of steganography, even though the recipient may not always be happy to discover what's hidden.

Trojan Horses

Trojan horse programs are often used by attackers to sneak viruses or other types of malicious code into an organization. To do this, a Trojan horse has an overt and a covert program. The overt program is what the user sees, such as a game or animation; the covert program is what is installed in the background that the user cannot see. The covert program is usually the virus or some malicious back-door program that the attacker wants to install on a system to gain entrance to it.

Trojan horse programs are similar to traditional stego in that there is an overt and covert feature, and the program runs in such a way that the true intent of the program is hidden from the user.

Trojan horse programs are slightly different from traditional steganography in that, with stego, one party manually puts the secret message in a file and the other party has to extract it manually. There is no way to have the content automatically run when it gets to the recipient. Stego uses the overt file as simply a place to put a payload, but the payload is passive. In this sense, Trojan horses are a specialized subset of stego because they can be hidden only in executable files and will always actively do something against the destination host.

Another big difference between Trojan horse programs and stego is the intent of the communication. With stego, there have to be two parties involved, the sender and the receiver. Both of these parties are aware of the scheme and are using stego to bypass some third-party observer. With Trojan horse programs, there is only one person who is aware of what is happening: the attacker or the sender of the malicious code. The recipient has no idea of what is happening and has no idea of the true intent of the communication.

Covert Channels

When two parties communicate covertly over normal communication channels they are, in essence, using covert channels of communication. The goal is to use normal data objects but modify them slightly so that they can be used to communicate information secretly; however, the modification should not make the object being sent over the channel look unusual. Covert channels are considered a subclass of stego.

With covert channels two parties would use resources that are available to them to signal to each other without anyone else knowing they are communicating. In the noncomputer world, an example of a covert channel would be the potted plant placed on his balcony by FBI Agent Fox Mulder in the *X-Files* to signal to a source that he needs to meet at an agreed-upon place to discuss a case.

In the realm of computers, covert channels work similarly.

Let's say Bill and Michelle work for the same government agency and have been secretly meeting for lunch to discuss their plans to steal and sell state secrets. They know that if they were seen leaving the office together it would arouse suspicion. They also know that their agency monitors all communication and that encrypted messages are not allowed.

Because they work for the same organization they both have access to the same file server. On the file server are several folders, including one called Research. Each research project file in this folder has a code name. Everyone in the agency can see all of the files; they just can't access them because they are password protected. Bill and Michelle come up with a plan; they agree that if a project file called Alpha1 appears on the server in the Research folder, they will meet that day in an agreed-upon spot in an out-of-the-way Washington, D.C. park.

Covert channels are similar to stego in that both parties know they are communicating and what they are communicating is known only to them. The big difference is that no overt file is used. Normal data is transmitted, and the covert message is not actually hidden as with traditional stego. The hidden message is the use of the covert channel itself.

Easter Eggs

Easter eggs are a hybrid between Trojan horses and stego. An Easter egg is a hidden "feature" such as an animation or video that developers of an operating system or application sneak into a program. At some point in time the programmers reveal the existence of the Easter egg to the public. Easter eggs are usually just for fun.

NOTE More than 6,000 different Easter eggs for a variety of operating systems and application can be found at www.eeggs.com.

Easter eggs operate very similarly to stego in that someone inserts the covert data into the overt program and someone has to follow a specific set of steps to remove it. These steps usually involve opening up an application, going to a certain area of it, and typing specific words or commands. Other common Easter eggs involve making a modification to an application's configuration file and then starting up the application. The intent is not malicious, as with most Trojan horses, and these programs do not automatically run without the user's consent.

Hardware Keys

A big problem that software developers have is copy protection of their software. There is nothing stopping someone from making a copy of a piece of software and giving it to 20 other people or installing a single copy on dozens of computers.

One technique that has been used to stop these practices incorporates a hardware key (called a *dongle*) that has to be connected to the back of the computer, usually through the parallel port, to run the software. This works, but it is inconvenient for the end user. In addition, these hardware devices can be replicated.

An alternative approach is to use a software dongle. In this scenario, a program that can be run only once inserts some hidden information on the hard drive, usually in a hidden sector so that it cannot easily be copied. When the actual software program is being installed, it looks for the hidden information. If it finds it, the software gets installed; if the software doesn't find the file, the program will not be installed.

This software-based steganography provides a nice solution to limiting the number of installations of a piece of software.

Security and Steganography

Computer and network security have certain core standards that any secret communication method should address. Though no one method addresses all security requirements, steganography does satisfy several of these requirements, sometimes in conjunction with other technologies such as crypto.

Confidentiality

Confidentiality is a basic aspect of network security; it deals with keeping your secrets secret and making sure that any unauthorized person cannot gain access to or read information on your network.

Confidentiality is at the heart of what steganography does. Steganography, though, accomplishes confidentiality in a slightly different manner than cryptography. With cryptography, an unauthorized person can see the information but cannot access it. Because he or she can tell that there is information being protected, the unauthorized person may try to break the encryption. With steganography, because the data is hidden, any unauthorized party does not even know there is sensitive data there. From a confidentiality standpoint, steganography keeps the information protected at a higher level.

Survivability

The main activity of communication is that one party transmits information and the other party receives it. The completion of this cycle represents the feature of survivability. Even when data is being hidden in a message you have to be sure that whatever processing of the data takes place between sender and receiver does not destroy the information. You must ensure that the information is not only received by the recipient, but also extracted so that the message can be read. When using steganography it is critical to understand the processing a message will go through and determine whether the hidden message has a high chance of survivability across a network.

Look at a nontechnical example of low message survivability. Phil wants to communicate with Mary so he creates 20 postcards with numbers written on them. The message is encoded based on the order in which the postcards are sent. Phil puts the postcards in the correct order to reveal the message he wants to communicate. He goes to the post office and every hour he mails out a postcard. From Phil's perspective the post cards were mailed in the correct order to reveal his secret message to Mary. The chance that these postcards will arrive in the same order in which they were sent, though, is very low. Therefore, even though this technique uses a form of steganography, it has a very low survivability and therefore should not be used to communicate hidden messages.

This technique can be adjusted to increase the survivability. What if Phil mails one postcard a day? This increases the survivability a little, but it is still not ideal. What if he mails a postcard once a week? Now he is approaching a more acceptable level of survivability. If Phil sends one postcard a month there would be a very high survivability rate; however this method is very impractical because sending one postcard a month would take years to get the message across to Mary. Even though there are things you can do to increase survivability you have to make sure that the end result is practical.

For a technical example of survivability, look at some methods used to hide information in TCP/IP headers. If my technique is going to be used on a local network and will not pass through any routers, then I can use the TTL (or time to live) field to hide my information. If I then take this technique and use it across the Internet, I will have a survivability issue because each router will decrement the TTL by 1. For greater survivability, I could use a field such as the IP ID because this field does not get modified as it is processed by routers.

No Detection

It makes no sense to perform data hiding if someone can figure out how or where the information is hidden. If someone can easily detect where you hid your information and find your message, it defeats the purpose of using steganography. The way that steganography is usually performed to make it hard to find the hidden data is to do it in such a way that there is little change to the properties of host file.

Therefore, the algorithm that is used must be robust enough that, even if someone knows how the technique works, he or she cannot easily find out that you have hidden data in a given file. A robust algorithm is one where the insertion method is hard to detect and hard to destroy.

Visibility

When you hide data you want it to be undetectable, so you must make sure that people can't see any visible changes to the host file in which the data is hidden. If I hide a secret message in an image and it distorts the image in such a way that someone can tell it has been modified, my steganography has been unsuccessful.

For example, I take a Word document that contains one page of text and is 200k in size, and I hide my data in the file, making the size of the file 20MB. Anybody can clearly see that there is something very unusual about that file. Drawing attention to a file because of some discernible characteristic defeats the purpose of using steganography in the first place.

Principles of Steganography

Steganography involves hiding data in an overt message and doing it in such a way that it is difficult for an adversary to detect and difficult for an adversary to remove. Based on this goal, three core principles can be used to measure the effectiveness of a given steganography technique: amount of data, difficulty of detection, and difficulty of removal.

- Amount of data suggests that the more data you can hide, the better the technique.
- Difficulty of detection relates to how easy it is for somebody to detect that a message has been hidden. There is usually a direct relationship between how much data can be hidden and how easy it is for someone to detect it. As you increase the amount of information that is hidden in a file, you increase the chance that someone will be able to detect that there is information hidden in the file.
- Difficulty of removal involves the principle that someone intercepting your file should not be able to remove the hidden data easily.

Types of Steganography

There are two general ways in which you can categorize steganography techniques: by type of host file and by how the data has been hidden. This section briefly looks at these two categories; they will be covered in more detail in Chapter 6.

File Type

File type categorization breaks down steganography based on the type of host or overt file in which the data is hidden. Different file formats have different properties that control how the data can be hidden in the file. For example, most techniques for hiding data in .bmp images place the information in the least significant bits of each pixel. How you pick the bits to use varies somewhat, but most techniques work in a very similar manner. Because of this, knowing the host file type can give you an idea of where the data might be hidden.

NOTE Categorizing stego techniques based on the hidden file type is not useful because you are always hiding binary information. Whether that binary information is an .exe or .doc file does not really matter, nor does it provide a relevant way of characterizing stego techniques.

Method of Hiding

Breaking down stego techniques based on hiding method is the preferred approach. There are essentially three ways to hide data: injection, substitution, and generation.

- *Injection* finds areas in a file that will be ignored and puts your covert message in those areas. For example, most files contain an EOF or end-of-file marker. When playing an audio file, the application that is playing the file will stop playing when it reaches the EOF because it thinks it is the end of the file. You can inject data after the EOF marker that does not have an effect on the sound of the file.

- *Substitution* finds insignificant information in the host file and replaces it with your covert data. For example, with sound files each unit of sound you hear is composed of several bytes. If you modify the least significant bit it will slightly modify the sound, but so slightly that the human ear cannot tell the difference.

- *Generation* creates a new overt file based on the information that is contained in the covert message. For example, one generation technique will take your covert file and produce a picture that resembles a modern painting. This is done by substituting a patch of green for every 0 and substituting a patch of yellow for every 1. The picture is created solely based on the bit sequence of the covert file.

The different types of steganography based on the method of hiding are discussed in greater detail in Chapter 6.

Hands-on Steganography

At this point it would be helpful to walk through a simple example of designing a basic stego technique so that you can see exactly how you hide data in a file.

As you know by now, stego requires two files, a covert file and an overt file. I'll begin with the covert or secret message. Anything that you hide needs to be translated into binary. I'll use an encoding scheme that takes the ASCII equivalent to text and converts it to binary. To keep it simple, I'll create a covert message of HI. The letter H is 48 hex and I is 49 hex. Converting 48 to binary it becomes 01001000 and 49 becomes 01001001. Putting the two pieces together yields this covert message, where the series of bits on the left correspond to the letter H and the bits on the right correspond to the letter I:

0100100001001001

For the overt file I'll use a .wav file. It's important that you understand how an audio file is constructed. First, a bleep is a given pitch that lasts for a half second. You put enough of these bleeps together, and you can produce music and sounds. Each bleep is made up of eight bits, so a given bleep would look like this:

11010001

Audio files are created by stringing a bunch of these individual bleeps together to form a song. The left-most bit is the most significant bit or the one that is most audible to the human ear, and the right-most bit is the least significant and least audible. If you change the left-most bit it will have a significant impact on the pitch. If you change the right-most bit it will have minimal impact. In fact, you can change the two least significant bits and have a minimal impact on the overall sound.

The basic stego technique would take the 2 least significant bits from each bleep and replace it with 2 bits from the hidden message. To hide a 16-bit message you would need to find 8 bleeps and overwrite the least significant 2 bits of each bleep with a message. Though this is not a highly elegant solution, it can be fairly effective and shows you a basic steganography technique.

Putting All the Pieces Together

Because cryptography and steganography complement each other, it is usually recommended that they be used together for a higher level of security. After a secret message is written, it would first be encrypted, then hidden in a host file.

It should be noted that by using an encrypted message, though the message may be more secure, it could make the steganography technique more detectable. Here's how this works. It is fairly easy to determine whether a given segment of text is encrypted by plotting a *histogram* (a graph that depicts how often each character appears). Figure 3.1 shows a plot of nonencrypted ASCII text, and Figure 3.2 shows a plot of encrypted ASCII text. In these graphs, the y axis is frequency and the x axis is the ASCII value for each character.

The nonencrypted text has values of zero except at 10, which is line feed, 13, which is carriage return, 32, which is a space, and 97-122, which is a-z. The encrypted text, however, is equally distributed across all ranges and has a fairly flat distribution. It is also interesting to point out that for nonencrypted text, the highest frequency of character occurrence is around 200 and for encrypted text, no character occurs more than 14 times. This demonstrates how the encryption flattens out the distribution.

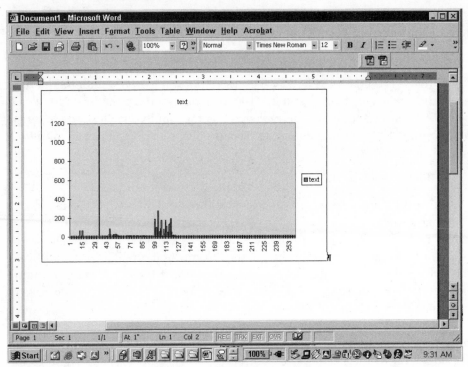

Figure 3.1   Nonencrypted ASCII text showing an unequal histogram. Notice the peaks of certain values.

If you have an idea that data might be hidden in the host file, you can run a histogram on this data and, depending on the results, have a good idea whether encrypted data is hidden in the file. The data would still be secure, but the extra layer of protection that you get by using steganography would be lost. You could argue that this is still better than using steganography without encryption. In that case, if you know where the data might be hidden, you would be able to read the message because there is nothing protecting the actual security of the message.

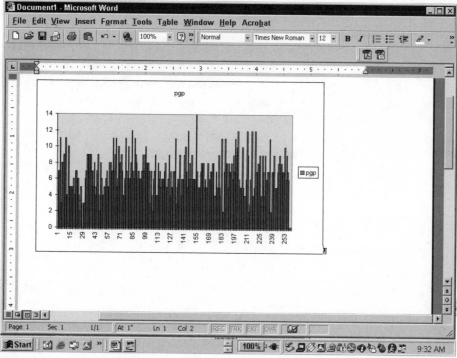

Figure 3.2 Encrypted ASCII text showing a very flat histogram. Notice that all characters appear about the same number of times; therefore there are no peaks.

NOTE One characteristic that steganography and cryptography share is that once people figure out how to break current techniques, new techniques need to be developed. With cryptography, a cycle develops in which one side keeps devising new techniques and the other side keeps figuring out new ways to "crack" them. This same cycle is starting to take place with steganography. Chapter 8 will explore how both crypto and stego can be cracked.

Looking Ahead

In the next chapter you'll take a look at digital watermarking and its relationship to steganography. Where stego is used to hide secret messages in media files, often by those who have an illegal reason to do so, digital watermarking is a tool of corporate America to defend itself against copyright abuses.

Digital watermarking hides copyright information in places such as software or music files. In Chapter 4 you'll see just how this works and what the technology has in common with other forms of stego.

Digital Watermarking

With the need to increase sales via the Internet, companies with Web content, such as e-magazines, face an interesting dilemma. On one hand, these companies want to post their pictures on their Web sites, for example, to sell more magazines. On the other hand, they want to make sure that nobody can steal their images and post them on other Internet sites. Because browsers download images for users to view them in Web pages, companies can't stop people who view their sites from downloading images.

By means of digital watermarks, online content providers can embed visible marks in their image files that flag the content as their property. Digital watermarks are almost impossible to remove without seriously degrading an image, so this helps to protect their content from piracy. Of course, some sites might post a digitally watermarked image, even though doing so is flagrantly illegal. This points to the other way in which digital watermarks are useful: Companies that use watermarks regularly scan sites looking for their unique digital signature in images. When they find these sites, they send their lawyers after the perpetrators.

In this chapter, you'll find out what digital watermarking is, how it's related to stego, and how it's being used.

IT'S AN ART

Randy Marx didn't like his job. His boss, Mr. Belgin, was a crook who paid his workers bottom dollar. The company made cheap products and wasn't beneath ripping off other companies' designs.

Even though Randy had a degree in design from a decent college, he wasn't given the least say in artistic decisions about laying out the calendars, coffee cups, and notepads his company printed in a sweatshop in Taiwan and sold by the thousands. He was a grunt worker, handling graphic design jobs with such fast turnaround that he didn't have time to do a decent job.

But his boss's latest stunt really burned Randy. Mr. Belgin had walked into his office the day before, handed him a computer disk and a set of 8" x 10" photos, and told him to use the photos on the disk to design a calendar for a new line of artsy products. When Randy opened one of the electronic files he noticed two things simultaneously. First, the photos were by a somewhat well-known photographer Randy admired—one whom Mr. Belgin would never pay the going rate for his museum-quality photos. Second, there was a digital watermark in the electronic files.

Mr. Belgin wanted him to use the electronic files for layout, but the actual calendars would be printed from the photo prints—prints Mr. Belgin had probably bought for a few bucks somewhere, but to which he certainly didn't have rights. The digital watermark on the electronic files was a dead giveaway— if the company had bought the rights to use the photos the stock photo company certainly wouldn't have provided digitally watermarked files. There was no way to remove that watermark without degrading the picture quality. Lots of companies put digital watermarks in their images to protect them from just this kind of piracy.

Mr. Belgin must have downloaded these from the Internet, then realized he'd have to fork over the few bucks for the printed photos and use the electronic files for position only in the layout.

Randy quit his job that afternoon, and he was very interested to read in the paper about six months later that his ex-boss had been sued by the artist for theft of intellectual property. Because Mr. Belgin couldn't prove where he got the images, he lost the case.

What Is Digital Watermarking?

According to Dictionary.com, a watermark is "a translucent design impressed on paper during manufacture and visible when the paper is held to the light." If you have an important printed document, such as a title to an automobile, you want to make sure that someone can't just print out a copy of the title on their laser printer and pretend to own your car. A watermark on such a document validates its authenticity. You can see watermarks on all kinds of documents, from diplomas to the paper money issued by most countries.

> **NOTE** A watermark isn't always that obvious. You may have seen a clerk in a store hold a bill up to the light to verify the watermark. Of course, holding paper to the light is awfully low tech and displays an obvious suspicion on the part of the clerk about the customer that could be offensive. Many stores now provide a highlighter-type of pen that allows the cashier to verify the watermark without squinting into the light.

An electronic watermark is an imprint in a document file that you can use to prove authenticity and to minimize the chance of someone counterfeiting the file. Watermarking is used to hide a small amount of information in an image and to do it in a way that doesn't obscure the original document.

Typically a watermark is visible only to those who know to look for it. The trick with watermarking is to provide a subtle element that doesn't overwrite anything else in the image, but that is significant enough to validate the image.

Exploring Uses for Digital Watermarking

Copy protection has always been a problem for businesses that deal in images or audio recordings. Now that so much content is stored in digital form and so many people have access to it via the Internet, protection of visual and audio material has become even more challenging. After all, if possession is nine-tenths of the law, how can you give somebody a copy of a file but still prove that you are the owner?

This is where digital watermarking becomes critical. Digital watermarking provides a way of protecting the rights of the owner of a file. Even if people copy or make minor transformations to the material, the owner can still prove it is his or her file.

So what does a digital watermark look like? Figure 4.1 shows an example of an image that has a digital watermark applied to it.

You can still view the image and see that it contains a view of a beautiful beach. If anyone tries to steal the image and post it on a Web site as his or her own, people would be tipped off by the (not so) subtle watermark printed across the entire image.

Companies that rent or sell stock photos—for example, to an advertising agency putting together a print advertisement—use watermarking all the time. Each electronic stock image would contain a digital watermark; an ad agency could preview the images, but not use them in a real advertisement until they buy the image and receive a copy with no watermark embedded.

Figure 4.1 Notice a visible watermark in the form of light gray lettering in the background of the image. The image is still visible, but it is also obvious to whom the image belongs.

It is important to note that even though digital watermarking is typically used with images, it can also be used with other types of files. Microsoft Word actually includes a feature for embedding watermarks in files, as shown in Figure 4.2.

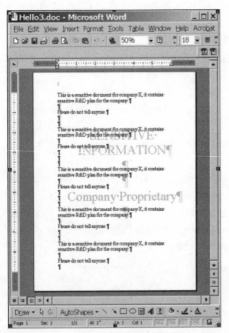

Figure 4.2 A watermark applied to a word processing document that still allows you to read the text.

This technique works for printed documents, but it is not very robust for sending document files to someone and protecting them. Using the same feature in Word, the recipient could easily remove the digital watermark.

NOTE A better approach for applying watermarks to Word files is to apply the watermark and then convert the document to PDF or some other format that cannot be changed by the recipient.

Properties of Digital Watermarking

Digital watermarking hides data in a file, and that act of hiding data makes it a form of steganography. It is a very limited form, though, and is appropriate only for protecting and proving ownership, not for transmitting information.

Digital watermarking inserts a small amount of information throughout a file in such a way that the file can still be viewed. If the watermark is ever removed, the image would be destroyed.

When using digital watermarking the goal is to find information in a file that can be modified without having a significant impact on the actual image. The important thing to remember is that when you apply a digital watermark to a file, you are modifying the file. Essentially, whenever you modify a file at the bit level you introduce errors into the file. As long as the errors are low, the overall impact on the file will usually be minimal.

NOTE Most files can tolerate minor changes, but some files have zero tolerance for errors. With zero-tolerance-for-error files, a bit change, no matter how minor, causes the file to be unusable.

Adding anything to a file is referred to as adding *noise*. Most file structures are designed to have a high tolerance for noise. Because they can accommodate some noise, digital files are perfect hosts for digital watermarking and steganography.

The one category of files that has a low tolerance for noise or errors is compressed files. Compressed files have been put through a process that removes any redundancy, thereby reducing the size of the file. Introducing any errors to a compressed file will render it unusable.

CIRCUMVENTING DIGITAL WATERMARKS

How can you get around a digital watermark? Here's one way. Take a look at the image shown in Figure 4.3, which contains a digital watermark.

Figure 4.3   Note the watermark copyright information in the bottom left-hand corner.

Can't see the watermark? Look at the bottom of the file. There is a single line that contains the watermark. How effective is this watermark? Someone could easily go in and remove the digital watermark without affecting the quality of the image by cropping the picture. That would result in the image shown in Figure 4.4.

Figure 4.4   The same image with the watermark cropped.

This image is missing a little bit off the bottom, but it is still a great picture of the beach. The moral? Where you place your watermark can be key to its effectiveness.

Figure 4.5 What makes this image unique is what you cannot see by looking at the image. Even though a watermark has been applied, there is no visible sign.

Types of Digital Watermarking

From an embedding standpoint, there are two general types of watermarks: invisible and visible. Figure 4.5 and 4.6 are copies of the same image. Both images have watermarks embedded in them; however, the watermark in the first figure is invisible, and the one in the second figure is visible to the eye.

Remember, unlike steganography, it does not matter if someone can detect a digital watermark (in fact, you usually want the watermark to be detectable to a would-be thief to deter tampering), as long as it cannot be removed.

NOTE Visible and invisible are two categories that have been applied to watermarks. Other categories for watermarks have been proposed. For example, one way that some people differentiate digital watermarks is by the robustness of the watermark and how easy it is to remove. From my perspective, this is not a category of watermark; it is simply a rating scheme to determine the quality of the watermark. For my money, visible and invisible types of watermarks are the categories that are worth a closer look.

Figure 4.6 In this image it is more obvious that a watermark has been applied.

Figure 4.7 If you put an image under a very high-powered microscope you could see the individual dots of color that make up the image.

Invisible Watermarking

With invisible watermarking you are applying a pattern to a file or an image in such a way that the human eye cannot detect it, but a computer program can. When you look at an image what you are really seeing is a bunch of little dots of color called *pixels* arranged in a way that forms an image.

If you take a small section of the image of a beach in Figure 4.1 and blow it up you would be able to see each pixel, as shown in Figure 4.7.

This figure shows 16 pixels that are taken from a portion of the sky. The smaller the pixels, the more detail a given picture can contain. The resolution on a computer screen is measured in pixels; if you change from 400×680 resolution to 1024×768, the image on your screen will be of much better quality.

Actually, there are more colors than the human eye can interpret in graphics files. With an invisible watermark you change certain pixels in a way so that the human eye can't tell that anything is missing; however, a computer program can.

Take a close look at the pixels shown in Figure 4.8.

Figure 4.8 Even though each of the circles looks as if it's made up of the same color, they are actually all different.

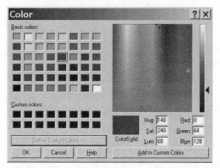

Figure 4.9 The Color Properties dialog box showing the RGB or red, green, blue values for the first circle in Figure 4.8. Notice that the values are different for each of the circles.

Concentrate on the first row in Figure 4.8. Even though all the pixels in the first row seem to use the same color, each pixel is actually slightly different. Figures 4.9 through 4.12 show the color palette setting for each pixel on the first row starting at the left and working toward the right. Notice that the RGB (red, green, blue) setting in this dialog box is different for each pixel. Yet, even though these pixels are different from a computer's perspective, the change in the image is so minimal that the human eye cannot pick it up.

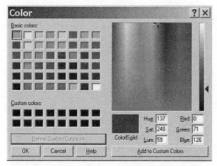

Figure 4.10 The RGB values for the second circle in Figure 4.8.

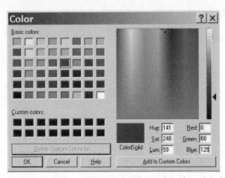

Figure 4.11   The RGB values for the third circle in Figure 4.8.

The other important thing to remember about an invisible digital watermark is that the smaller the pixels, the less chance there is that someone will be able to discern changes to them.

To demonstrate an invisible watermark I took the 16 pixels of the sky and applied an invisible watermark to the image. I then went through and gradually converted the invisible watermark to a visible one so that you could see the transformation. Starting at the top left column and working down you can barely see any difference between the pixels, but if you look very carefully at the bottom of the left-hand column, you can see a slight difference. Starting at on the right-hand column and working down, you can see that the watermark is becoming more and more visible (see Figure 4.13).

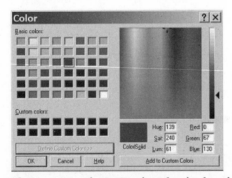

Figure 4.12   The RGB values for the fourth circle in Figure 4.8.

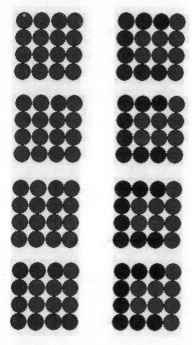

Figure 4.13 By slowing increasing the intensity of the invisible watermark, it becomes visible.

The strength of invisible watermarks is that the image quality is not degraded. By looking at the image, people can't tell that there is a watermark, yet your digital image is still protected. Invisible watermarks are effective, though, only while the image is in digital form. If I take a digital image that has an invisible watermark, print out the image, and then rescan it, the watermark has essentially been removed.

Visible Watermarking

Like an invisible watermark, a visible watermark makes slight modifications to an image. In this case, the transformation is such that the image can still be seen, yet a watermark image appears in it. One of the advantages of visible watermarks is that, even if an image is printed and scanned, the watermark is still visible.

A visible watermark image will usually make use of a light grayscale tone or simply make the pixels that contain the watermark slightly lighter or darker than the surrounding area.

Figure 4.14 Simple example of a watermark created by making modifications to certain pixels.

The trick is to make sure that the watermark is applied to enough of the image so that it cannot be removed. One challenge with visible watermarks is to make sure that when you apply the watermark, the original image is still visible. If you apply too much of a watermark, all you will see is the watermark and little of the actual image.

Complex mathematical formulas can be used to make watermarks more robust, but at a general level a watermarking program finds a group of pixels and adjusts the pixels in a way so that the watermark can be seen but the image is not destroyed. The usual way of performing this operation is to make the color of specific pixels darker.

In Figure 4.14 you can see a group of pixels in which the word ERIC was embedded by darkening the colors of certain pixels.

Goals of Digital Watermarking

Before I compare digital watermarking with other forms of steganography, it is important that you have in mind the goals of digital watermarking.

Digital watermarking has the following characteristics:

Does not impair the image.   This is mainly a concern with visible watermarks; even though you can see the watermark it must be done in such a way that you can still see the underlying image. If the watermark blocks large portions of the image or the entire image, it is not an effective watermark.

Cannot be removed.   There is no point in watermarking an image if someone can easily remove the watermark. The typical litmus test with digital watermarks is this: If the watermark is removed, then the image should be impaired or destroyed.

Embeds a small amount of information. Digital watermarking is usually done to mark an image or to prove ownership. Therefore, only a small amount of data needs to be embedded in an image.

Repeats data. Even though only a small amount of data is being embedded in an image it should be done in more than one place. This helps to ensure that it cannot be easily removed.

Digital Watermarking and Stego

Digital watermarking is one form of stego, but it has some unique characteristics. Table 4.1 shows the similarities and differences between digital watermarking and other forms of stego.

Though the basic premise of embedding one thing in another is common, the motive of hiding data is usually not present in watermarking, and the uses of watermarking are quite different than those of most other forms of steganography.

Table 4.1 Digital Watermarking versus Stego

CHARACTERISTIC	STEGANOGRAPHY	DIGITAL WATERMARKING
Amount of data	As much as possible	Small amount
Ease of detection	Very difficult to detect	Not critical with visible watermarks
Ease of removal	Important that someone cannot remove	Important that someone cannot remove
Goal of an attacker	To detect the data	To remove the data
Goal of user	To hide information in a file so that someone cannot detect it	To embed a signature so that ownership can be proved
Current uses	Corporate espionage, covert communication by executives, drug dealers, terrorists	Protecting rights of owners of digital images, video or audio content

Uses of Digital Watermarking

There are many uses for digital watermarking, but most of them revolve around protecting intellectual property and being able to prove that a given digital file belongs to you. Artists and companies that want to display images a customer can preview online before buying often use watermarking to differentiate between the preview version and the purchased version.

> **NOTE** Audio and video content protection methods use their own form of watermarks, but the principle is the same: a small modification that can be recognized to identify the file.

Most of the products that are on the market today focus on three areas: audio, video, and still images or pictures. Table 4.2 lists many of the programs available for performing digital watermarking and includes a brief description of each.

Table 4.2   Digital Watermarking Products

PRODUCT	COMPANY	WEB SITE	FORMAT	DESCRIPTION
AudioMark	Alpha Tec Ltd	www.alpha-tecltd.com/	Audio	Inserts and retrieves inaudible watermarks in audio files
Digimarc Watermarking Solutions	Digimarc	www.digimarc.com	Image and documents	Patented technology that inserts and retrieves watermarks from a variety of file formats using a suite of products
EIKONAmark	Alpha-Tec Ltd	www.alphatecltd.com/	Image	Inserts and retrieves invisible watermarks in still images
Giovanni	BlueSpike	www.bluespike.com	Audio, image, and text	Inserts and retrieves watermarks into image, audio, and text using cryptographic keys

PRODUCT	COMPANY	WEB SITE	FORMAT	DESCRIPTION
SysCop	MediaSec Technologies	www.mediasec .com	Audio, image, and video	Watermarking technology for audio, image, and video
Verance	Verance	www.verance .com/verance .html	DVD-audio	Patented technology for inserting watermarks into DVD-audio and SDMI Phase 1 files
VideoMark	Alpha-Tec Ltd	www.alphatecltd .com	Video	Inserts and retrieves invisible watermarks in video
VolMark	Alpha-Tec Ltd	www.alphatecltd .com	3D images	Inserts and retrieves 3D watermarks in grayscale and 3D images and volumes

Removing Digital Watermarks

The main goal of digital watermarking a graphic image is to make sure that someone cannot remove the watermark without seriously damaging the image.

NOTE Various signal processing techniques can be applied to an image to change its formatting without destroying its appearance. A good example of this is taking an image that is in one format and converting it to another format. For example, if a .bmp is converted to a JPEG file and then back to a .bmp, the two images would look the same, but the bit-by-bit composition of the images would be different.

One tool used to attack digital watermarks is Stir Mark, written by Fabien Petitcolas. Stir Mark is used to test the strength of digital watermarking technologies. You can add your own tests to the program, but it comes with three standard tests:

PSNR test. PSNR stands for the peak signal-to-noise ratio, which is essentially the peak signal versus the mean square error. The equation for PSNR is PSNR $= 20 \log_{10} (255/\text{RMSE})$, where RMSE is the root mean squared error. Typical values for PSNR are between 20 and 40. Remember, when you are applying a digital watermark or any form of stego to an image, you are introducing errors. This test measures the PSNR before and after watermarking to identify such errors.

JPEG test. JPEG images are a compressed image format, one reason why this format is typically used on the Internet. A .bmp file that is a couple of megabytes in size would most likely be a couple hundred kilobytes in size when converted to JPEG. Because JPEG is a compressed format, when other formats are converted to JPEG they often lose information. This test converts various formats to JPEG to see the impact of the conversion on a watermark.

Affine test. This test performs an affine transformation across the image. An affine transformation requires that two properties of an image must be maintained after the transformation: Any point that lies on a line still must be on that line after transformation, and the midpoint of the line must stay the same. The transformation is performed to see what effect, if any, this action has on a watermark.

What follows is part of a report generated by Stir Mark. Here you can see the different tests and how changing the input values for each of the tests can have an impact on the certainty of the detection. For example, with the PSNR tests an input value has to be provided that tells the program what percentage of noise it should use. You can see how the certainty changes with the various percents of noise.

```
Test_PSNR — Sat Nov 02 00.37.30 2002

Test_PSNR    0    Images/Set1/Sample    Certainty:    57.1169    1.#INF dB
Test_PSNR   10    Images/Set1/Sample    Certainty:    59.5881    39.5346 dB
Test_PSNR   20    Images/Set1/Sample    Certainty:    61.2351    35.1198 dB
Test_PSNR   30    Images/Set1/Sample    Certainty:    63.7055    32.0288 dB
Test_PSNR   40    Images/Set1/Sample    Certainty:    65.3515    29.079 dB
Test_PSNR   50    Images/Set1/Sample    Certainty:    67.8198    27.4019 dB
Test_PSNR   60    Images/Set1/Sample    Certainty:    69.4646    25.5721 dB
Test_PSNR   70    Images/Set1/Sample    Certainty:    71.9341    23.9908 dB
Test_PSNR   80    Images/Set1/Sample    Certainty:    73.5774    23.0663 dB
Test_PSNR   90    Images/Set1/Sample    Certainty:    76.0416    21.8534 dB
Test_PSNR  100    Images/Set1/Sample    Certainty:    77.6834    21.1355 dB
```

Figure 4.15 The original image with no modifications.

In most cases, as Stir Mark performs its transformations and removes a watermark, the resulting image is destroyed. It's worth looking at several images after transformations have been performed. I've used the sample image set that comes with Stir Mark. Figure 4.15 shows the original Lena image.

Looking at the PSNR output, you can see that even when you change the input values, this test reveals a minimal impact on the actual image. Figure 4.16 is an image with a PSNR of 0, Figure 4.17 has a PSNR of 50, and Figure 4.18 has a PSNR of 100 percent.

Figure 4.16 Image after 0 percent noise has been added to it.

Figure 4.17   Image after 50 percent noise has been added to it.

Figure 4.18   Image after 100 percent noise has been added to it.

By examining these images carefully you can see that when you increase the peak signal-to-noise ratio the image begins to look more and more faded and you lose some sharpness. As you can also see, the quality of the image is still fairly good in all the examples.

The affine transformation test keeps the image intact but makes it look like it was slightly offcenter when printed, as shown in Figures 4.19 and 4.20.

Figure 4.19 After the transformation a visible change has been made to the image.

Figure 4.20 By changing the input to the transformation a different visual effect can be seen.

The biggest effect comes when direct noise is applied to the image. Figure 4.21 shows 20 percent noise, Figure 4.22 shows 60 percent noise, and Figure 4.23 is an image with 80 percent noise applied.

Figure 4.21   When you apply noise to the image it becomes distorted.

Figure 4.22   As more noise is added, at the 60 percent level, the image can be seen only faintly.

Figure 4.23   At 80 percent noise you can barely see the image.

As you can see, the more noise that is inserted in an image, the less clear it becomes.

Looking Ahead

Digital watermarking is an exciting and complex field. Most people consider it a subset of stego, but remember the key differences. Digital watermarking is concerned with hiding small amounts of data in many places across an image and doing it in a way that destroys the image if the data is removed. Other forms of stego are concerned with hiding data entirely.

In the chapters that follow I'll go beyond the basics of stego to show you the impact it is having on our society, how it is generated, and how it can be detected.

The Hidden Realm of Steganography

Steganography at Large

People with secrets sometimes live on the shady side of life. It's a logical conclusion, therefore, that secret communication, including steganography, is used by those who deal in illegal or undercover activities.

In this chapter, I want to take you by the hand and lead you around the globe to get a feel for some of the ways that people are using secret communication and the impact it has on our increasingly global society.

HIDDEN SHAME

It wasn't unusual for government agencies such as the FBI and CIA to help each other out now and then. So when Joey got the call inviting him to the Tampa, Florida FBI field office to give a presentation on steganography, he checked with his boss and then booked a flight for the following week.

The morning he was to give his presentation was a warm, sunny one with just a hint of a sultry breeze. Joey strolled from the hotel to the FBI offices, which were located in the local police station. Joey grabbed a coffee from a Starbucks on his way, being way too familiar with the bitter, overbrewed java served at most police stations. When he walked in the police station he flashed his badge, and was shown into a room at the back of the building. Four FBI agents sauntered in, and one came up to Joey to introduce himself.

"Bob Carlos," he said as he shook Joey's hand. "Welcome to Tampa. Say, I hope you don't mind, but a few of the police detectives that work in the building wanted to sit in on your talk."

(continued)

HIDDEN SHAME *(continued)*

"No problem," Joey replied, taking a last sip of his coffee before throwing the cup into a nearby wastebasket. The last few people filtered in as Joey and Bob made small talk about the weather and interagency trivia.

Joey began his presentation a few minutes later, explaining how steganography works and showing slides with sample images that contained hidden data. As he talked, he noticed that two of the detectives seemed a little ill at ease. When Joey had shown the last slide and the lights came on again, he signaled that he was ready to take questions from the group.

One of the anxious detectives' arms shot up immediately. Joey scanned the nameplate pinned to the guy's chest and realized this was the Chief of Detectives, Larry Martinez.

"Is this on the level?" he asked Joey with an incredulous look on his face.

"Absolutely," Joey responded.

Larry then launched into a story about a child pornography case they'd dealt with a couple of months earlier. They had gotten a search warrant and taken the guy's computer to look for evidence, but they didn't find anything. "But that computer was full of pictures—about a few hundred image files. It seemed odd at the time, but we couldn't make anything of it. The case got thrown out for lack of evidence. Now I'm thinking maybe this stego thing..." His voice trailed off, not sure if he was on to something or not.

After several more questions the group broke up, and the Chief pulled Joey aside. "You got time to take a look at some of the files we copied off the perp's computer in that child porn case?"

"Have somebody buy me another Starbucks Grande and I'm yours for the afternoon," Joey quipped.

The Chief sent out for the coffee, then had the department assistant get the computer discs from the evidence drawer. The Chief sat Joey down in his own office to use the computer there.

What Joey saw made his jaw drop. There had to be 400 image files on the discs in a variety of formats. Joey quickly went online, downloaded a stego tool, and went to work. Within an hour he had extracted enough evidence from the files to take to a judge and ask to get the case reopened.

A month later Joey returned to Tampa, this time to appear in court as an expert witness at an evidence hearing. Because the judge wasn't that computer savvy, Joey explained carefully about steganography and the image files. He showed some stereogram images from the newspaper (those images that appear to change when you stare at them long enough) to help the judge understand how data could be hidden in an image, but not be readily apparent.

After Joey's testimony was over, the Chief of Detectives took the stand and explained how they had gone by the book to digitally sign the suspect's computer system when they impounded it to ensure that nobody could be accused of planting evidence. Between Joey's testimony, the extracted data from the image files, and the Chief's explanation of their procedure, the judge was convinced there was ample reason to reopen the case.

A week later, the accused and three of his cohorts sat behind bars, awaiting trial without bail, and a large child pornography network was shut down.

The Internet: A Climate for Deceit

Former Interpol Secretary General Ray Kendall has said, "Interpol has been pressing for years for cooperation with the private sector as technological advances make it clear crimes such as money laundering, electronic fraud and industrial espionage would boom in the Internet age. Frankly, we are not prepared for this explosion."

The reality is that cybercrime is happening internationally among organized criminal groups, corporations, and governments, as well as at the individual hacker level. Besides simply communicating about their various activities, one of the most frequent uses of the Internet by organized crime and terrorists alike is to launder money, which involves secret communication about that money as well as the financial transactions that move it from account to account.

The Internet provides the perfect climate for criminals for several reasons.

It's fast.   Transactions can be carried out quickly, before law enforcement has a chance to make a move.

It's anonymous.   It's very easy to get an account with an ISP or an email address with phony credentials (in fact, few credentials are required at all). Once you do, you are faceless, and you can conduct your transactions from a phone booth or an airplane. With a little effort, you can ensure that these transactions are virtually untraceable.

It's unregulated.   There is no government of the Internet. In addition, because of its international nature, no one country's laws prevail online, and no one group polices the mean streets of the cyberworld.

Take a moment to consider these and other features of the Internet that make it the perfect playground for the criminal mind.

The End of the Paper Trail

Law enforcement likes nothing better than a paper trail of cash deposits. Large bank deposits are often the perfect tip-off to a crime or money laundering scheme implemented by organized crime or terrorist groups. Unfortunately, the Internet puts an end to the paper trail.

Online you have the ability to send money to dozens of recipients through many small electronic transactions, foiling the attempts of law enforcement to follow the big-deposit money trail. And, you can switch money around from place to place without ever showing your face to a bank teller.

Even more frightening is the fact that, as criminals become more Internet savvy, they are devising their own online banking subculture that circumvents the mainstream financial world. Imagine a huge organized crime banking network where money can change hands completely undetected. These transactions call on tools such as encryption and steganography to communicate and protect their activities from prying eyes.

The future of the online financial world, including the use of smart cards that can send virtual cash directly from one person to another, is downright scary to law enforcement. Once criminals can exchange large amounts of cash with no financial institution serving as an intermediary, and without carrying suitcases of cash across borders, the very existence of a criminal element will become much more viable.

Your Jurisdiction or Mine?

The global nature of e-commerce and the Internet is causing chaos for those trying to track cybercrimes. That's because it's often hard to determine just exactly where a crime is committed and whose law applies.

This confusion begins within national boundaries. For example, in the United States individual states have their own laws in addition to federal law. Wisely, the United States enacted section 1343 of the Federal Criminal Code in 1952, which included a wire fraud provision. This provision, which has been extended to cover the Internet in practice, makes it a federal offense to use any part of the telecommunications system to commit any element of a criminal act. In practice, it's this provision that, in many cases, makes pure online crime, such as identity theft, a federal case.

IS CYBERCRIME TERRORISM?

The Anti-Terrorism Act created in the wake of September 11, 2001, included crimes covered under the Computer Fraud and Abuse Act of 1986 in its definition of terrorism. This made hacking and denial of service attacks terrorist acts. Cindy Cohn, legal director of the Electronic Frontier Foundation, expressed the sentiments of many when she said, "It may not be something we like, but breaking into a computer or defacing a Web site isn't terrorism. It's not right in our society to equate low-level offenses with our highest level of offense. There's no link to terrorism here."

If brought under such a broad piece of legislation a hacker or spammer's activities could land him or her in prison for life, whether the deed is done as a harmless prank by a teenager or as an attempt to bring an industry to its knees by a terrorist.

When the Internet is used to plan an offline crime, jurisdiction gets muddied. If a New York bank is robbed by transferring funds from customer accounts to a Delaware bank account, but the thief used a computer in New Jersey to steal the bank's security system password and make the transfers, where was the crime committed?

Internationally things get even more chaotic, especially when money crosses borders with no overriding judicial system to make the call. Cybercriminals know this, and they take advantage of the fact that the international legal community uses different standards, different enforcement practices, and different rule books when it comes to online crime.

In fact, some countries offer jurisdictional refuge, intentionally or unintentionally. In some places, such as Germany, identity theft is simply not held to be as serious as it is in other countries. At one point, the Phillipines had no law against those who disseminate computer viruses. Some countries have laws against publishing racial slurs online, while the United States protects the publishing of such material online under its First Amendment. If you perform illegal activities through ISP accounts within some countries' borders, you are protected by a lax attitude to such activity. For example, to safely open a drop-off email account where ill-gotten information can be deposited, all a criminal has to do is get an email address in a country that considers punishing such activity not worth its time or effort.

Still other nations knowingly harbor people who are terrorists or who use the Internet to commit crimes, as a way to support their own economies. Afghanistan and Pakistan have been accused of such a stance with terrorists, for example.

Finally, corporations' own private networks have proven to be a likely place for criminals and terrorists to hide information. Because these networks are privately controlled, the FBI must seek cooperation from those corporations to access data that may be transmitted via a back door to their networks.

NOTE Some have suggested that high seas conventions, which provide for jurisdiction over crimes committed in international waters by a commission of interested nations, might be a good model for cybercrime jurisdiction.

Searching for Identity

When you opened your account with an ISP, what proof of identity did you provide? A driver's license number? A faxed copy of your birth certificate? A notarized affidavit from your kindergarten teacher? Nope, you probably provided your name, address, and a credit card number. Oh, and perhaps your favorite dog's name for a security question the ISP could ask if you forgot your password.

LOVE BUG ATTACK

One example of the damage that can be done to the world's computers from a safe haven is the Love Bug virus, spread in 2000. The virus ate computer files and absconded with thousands of passwords in only two hours, causing havoc. All the ATMs in Belgium shut down; 70 percent of the computers in Germany, the Netherlands, and Sweden were disabled; and England's Parliament and the U.S. Congress had to shut down their email systems for a time.

Law enforcement was not spared. Some estimates say that as many as 80 percent of federal agencies were bereft of email for a time, an important tool for staying in touch with operatives all over the world. The U.S. Defense and State Departments, NASA, and the CIA were also victims.

Where did the Love Bug come from? The Philippines, where no cybercrime laws existed. The young student who was found to be the father of the bug was finally charged with theft and credit card fraud, not cybercrime. Because of legal technicalities between the Philippines and other countries, the student couldn't be extradited and was never held accountable for as much as $10 billion in damages resulting from his acts.

The fact is that there is no strong system for authenticating who you are dealing with online. For all you know, the person who sells you something on eBay is doing so from a jail cell, and for all your ISP knows, you are an international terrorist planning to use your online account to send secret plans through hidden messages in JPEG files.

Because identity is so elusive online, the Internet is a perfect place for crime. You can use phony identities, steal others' identities, and change identities at will. In fact, hanging around public sites can be a cybercriminal's best defense. They lurk on Yahoo!, use Hotmail, and hang out in online cafes where their activities are lost among those of the crowd of people chatting and sharing information. And they stay one step ahead of any particular country's legal apparatus.

This lack of identity makes the use of stego even more secure for the criminal—after all, even if a cybercop actually could detect the hidden message you send, he or she may never be able to track down the sender.

FUNNY BUSINESS

Andy was no stranger to the criminal justice system. He was often called in by law enforcement as an expert witness on computer crime. When he got the call that Saturday afternoon, it sounded like an interesting case.

The caller, a Sergeant McGee, told him that a woman named Marsha Lurlee had filed Chapter 7 bankruptcy for her import business a few months ago. She'd stiffed her employees out of a few months' pay and all their pension money. One of the employees, Pete Mazzoni, had hired a lawyer and rallied the other employees to start an investigation.

They had an idea that Ms. Lurlee wasn't disclosing everything about the company's finances. If they could just prove that she was hiding information about the company, they'd have the basis for an indictment of fraud. Pete and his lawyer talked to the police and a judge, got a search warrant, and gave Marsha's home the once-over, looking for evidence.

The day after the Sargeant called, Andy went to police headquarters, where the suspect's business and home computers had been taken after they were seized as evidence.

"All we need is to know if she's trying to hide something," said Pete Mazzoni's attorney, Linda Lewis, a woman of 40 or so dressed in a business suit. Andy sat down at the home computer and started to look through the folders on it.

At first there was nothing out of the ordinary, and he was beginning to think he wouldn't be able to do a thing for Ms. Lewis. But he switched to the business computer, and after about a half an hour, he came across something. What he found brought a smile to his face.

Looking at a list of files he spotted two stego programs on the system. One of them, J-Steg, was used to hide data in JPEG files. When he explained what he'd found to Ms. Lewis, she grinned from ear to ear. The mere fact that there were programs on the computer designed to hide data was enough for her. "Got her!" she exclaimed.

But Andy wanted more. He started looking through the JPEG images on the hard drive—and there were dozens. As he extracted the data from image after image, the picture came clear: Ms. Lurlee had been embezzling from her company for years. The hidden data even told them where the money was stashed. Case closed.

Corporate Espionage

As we're all becoming more and more aware in this age of Enron and Worldcom scandals, companies have their own secrets to protect. Some are legitimate, such as the formula for a new drug or the code for proprietary software, and some are a part of their own deceptive practices. Stealing such information has become a business in and of itself, and it is practiced by everybody from disgruntled ex-employees to professional information brokers.

Who's Playing?

Information theft in the United States costs approximately $59 billion a year, according to a recent survey by the American Society for Industrial Security, PricewaterhouseCoopers, and the U.S. Chamber of Commerce.

Though some thefts of corporate secrets are simply random acts of revenge by employees, organized corporate espionage is more typically performed by groups of people who make it their business to break into your business.

In general, corporate espionage is performed by three distinct sectors:

Freelance.   This is the independent hacker who steals and sells to highest bidder.

Outsourced.   In this scenario, a company or government hires an information broker or investigative agency to steal information from competitors. They may send crackers into a company's computer system; bribe an employee to steal information; or even hire away a senior employee who brings the goods along with him or her on the first day of work.

State-sponsored.   Many governments use intelligence resources to discover information and plans for secret projects at foreign companies, then offer that information to industries in their own countries to give them a competitive edge.

Information Attacks

Information attacks involve taking confidential information from an organization or individual. Methods may range from talking some unsuspecting employee into faxing a data sheet on an unreleased product, to somebody posing as an employee to access company pass codes, to hacking into sophisticated computer systems.

A glance at some of the statistics on this form of attack is frightening. Colonel Thaddeus Dmuchowski, Director of the Army's Information Operations Assurance Office, recently addressed the topic of computer intrusions in a presentation to the National High-Performance Computing and Communications Council. He reported, "Between 2000 and 2001, the Army Computer Emergency Response Team counted a steady rise in reported incidents, from 5,616 to 14,641. The number of IT systems intrusions jumped from 64 to 98." These numbers are probably on the low side because concern about public image and consumer confidence causes many information attacks against organizations every year to go unreported.

The most common types of information stolen are research and development data (49 percent), private customer information (36 percent), and financial data (27 percent), according to a Trends in Proprietary Information Loss Survey by the American Society for Industrial Security.

These are not inexpensive assaults for companies: R&D theft typically has a $404,000 per-incident cost. Financial data theft costs about $356,000 per incident.

And what methods are these attackers using? Robert M. Wright of the NIPC's Special Technology Application Unit said at a recent conference, "Today's insiders are bringing in their own tools, such as key-chain hard drives, anonymous-remailer software, peer-to-peer applications, infrared and radio wireless devices, and steganography—messages hidden within digital images."

System Attacks

If stealing secrets isn't destructive enough, there are people and groups who go after organizations and their data with a broader brushstroke. Aimed at shutting down an organization at least temporarily and often costing it millions of dollars, actions such as denial of service attacks or transmission of destructive viruses can cause corporate chaos.

MessageLabs Inc., a managed services provider, predicts that one-half of all emails will be infected with a virus by 2013. Some of these viruses are the work of adolescent and misguided hackers, but more and more viruses are being used in formal attacks to undermine companies, industries, and even societies. The potential threat that terrorist groups might use such tools to undermine the information infrastructure of our world is very real.

Technology is aiding these criminals in their attacks. For example, flash worms now exist that can infect a network in as little as 30 seconds. Extrapolating from this, you can imagine a scenario where a million of the 12 million or so servers that form the backbone of the Internet could be infected in just 15 minutes.

NOTE Who else should we be wary of? Well, according to one Naval Postgraduate School study from 1999, religious extremists are most likely to pursue sophisticated tools for attacks to create mass disruption.

Playing Spy

Governments are not standing on the sidelines when it comes to information crime. Some are legislating against it, others are actively involved in committing it, but few are sitting the game out.

Big Brother—With an Attitude

Surveillance by governments is nothing new; today these surveillance systems are rushing to keep up with secret communication technologies that detect and transmit private messages and files. There have long been rumors of a global surveillance system set up by the United States during the Cold War. This system, called Echelon, is reportedly also used by other countries including England, Austrialia, and Spain. Echelon tracks communications via cellular, satellite, fiber optics, and other media. Though the United States has never confirmed the existence of Echelon, it has at times been accused of using it to steal foreign company information and share it with U.S. companies.

Konrad Kramer, a reporter for the Austrian newspaper *Kurier*, wrote in an article dated November 9, 1999: "The U.S. Secret Service NSA listens in—if its spies consider this necessary—with the help of Echelon. It can tap any kind of electronic communication. The most important target of the Secret Service is the Internet with its information channels that are difficult to follow."

The United States isn't the only country with surveillance systems in place. For example, in Britain various laws have been proposed that define the monitoring capabilities of its law enforcement agencies relative to phones, pagers, and corporate intranets. During debates over one such regulation, some proponents pointed out that covert surveillance and communication have existed for years, and the regulation simply provided for external supervision of these activities. Opponents cited the dangers in provisions for jailing those who refused to give up private keys to encrypted data.

LAISSEZ FAIRE?

Al St. John had worked for the Communications Security Establishment, Canada's largest spy network, for 10 years. He'd seen things change in that time. Russia was no longer the bad guy.

These days he spends most of his time at international trade and commerce conferences eavesdropping on conversations between big wigs from major corporations. The business of spying has become one with big business.

Al found he could pick up some very useful information at these conferences. Once he'd overheard a conversation about a major Korean firm that was angling to wrest a major contract from one of Canada's largest software firms. He'd gotten a message to his home office, and the Korean company was headed off at the pass. Another time he "borrowed" plans for a soon-to-be-released high-tech product from the hotel room of the CFO of a German company. The Germans were racing to bring the product out before the R&D department of a major Canadian university could perfect its prototype in partnership with three large manufacturers. The CEO of that German company almost had a heart attack when he heard that the Canadian prototype was being shown to prospective customers three weeks before his company's product hit the streets.

Today Al was working on gathering information about a deal between the Japanese government and a French transportation company to supply new high-speed trains to Japan. Al's boss thought a Canadian company might be interested in stepping into the negotiations to get a piece of the action. When the two men who'd been discussing the deal over drinks in an Austrian hotel lobby got up and left, Al just wandered over, picked up a cocktail napkin with some quick notes about the deal, and pocketed the goods. He walked straight to the business office of the hotel and got the numbers scanned. Then, he took the disk with the scanned file back to his hotel room, downloaded an audio file from the Internet, and hid the scanned file in it.

By dinner time the preliminary numbers on the deal with Japan were in the hands of Al's unit boss, who was already on the phone briefing the Canadian industry giant.

Information Crime and the Law

Generally speaking, a great many of today's legal battles related to information fall largely into one of two areas: the acts of governments in using surveillance on their own citizens or citizens of other countries and the threat to civil rights inherent in that surveillance; and the use of digital watermarking and encryption to protect intellectual property.

Who's Watching Whom?

The world is on an organized manhunt, and governments are trying hard to get and use their power to follow criminals wherever they go, including the places that technology can take them. The Combating Terrorism Act of 2001, which came out days after the attacks of September 11, 2001, allows 48-hour surveillance of suspected individuals or groups without the approval of a judge. This may help law enforcement to move quickly enough to locate terrorists, but it brings up some frightening questions about our personal liberties and privacy.

Countries such as the United States and England have been trying to pass laws on encryption that, in some cases, give their governments the right to jail people who will not give up their private keys to encrypted data on demand. This raises more questions. How do we implement the dissemination of government keys? Do we trust all governments to have this power over their citizens? Who, exactly, gets to see cross-border communications?

Protecting Ideas

Use of technology to stop ordinary citizens from violating intellectual property and copyright laws is another area of hot debate. The Internet has made it possible to copy and disseminate everything from novels to music and videos in the blink of an eye. Some argue that this takes the bread out of the mouths of the artists and companies who produce this material; others say that this is part of the openness of a digital age that is based on freedom of information exchange.

In the United States, there have been several proposed laws to address copyright violations that involve technologies such as digital watermarking to embed copyright controls in files. South Carolina Democrat Senator Fritz Hollings' digital rights management proposal to forcibly implant copy protection technology in nearly every PC and electronics device is one example. As you might expect, this bill is backed by copyright holders such as Walt Disney Co. but fought by technology firms.

Of course, if you create a standard somebody will violate it, and so the use of phony watermarks has begun. Senator Joseph Biden proposed an anti-counterfeiting bill that makes trafficking in a fake watermark or digital signature illegal. This bill permits a company whose watermark is misused to sue for damages of not less than $2500 and not more than $25,000.

Dan Burk, intellectual property law professor at the University of Minnesota, has said, "If Biden's proposal were to become law, it would be a real problem for researchers working on steganography. This bill doesn't say 'digital watermark,' but the language about numbers, codes, and symbols may be broad enough to cover steganography, which suggests that it was altered in an attempt to plug a hole left in the original DMCA (Digital Millennium Copyright Act of 1998)."

The Consumer Broadband and Digital Television Promotion Act was an attempt to forcibly embed copyright protection in electronic devices such as cell phones and digital cameras. The implications of such legislation on programmers and those who distribute code for free are serious. If digital devices had a copy protection chip, no program that wasn't registered and identifiable could be run. One of the serious problems with such legislation is that, if it were enacted in the United States but not in other countries, it would effectively sever trade ties for electronic and digital device sales and cause serious damage to the technology sector. Restrictions on software that is distributed freely, such as the open source Linux operating system, would effectively put these programs out of business.

In the case of some of the legislation discussed here, use of steganography could be at risk if a stego program is not properly "registered." A world where devices and technologies geared toward keeping communication secret must be registered would seem, on the surface of it, to be a world where secret communication is in serious danger of extinction.

Enforcement: A Tough Nut

In addition to jurisdictional confusion that makes it difficult to even identify which law is at work in a particular crime, it is simply difficult to find the criminals—and sometimes it is even difficult to find the crime. The daunting task of monitoring all online activity is one that law enforcement at every level and in every country is ill equipped to handle.

The Challenge

William Gurley wrote this on News.com, on October 2, 2001: "There are an increasing number of ways to move files on the Internet. To name a few: e-mail, FTP, instant messaging, chat, file lockers, Napster, and Gnutella. In the next few years, the number of e-mails and instant messages sent each year will be measured in the trillions (for each). Peer-to-peer file transfers will easily number in the billions. How do you monitor all of this? Where could you even store the log data? The pin is small, the haystack is large, and astute cryptographers can use steganography to increase the size of the haystack."

And how are our government agencies responding to this challenge? According to a Wired News story in 2001, "The FBI has openly admitted that its agents have difficulties collecting evidence from computers. FBI Director Robert Mueller told a House committee this summer that the agency lacks the technology skills and understanding that would allow agents to conduct complete computer forensics searches."

In response to the challenge, Robert Mueller then announced a reorganization of the FBI in May of 2002 that made high-tech crimes one of its top priorities. It even established a Cyber Division to focus on online crime and misuse of information by the criminal element. Mueller noted that when it comes to technology, the FBI was "years behind the time."

Yet, when faced with the technology of steganography, which makes every photo, piece of music, and video file flying around the Internet a potential transport mechanism, how can any government or law enforcement agency ever hope to keep up?

Enforcing the Unenforceable

Being able to locate information is one issue; being able to use it to enforce a law is another. Privacy groups are hovering close to law enforcement at every turn, trying to protect the balance between surveillance and invasion of privacy.

The FBI diagnostic tool called Carnivore was developed to help the agency sniff out specific illegal messages in the sea of communication that is the Internet. The software works like the commercially available sniffer software often used by ISPs to review online activity among their members for inappropriate behavior. ISPs have to cooperate with the FBI to install Carnivore on their servers, and the FBI must have a court order to request that they do so. The problem is that Carnivore often scoops up more than the target's communications. This has led to some concern that an individual who trusts that his or her communications via his or her ISP are secure may, in fact, have those communications intercepted by a government agency.

TAKING THE TEETH OUT OF CARNIVORE

A graduate student named Alex Iliev has proposed a modification to the way the FBI is allowed to collect data from groups such as ISPs. Because Carnivore tends to take in huge chunks of information, some totally irrelevant to the case under investigation, innocent individuals' privacy is at risk from such eavesdropping systems. Therefore, Iliev has suggested that redesigning the system to allow access to discrete packages of information would be a better protection of civil rights. Judges would use digital signatures to grant access to programmed "vaults" of data, cutting down the possibility of information fishing expeditions.

The Growing Science of Computer Forensics

One key part of enforcing laws related to information theft and the Internet in the world today is the science of computer forensics. Forensics specialists use techniques to uncover data that exists on a computer drive or to recover damaged or encrypted files to provide evidence of a wide variety of crimes, from murder to terrorism.

Computer forensics experts are used by government agencies, lawyers in criminal proceedings, insurance companies on the lookout for fraud, and corporations hunting the misuse of confidential information or embezzlement.

Computer forensics experts hunt down evidence by detecting damaged or hidden files and opening password-protected or encrypted files. In some cases, unallocated areas of disks are searched; though these areas may not currently be occupied by data, it is still sometimes possible to retrieve previously stored data. In addition, there are methods of hiding data in small unallocated areas at the end of files, referred to as *slack space*.

Part of good forensics procedure is to ensure the viability of evidence that is discovered—that is, that nobody has tampered in any way with it as it is retrieved or recovered. This involves using digital signatures to mark the content when it is retrieved; any change made after the digital signature would be evident.

One area of forensics deals with trying to figure out what happened to data by recreating the evidence. In many cases, this involves trying to recover information that has been deleted from a system. When files are deleted there is a trail that can be used to try to retrieve the deleted data. Steganography turns forensics on its ear. Not only is there no longer a trail because the files are hidden in other information, but anything on the system could now be considered evidence because any file could contain hidden information.

Most forensic programs and procedures that are used today do little to account for hidden files. This is a perfect example of how a better understanding of the criminal element can help investigators be more successful in solving cyber crimes.

Looking Ahead

In this chapter you got a look at the state of information crime in the world today and some of the challenges that law enforcement faces in tracking violations and bringing the criminals to justice. Now that you understand the landscape for the use of stego, including cybercrime, it's time to introduce you to the specifics: the nuts and bolts of using stego.

CHAPTER 6

Nuts and Bolts of Steganography

There are many different ways to hide data in a file. This chapter will provide an overview of how you hide data in different file formats—images, sound files, Word documents, text files, and so on—using a variety of techniques. You'll discover the tricks of the stego trade and examine potentially untapped areas for hiding information.

In this chapter, you'll use some common stego tools and even write algorithms of your own. These tools are all easy to use. It is important to remember that even though the tools might seem simple, the techniques are very powerful and, in some cases, very difficult to detect.

COUNTER INTELLIGENCE

It's standard procedure for government intelligence agencies to go on fishing expeditions when there's a big political gathering coming up in a foreign country. They send operatives to the host country to get wind of any extremist political groups that might disrupt the proceedings, as well as to pick up any tidbits they can about other countries' agendas to help their side at the bargaining table.

It wasn't unusual that the CIA had a man in Belgium keeping his ears open several weeks before the Arms Treaty summit that was coming up in Brussels. After all, presidents from three major European countries would be there, along

(continued)

COUNTER INTELLIGENCE *(continued)*

with the Secretary of State of the United States. The agent the CIA planted, code named Cocoa, had been sending back intelligence about the other countries' representatives and security arrangements for the summit with regularity.

So when Cocoa's U.S. contact called one Monday morning to report that the messages had suddenly stopped, the Assistant Director in charge of the operation got a bad feeling. Agents of other governments must be watching Cocoa a little too closely, the AD guessed, so the agent had been forced to stop all communications.

The Assistant Director picked up his phone and punched in an extension— the cryptanalysis unit. What the AD needed was to give his agent a way to communicate without anybody knowing what was going on, and these guys wrote the book on that.

The next morning Sarah Bendel caught a plane to Brussels. She'd thrown a change of clothes in a suitcase and got the first flight out, understanding the urgency of the situation from the strained tone in the Assistant Director's voice. As she sat in the back of the taxi watching the dull modern buildings that were taking over Brussels flash by in the rain, she mulled over an idea about how she might set up a communications method for Cocoa.

An hour later, after she'd had time to check her hotel room for listening devices, there was a knock at her room door. Cocoa, a tall, elegant, balding man in an impeccably tailored suit, strode into the room. Pouring him a glass of ginger ale from the mini-bar, Sarah started to outline her plan.

First, they had to find something Cocoa was interested in, something that he browsed the Internet for on a regular basis. She needed that hook because she didn't want to raise the suspicions of anybody watching Cocoa by having him begin to perform unusual online activity. It turned out that Cocoa had a passion for stamps, and he often surfed the Web to visit stamp collecting sites.

She got to work setting up a Web site where people could submit stamp images and post comments about stamps. Then she populated its discussion boards with phony messages from dozens of false email accounts. She taught Cocoa how to use a simple stego program to hide the goods in image files. All Cocoa had to do was post a few routine messages. Then, when those watching him were lulled into thinking this was just a hobby, Cocoa would begin to post messages, including photos of various stamps (all the pictures he already had on his computer), that had some very interesting information stored in them.

Sarah flew back to the States the next day and began retrieving Cocoa's messages that very night.

Types of Steganography

Over the years, people have categorized steganography techniques in different ways. Throughout my career in stego I have relied on two different schemes, which I'll call the original scheme and the new scheme. The new scheme is more comprehensive and general, and it better addresses some of the tools that have come out in recent years. Just as a car mechanic has to know how to work on older model cars, those trying to create and detect stego should know how both these methods of classification work.

NOTE There are hundreds of tools that implement steganography, and a complete list can be found at www.stegoarchive.com/.

Original Classification Scheme

My original classification scheme breaks steganography down into the following three groups:

- Insertion-based
- Algorithmic-based
- Grammar-based

This scheme focuses on how data is hidden. Note that as new techniques have been developed, they do not clearly map into this scheme.

Insertion-Based

Insertion-based steganography techniques work by inserting blocks of data into a host file. Using an insertion-based technique, data is inserted at the same point in every file. This type of technique works by finding places in a file that can be changed, without having any significant effect on the host file.

Once these redundant areas are identified, the data to be hidden can be broken up and inserted in them and will be fairly hard to detect. Depending on the file format, this data can be hidden between headers, in color tables, in image data, or in several other fields.

A very common way to hide data is to insert it into the least significant bits (LSB) of an 8-bit or 16-bit file—for example, a 16-bit sound file. With sound files, one can change the first and second LSB of each 16-bit group without having a large impact on the quality of the sound. Because data is always being inserted at the same point for each file, this can be categorized as an insertion steganography technique.

Algorithmic-Based

Algorithmic-based steganography techniques use some sort of computer algorithm to designate where in a file data should be hidden. Because this category of technique doesn't always insert data in the same spot in each file, it is possible that the process will degrade the quality of the file. If someone compared the original file to the one where data is hidden, that person might be able to see or hear a change in the file.

This category of techniques has to be examined carefully to ascertain whether a technique is detectable. Remember that one of the goals of stego is to make sure nobody can detect that data is hidden in a file. If you do not create an algorithm and seed number that place the data in nonessential locations, the hidden data could completely obliterate the original image file or result in an image that looks very unusual

For example, if you hide data in an image file you must provide a number to seed the stenographic technique. This number could be either a random number or the first five bytes of the file. The algorithmic technique would take the seed value and use it to determine where to place the secret data throughout the file. The algorithm could be very complex or as simple as this: If the first digit is 1, insert the first bit at location x; if the first digit is 2, insert the first bit at location y; and so on. If careful thought is not given to the algorithm that is used, it could result in a disastrous output file.

Grammar-Based

Both the insertion and algorithmic techniques would take the secret message and somehow embed it in a host file. Grammar-based steganography techniques require no host file in which to hide a message because it generates its own host file.

This class of technique uses hidden data to generate an output file based on a predefined grammar. In fact, the output file produced looks just like the predefined grammar.

For example, if you wanted a piece of text to sound like the *Washington Post* classified section, you could gather a large amount of source material from the classified section and render statistical patterns. The patterns would make it possible to mimic the output (the classified ad section).

This approach could be used to hide data from automatic scanning programs that use statistical patterns to identify data. These programs scan data looking for anything unusual. For example, in a typical classified ad, it would be odd to have the contents be all binary or Japanese. Such a program can scan for English type text, and anything that fits the profile would not be flagged by the scanning program.

NOTE There are different complexities or levels in which a grammar can be built. The higher the level of the grammar, the more it looks like the specified language and the greater the chance it will go undetected by scanning programs.

New Classification Scheme

The original classification scheme focuses on how data is hidden. This newer scheme deals with both how and where the data is hidden. This scheme is more comprehensive, and it is a better breakdown of modern data stego.

The new scheme breaks down techniques into the following categories:

- Insertion-based
- Substitution-based
- Generation-based

NOTE It is important to realize that even though both classification schemes have a category named insertion, the insertion-based category is different in the two schemes.

Insertion-Based

Insertion-based techniques find places in a file that are ignored by the application that reads the file. Essentially, you insert data in a file that increases the size of a file, but has no effect on the representation (that is, visual or audio reproduction) of the data.

For example, with some files there is a flag called an EOF or end-of-file marker. This flag signifies to the application that is reading the file that it has reached the end of the file and therefore the application can stop processing the file. You could insert your hidden data after the EOF marker, and the application will ignore it, though the hidden data is still in the file.

Another example of an insertion-based method works with Microsoft Word files. In Word markers in the file tell Word what data it should display on the screen and what information should not be displayed. This is used with features such as Undo, where information is still stored in the file but not displayed to the user.

Say that you create two Word documents. In one you type "This is a test." Now take a large Word document (say 80 or more pages to provide enough room for hiding) and enter the phrase "This is a test" at the end. Then, delete the contents until you are left with only the words "This is a test." Both documents look exactly the same, but if you check the file sizes, you will notice that they are different. In Figure 6.1 you can see that the document that once had additional information in it is larger than the other document where nothing was deleted.

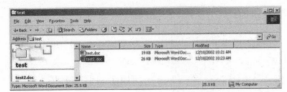

Figure 6.1 Examination of the file sizes for the two files that contain identical text.

Word documents are configured to contain begin-text and end-text markers. Anything that is between a begin-text and an end-text marker is processed, and anything between an end-text and a begin-text marker is ignored. You can insert as much data in the areas between the end-text and begin-text markers as you want and not affect the appearance of the document when viewed in Word.

The main attribute of insertion-based techniques is that you are only adding data to the file; you are not modifying or changing any of the existing contents of the file. The good news is that with insertion you can theoretically hide as much information as you want with no image degradation. The bad news is that at some point the file will be so large that someone is likely to notice. If you have a file that contains only the words "This is a test," and it is 5MB, you might as well name the file "Hey, There's Stego in Here."

Substitution-Based

As the name implies, with substitution-based stego you go in and substitute data for information that is already in the file, often referred to as overwriting. This method may seem straightforward, but you have to be very careful that you don't overwrite data in a way that would make the file unusable or visually flawed. The trick is to find insignificant information in a file—information that can be overwritten without having any impact.

For example, you can take the Word example discussed in the previous section and use a substitution-based technique instead of an insertion-based technique. In this case, any data that is between end-of-text and beginning-of-text markers has minimal impact on the document and could be overwritten. The difference is that with substitution, the size of the file has not changed.

There is a limit to how much data you can hide with this approach because you are limited to the amount of insignificant data in the file.

Generation-Based

Both insertion- and substitution-based techniques require a covert (hidden) and an overt (host) file. With generation-based techniques the covert file is used to create the overt file. This method addresses one of the issues with avoiding stego detection: If someone can obtain both the original file and the one with data hidden in it, they can tell that they have a different binary composition.

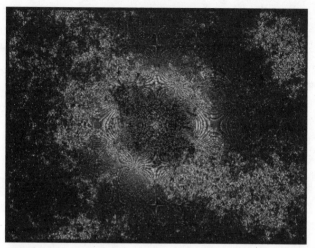

Figure 6.2   Example of a fractal taken from http://membres.lycos.fr/warey/fract/str08.htm.

The most common example of generation-based stego is where you use an overt file to create a fractal image. A fractal image has critical mathematical properties, but it is essentially a collection of patterns and lines in different colors. You could use your covert message to determine the angle, length, and color of each line. Figure 6.2 shows an example of a fairly complex fractal that was created using generation-based stego.

The important thing to keep in mind in using generation-based stego techniques is that the image that is generated has to fit the profile of the person using it to avoid detection. If somebody has never received a fractal file before, and he or she starts receiving dozens of such images, it may attract attention.

With generation-based stego the file created must have some predictable pattern that could be coded into an algorithm. For example, with a fractal the angles and length of the lines can be fed into an algorithm that is based on the input text and creates the overt image.

A picture of something as realistic as a car cannot easily be created with a generation-based technique. In most cases, random-looking images like fractals and English text are the two main media for generation-based stego.

Color Tables

An element you need to learn about to understand how data is hidden in image files is color tables. Color tables are used by several stego techniques to hide data.

All images are composed of dots called pixels. By putting all these pixels together, an image is formed. Each pixel gets its own color by combining varying percentages of red, green, and blue (RGB). Each of these three colors has a value that can range from 0 to 255. Zero designates that the color is present, and 255 designates complete saturation of that color. In the RGB color model there are a total of 256×256×256 = 16,777,216 possible colors. Here are values for some common colors:

- 255 0 0 is red.
- 0 255 0 is green.
- 0 0 255 is blue.
- 0 0 0 is black.
- 255 255 255 is white.

The RGB value for each pixel is stored in a color table. Each entry includes a row number and a value for red, green, and blue. A portion of a color table is shown in Table 6.1. The first number is the row number, which the pixel references to identify its corresponding color. The second number is the value for red. The third number is the value for green. The fourth number is the value for blue.

Products That Implement Steganography

In this section you'll look at several freeware, shareware, and commercial steganography programs and learn how they go about hiding data in a host file. The tools that you will work with in the following sections are as follows:

- S-Tools
- Hide and Seek
- JSteg
- EZ Stego
- Image Hide
- Digital Picture Envelope
- Camouflage
- Gif Shuffle
- Spam Mimic

Though there are hundreds of stego tools available, this section provides a sampling of insertion-, substitution-, and generation-based stego techniques. Most of the other tools that are available today are similar to these tools in functionality and usability.

Table 6.1 Sample Color Table

ENTRY NUMBER	R	G	B
0	24	104	155
1	41	100	65
2	24	120	179
3	33	83	49
4	82	132	90
5	65	125	90

S-Tools

S-Tools is a freeware program with a drag-and-drop interface that runs on most versions of Windows 95 or later. It can hide data in GIF or .bmp image files or in .wav sound files. It can also perform encryption with IDEA, DES, Triple-DES, and MDC. Compressing files is also an option.

S-Tools offers the ability to hide multiple secret messages in one host file. For all of the file formats, it hides data in the three least significant bits of each byte of data.

> **NOTE** Most of the stego tools that are available today give you the option to protect the data with a password, encrypt the data, or compress the data for additional security.

Using S-Tools with Image Files

For image host files, S-Tools works by distributing the bits of the secret message across the least significant bits (also referred to as LSB) of the colors for the image. The method used for hiding data in images depends on the type of image.

For example, the .bmp format supports both 24- and 8-bit color, whereas the GIF format supports only 8-bit color. Also, 24-bit images encode pixel data using 3 bytes per pixel, 1 byte for red, 1 byte for green, and 1 byte for blue. The secret message is hidden directly in the three LSB of the pixel data.

> **NOTE** The disadvantage to hiding data in 24-bit images is twofold: They are not that common so they may draw attention, and they are very large.

Note that 8-bit images are different from 24-bit images in that they are created with a reduced file size. These images use a color table (or palette) of 256 RGB values. This means the color table has 256 entries. The pixels are represented by a single byte, which specifies which RGB value to use from the color table.

To hide data in 8-bit images, S-Tools modifies the image to use only a 32-color palette instead of 256. The 32 colors are duplicated 8 times ($32 \times 8 = 256$), to fill the color table with duplicate entries. S-Tools can then use the duplicate entries to store the secret message in the three LSB for each RGB entry. Because each color in the modified image can be represented in eight different ways, information can be hidden in any of the redundant representations. This is the method used most often by S-Tools because most images are stored as 8-bit to save space.

NOTE This method will also work with grayscale images because they are almost always 8-bit color; the color table in this case contains 256 different shades of gray.

Using S-Tools with Sound Files

For sound files, data is placed directly into the three least significant bits of the file. This works with either 8-bit or 16-bit .wav files. Here's an example that shows how this works with S-Tools: Suppose that a sound sample had the following 8 bytes of information in it somewhere:

```
132     134     137     141     121     101     74      38
```

This is how this information would be represented in binary:

```
10000100 10000110 10001001 10001101 01111001 01100101 01001010 00100110
```

You want to hide the binary byte 11010101 (213) in this sequence. We simply replace the LSB of each sample byte with the corresponding bit from the byte you are trying to hide. The original sequence will change to:

```
133     135     136     141     120     101     74      39
```

In binary, this is:

```
10000101 10000111 10001000 10001101 01111000 01100101 01001010 00100111
```

The left-most byte is now 10000101, meaning that only the last bit changed to 1. This occurred because the data that needed to be hidden in that bit was 01, causing the last two bits of the original byte 00 to change. If the first two bits of the original byte had been 10, then both bits would have to change to get to 01. If the two bits of the original byte were 01, then none of the bits would have to change.

S-Tools Step-by-Step

Using S-Tools is very easy because of its drag-and-drop interface. Because of this ease of use and the powerful hiding techniques it employs, S-Tools is one of the most popular stego tools available.

If you'd like to try S-Tools out, locate the file on the accompanying CD, install it, and then follow these steps:

1. Open the program from the Windows Start menu.

2. Drag the image in which you want to hide data into the S-Tools window from the Windows desktop or an open folder. The image appears in the S-Tools window, as shown in Figure 6.3.

3. Drag the file that contains the message you want to hide into the S-Tools window and place it over the host image. The dialog box shown in Figure 6.4 appears.

4. Enter the pass phrase, and click OK.

5. At this point, a new image will appear that looks identical to the original image, except that data has been hidden in it. Save the covert file; you might also want to destroy the original image at this point so that nobody can locate it and compare the two.

Figure 6.3   S-Tools with an image loaded.

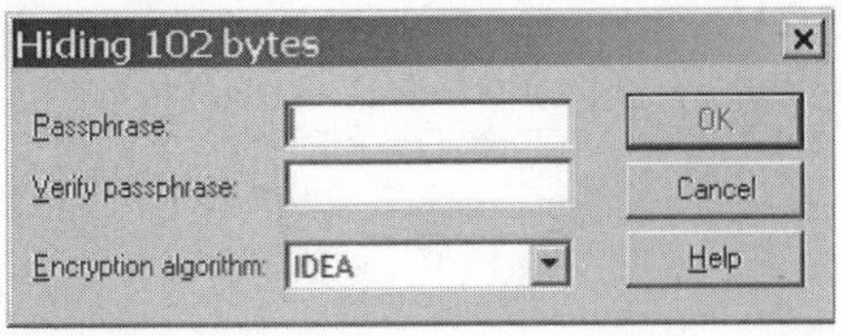

Figure 6.4   S-Tools prompting the user for a pass phrase.

Hide and Seek

Hide and Seek, Version 4.1, is a freeware program that runs under DOS. Hide and Seek hides data in GIF image files using the least significant bit of each data byte to encode characters. It then uses dispersion to spread the data (and thus the picture quality degradation) out a bit throughout the GIF in a pseudo-random fashion. A pseudo-random algorithm looks fairly random, but it is actually predictable to allow data to be extracted.

This method is fundamentally the same as the 8-bit method used by S-Tools. The only difference is that Hide and Seek reduces the color table to 128 colors and creates 2 duplicates (you'll remember that S-Tools reduces the table to 32 colors and creates 8 duplicates). Hide and Seek works only with 8-bit color encoding.

Noise is noticeable when using Hide and Seek with larger host files, but smaller files remain largely intact. The file to be hidden must also be short (no longer than 19K) because each character takes 8 pixels to hide.

NOTE Here's where the 19K file size for Hide and Seek comes from. There are 320×480 pixels in the maximum VGA display mode, thus ((320×480)/8), which equals 19200. This gets rounded down to an even 19000 for safe dispersion.

Hide and Seek actually consists of two executables, one for hiding and one for extracting data. Both programs run from a command prompt, and the user passes in the arguments for the filenames.

To hide data in a file you type "hide", followed by the covert filename, followed by the overt filename. Figure 6.5 shows a typical hide command.

NOTE Because Hide is relatively weak and easy to crack you can also provide a key that will lock the message and make it harder to crack.

Figure 6.5 Process for hiding information using Hide.

When you press Enter you will see a screen telling you to press any key when you're ready to proceed. You will then see the message image flash up on the screen as data is hidden in it.

When the data has been hidden you receive the following message: Done! You can use a command-line direction to save the file. Remember to delete your original file for safety, if necessary. If you don't want to take a chance that somebody can locate your original file and compare it to the one with hidden data, follow that direction.

J-Steg

J-Steg hides data in JPEG images. Hiding in JPEG images is quite different from all the other techniques. JPEG uses a lossy compression algorithm to store image data. That is why JPEG images are used on the Internet—because they are compressed, they take up less space.

A lossy data compression or encoding algorithm is one that loses, or purposely throws away, input data during the encoding process to gain a better compression ratio. When lossy compression is used, the messages stored in the image data will be corrupted. Because of this you would think that this file format could not be used to hide data.

To overcome this problem, instead of storing messages in the image data, J-Steg uses the compression coefficients to store data. Here's how this works. JPEG images use a Discrete Cosine Transform (DCT) compression scheme. The compressed data is stored as integers, and the compression involves extensive floating-point calculations that are rounded at the end. When this rounding occurs, the program makes a choice to round up or round down. By modulating these choices, messages can be embedded in the DCT coefficients. Messages hidden in this way are quite difficult to detect.

J-Steg has a simple built-in wizard that you can use to hide and extract images. When you first start the program, you can choose whether you want to hide or extract a file in a JPEG image on the opening screen. In this example, you will first hide data and then extract it, so you would select the Hide option and click Next. J-Steg then prompts you for the name of the file you want to hide, as shown in Figure 6.6.

When you proceed to the next wizard step, you see the window shown in Figure 6.7. Here is where you select the carrier file in which you want to hide data. This screen provides four options that determine how much data can be embedded and the level of detection.

- Both the compression quality and Huffman table (the table of values used to encode the compressed data) allow you to hide additional information in the file by applying different levels of compression.

- Smoothing makes the DCT coefficients look smoother and less detectable, but in doing so limits the amount of information you can hide. With color images you can obtain more detail, but it is also easier to spot discrepancies in the data.

- By converting an image to grayscale more data can be hidden. Because everything is gray it is much harder to detect slight changes to the file. Changes that would look obvious in a color image blend in nicely in a grayscale image.

On the next screen of the wizard you enter a name for the output file containing the hidden data.

Now that you have hidden data in a file, you need a way to extract the information. To do this, at J-Steg's opening screen you select the Extract option. The extraction process is simple: All you have to do is select the file that has data hidden in it in the screen shown in Figure 6.8, and J-Steg will automatically extract the information.

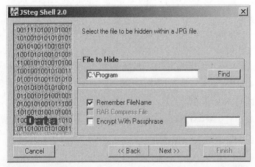

Figure 6.6   J-Steg screen to pick the covert file.

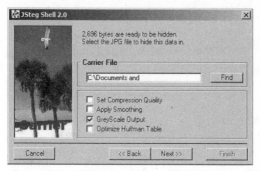

Figure 6.7   J-Steg screen for picking the overt file in which you want to hide data.

As you can see, J-Steg is probably one of the easiest stego programs to use. It takes little effort or understanding of the process to hide data, and the technique is fairly robust.

EZ Stego

EZ Stego is written in Java. This program hides data using the least significant bits of GIF images. It does this by storing the data in the color table, but the table is not modified as it is with S-Tools and Hide and Seek. With EZ Stego the color table is sorted by RGB colors, rather than reducing the color in the image and making duplicate color entries. This sorting is done in such a way that similar colors appear next to each other in the color table. This is critical to ensure that the output image will not be badly degraded.

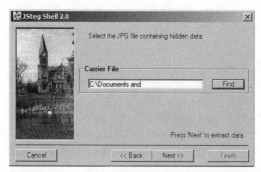

Figure 6.8   J-Steg prompting for the file that has data embedded in it.

Here are the steps that EZ Stego goes through:

1. It copies the color table from the image and rearranges the copy of the table so that colors that are near each other in the color model are near each other in the color table.

2. It takes the first pixel and finds the corresponding entry in the new sorted color table.

3. The program takes the first bit of data from the secret message and puts it in the least significant bit of the number corresponding to the row in the color table to which the pixel points.

4. EZ Stego then finds the new color that the index points to and locates that color in the original color table.

5. The program points the pixel to the row corresponding to the new color in the color table.

For this process, having the color table sorted correctly is crucial, so when the pixel points to a new entry in the color table, the corresponding color is very close to the original color. If this assumption is not true, then the new image will be degraded.

Image Hide

Image Hide is a stego program that has a very easy-to-use GUI. The program can hide data in a variety of formats. It does so in a similar fashion to the other techniques you've read about in this chapter, by replacing the least significant bits of the individual pixels of an image. It, however, does the embedding on the fly, which makes this program unique.

When you start the program you get an opening screen; from here you can open the file into which you want to embed data (see Figure 6.9). Highlight the area of this image in which you want to hide data, type the message, and then click the Write button.

At this point the data is hidden in the file, and the screen shown in Figure 6.10 appears. At this point, you can either hide more data or extract the data you already hid.

To extract the data that you already hid, you highlight the area on the screen where you hid it, then click Read. Your message appears at the bottom of the screen.

> **NOTE** Because Hide is a subsitution technique, it does not increase the size of the file; therefore, there are limits to the amount of data it can hide.

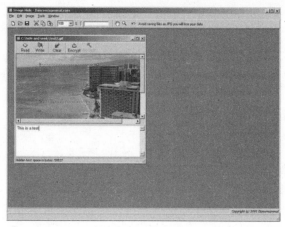

Figure 6.9 Opening screen for Image Hide with overt file loaded and covert message typed at the bottom.

Digital Picture Envelope

Digital Picture Envelope (DPE) is a stego technique that hides information in a .bmp file format. Even though you have read about other techniques for hiding information in .bmp files, what makes this technique unique is that it can hide large amounts of data in an image and do so without changing the file size.

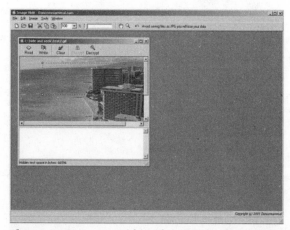

Figure 6.10 Image Hide with image loaded that contains embedded information.

The program comes with two mini-applications: one for embedding the information and one for extracting it. Digital Picture Envelope is based on a hiding technique called BCPS, which was invented by Eiji Kawaguchi of Japan. DPE can use 8-bit .bmp images, but to hide the maximum amount of data you would use it with true color or 24-bit images. The data is embedded in the bit planes (similar to pixels) of the images, which is what allows you to hide such a large amount of data. This technique is also called large-capacity stego.

NOTE It is important to note for those of us who do not read Japanese: Some of the prompts and error messages in this program are in Japanese. There are enough elements in English, though, that you can easily figure out what's going on.

To hide data in an image you start up the encoder application, shown in Figure 6.11.

To use the program you drag and drop the image in which you want to hide information onto the dummy image area of the program. You then copy the text you want to embed to the Windows clipboard, and you click the Embed button, shown in Figure 6.11. When you click that button the text that is being hidden will pop up in a window, as shown in Figure 6.12.

When you click Next, the program will then show both images, as in Figure 6.13. You can see how similar the images are.

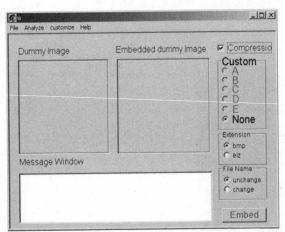

Figure 6.11 Digital Picture Envelope GUI for embedding information in a file.

Figure 6.12 Digital Picture Envelope screen showing a covert message.

NOTE You can use the Analyze menu, as shown in Figure 6.13, to have the program analyze the dummy image and tell you how much data you can hide in it.

To extract the message you hid, you have to use the Digital Picture Envelope Decoder. You start up the Decoder, open the picture that has data embedded in it, and then click the Extract button, as shown in Figure 6.14.

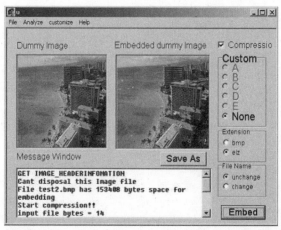

Figure 6.13 Digital Picture Envelope screen showing both the original image and the image that has data hidden in it.

Figure 6.14   Digital Picture Envelope GUI for extracting information from a file.

Camouflage

Camouflage is a relatively simple insertion technique that works across a variety of formats. It hides data at the end of a file, placing it after the end-of-file marker. The application ignores this information. Because Camouflage uses an insertion technique, you can hide large amounts of data, but that data is fairly easy to detect. What makes this program unique is that to use it you do not run a special application to hide and extract information. Once you've installed Camouflage, you simply right-click on the file you want to hide in Windows Explorer, as shown in Figure 6.15. On the Windows shortcut menu that appears, you have two additional options, one to Camouflage and one to Uncamouflage.

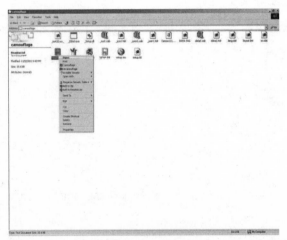

Figure 6.15   Shortcut menu showing options for Camouflage.

Gif Shuffle

Gif Shuffle is a program that hides data in GIF images. It does this by manipulating the color table of the image. The order of the color table does not matter for GIF images, but in your typical GIF image the table is not sorted. Gif Shuffle takes an image and sorts the color table, organizing it by similar colors. This is done by using the RGB or red, green, and blue values. A mod operation is then performed, and each piece of the covert message is hidden in the color table.

Gif Shuffle is a command-line tool that you use to both hide and extract a message. Because this technique manipulates the color map, there is a limit to the amount of data that can be hidden, so the program comes with a command-line option that shows you how much data can be hidden in a file. To see how much information can be hidden, use the S option shown in Figure 6.16.

Using Gif Shuffle you can hide a covert file, or you can pass text to the program in which the file will hide. To extract a message, type the name of the program, followed by the name of the file that has data hidden in it, and the message appears. Figure 6.17 shows the file covert.txt being hidden in a GIF image.

NOTE You can use the P option to protect the information you are hiding with a password and the C option to compress the data.

Spam Mimic

Spam Mimic is a generation technique that takes a covert message and uses an English grammar rule set to generate text that looks like spam. Spam Mimic creates a grammar tree showing the different possible words that can be used and, based on the covert message, selects words from it.

Figure 6.16   Gif Shuffle, showing how much data can be hidden in a file.

Figure 6.17   Using Gif Shuffle to hide data.

A simple example is the phrase "_____ went to the store." The blank could be filled in with several different words, such as he, she, it, and so on. By building a grammar tree with the covert message, the program picks what words will appear and generates the text. You can then use the technique in reverse to find the hidden message.

Spam Mimic is unique from the other techniques that you have looked at in that it runs from a Web site. Go to www.spammimic.com (shown in Figure 6.18) and type in your message.

After you click Encode, the program will generate the overt message shown in Figure 6.19.

One of the limitations of this program is the small area for entering text. You can actually type as much information in the box as you want and cut and paste long messages into the window, but the developers purposely kept the box small to discourage people from typing long messages. Another problem with the program is that when you type a long message, the output text starts to repeat itself and looks suspicious. With a more advanced grammar, or by varying the grammar, this problem could be avoided.

Figure 6.18   Spam Mimic's encoding screen.

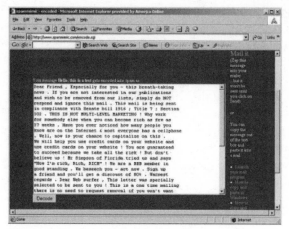

Figure 6.19   Spam Mimic's decoding screen.

The other problem with this technique is that the ratio of input to output text is very large. For example, if I fed the preceding paragraph into the program as my covert message the output message would be 12 pages long.

Rolling Your Own Stego

Now that you've seen several freeware and commercial products that implement stego and understand the techniques they use, you get to create your own. You'll explore all three types of techniques: insertion, substitution, and generation. You'll see that the number of approaches to stego you might come up with is limited only by your creativity.

For this section I concentrated on the functionality, not fancy GUIs. Elaborate GUIs may look nice, but they make it harder to compile code on different platforms.

NOTE All of the techniques presented in this section were developed specifically for this book. To make it easier for you to experiment, I have included all of the code in Appendix A and on the CD that comes with this book. I have also provided a fully compiled .exe for Windows that will let you experiment with these techniques without having to compile code. If you are working on a Unix platform, you should be able to compile the code cleanly because it is all command-line based.

Comprehensive Stego Program

What follows in this chapter is a description of nine brand new stego techniques for hiding data. The source code for each technique is included in Appendix A. To make the program easier to use, a command-line program was developed that allows you to run all of the different techniques discussed here. By specifying different command-line options you control which technique is used. (This was written as a command-line tool to make it easier for you to port it between different operating systems.)

Figure 6.20 shows output from running the tool. The tool provides an interface for using all of the techniques that follow.

Essentially, for each technique discussed here, there is a number for hiding information and a number for extracting information (see the list that follows). For example, r17 will encode information, and r18 will extract the information with the wav-sine technique. The following are the different routines supported by this program; all of the techniques are discussed in the text that follows in this chapter:

1. HTTP Insertion encode
2. HTTP Insertion decode
3. EXE Stuffer encode
4. EXE Stuffer decode
5. RTF Insertion encode
6. RTF Insertion decode
7. WAV Creation encode
8. WAV Creation decode
9. WAV Twiddle encode
10. WAV Twiddle decode
11. WAR Create encode
12. WAR Create decode
13. DOC Stuffer encode
14. DOC Stuffer decode
15. HTTP_VARY Insertion encode
16. HTTP_VARY Insertion decode
17. WAV_SINE Creation encode
18. WAV_SINE Creation decode

Figure 6.20   Output from running the comprehensive stego tool.

The following are parameters for using this program:

File names must be less than 80 characters

C <covert filename> Current: covertFile.txt

c <decoded filename> Current:

O <overt filename> Current: overtFile.txt

o <final overt filename> Current: overt2File.txt

r <1-?? hidding routine> Current: 0

v <1-255 variable>   Current: 0

? Display this message

The following are some examples of using this program to embed or extract information based on the preceding list:

Example, to HTTP_WS encode:

    stego.exe -r 1 -C covertSmall.txt -O overtBig.html -o out.html

Example, to HTTP_WS decode:

    stego.exe -r 2 -c covert2.txt -o out.html

Example, to exeStuffer encode:

> stego.exe -r 4 -C covertMedium.bin -c covertMedium2.bin -O stego.exe
> -o stego1.exe

Example, to exeStuffer decode:

> stego.exe -r 5 -C covertMedium.bin -c covertMedium2.bin -O stego.exe
> -o stego1.exe

This tool is meant as a prototype of a proof-of-concept tool. The .exe and source code are provided so that you can try out techniques and make any modifications that you would like.

Technique Structure

To describe each technique I will use the following format:

- An *overview* of the technique highlighting the type of technique with an overall simplicity and ease-of-detection rating. This rating ranges from 1 to 5, 1 being the lowest and 5 the highest.

- The *idea* explaining the concept behind how data is hidden using this technique.

- A *detailed description* of the idea.

- A *logic flow diagram*, which is a typical part of the design of a technique and is developed before you code.

- *Areas of improvement* for the technique that will make it more robust and harder to detect.

WAV Creation

For the first set of examples, you'll take a single technique and file type and learn how to create a stego technique using creation, modify it to do insertion, and finish by showing how it can be done with substitution.

In this example you work with a stego technique using .wav audio files.

Overview

Type: Creation

Simplicity: 1

Ease of detection: 1

Idea

With this first technique you are going to look at ways to hide data in sound or .wav files. Sometimes simple techniques provide powerful results. For a .wav file the simplest way to hide data is to take covert data and use it to create a new .wav file. (Now, this .wav file is not going to sound that great, but it's a good technique for you to start with.)

Details

With this technique you take a secret message and convert it to the data portion of the overt file. In order to do this, you have to understand how .wav files work.

A .wav file has three areas of information in it: RIFF, FORMAT, and DATA.

The RIFF chunk is composed of 12 bytes of data. The breakdown of the bytes in this portion of a .wav file is as follows:

- Bytes 0–3 are the RIFF bytes and contain ASCII characters.

- Bytes 4–7 contain the total length.

- Bytes 8–11 specify the .wav format and are ASCII characters.

NOTE When you are counting bytes in files or network traffic you always start counting at 0, not 1. Therefore, 12 bytes of data means that when you start at the beginning of a file, the first byte is 0 and the last byte is 11.

The FORMAT area is 24 bytes in length, and the bytes are broken down this way:

- Bytes 0–3 are the format or "fmt_" bytes and contain ASCII characters.

- Bytes 4–7 are the length of FORMAT chunks, which are always 0×10.

- Bytes 8–9 are always 0×01.

- Bytes 10–11 are for mono versus stereo:

    0×01 = Mono

    0×02 = Stereo

- Bytes 12–15 are the sampling rate listed in Hz.

- Bytes 16–19 are the bytes per second of the playback.

- Bytes 20–21 are the bytes per sampling interval—that is, 1,2, or 4.

- Bytes 22–23 are the bits per sample.

The DATA area is not a set length because it contains the actually data, or code, that the .wav file actually uses to create the audio sound. The beginning part of this area does have some preset fields that breakdown this way:

- Bytes 0–3 point to the data and are in ASCII characters.
- Bytes 4–7 are the length of data that follows.
- Bytes 8–end are the actual data.

The first step in creating this stego is to create a file that has the proper RIFF, FORMAT, and DATA bytes set; then paste your covert data into the data portion.

Logic Flow

The diagram in Figure 6.21 shows the logic flow that was used for both the encoding and decoding of this technique.

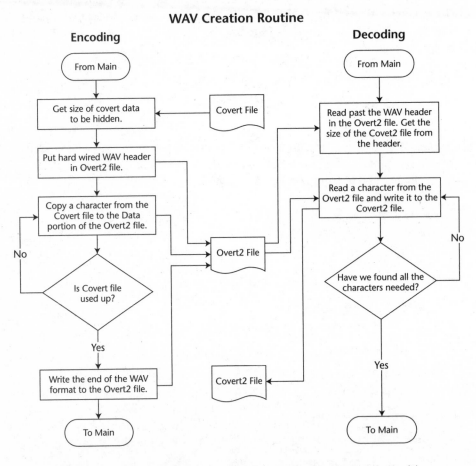

WAV Creation Routine

The WAV header file is hard wired (same for all Overt2 files) with the exception that the size of the Covert file must be put in the header.

The size of the data block in the WAV file is stored in the WAV header.

Figure 6.21 Logic flow diagram for the .wav creation technique.

Areas for Improvement

This technique is fairly basic and makes no attempt to be stealthy. It is included to show how a stego technique can be used to create a host file. With this technique you can randomize the data or encrypt the information to make it harder for someone to pull out the covert file; however, this does not really address the heart of the problem. The way to improve this technique is to make the file sound more like a legitimate sound file. The next two techniques modify this technique to make the resulting file sound more legitimate.

wav-Sine Creation

In this example, note an improvement over the previous technique as you create an insertion-based stego technique using .wav audio files by mimicking a sine wave.

Overview

Type: Insertion

Simplicity: 2

Ease of detection: 3

Idea

This technique expands on the previous one to make it more robust. A secondary goal here is to show you how to create an insertion technique. The first thing you do with this technique is create a legitimate sound file. Then you take covert data and insert it into certain portions of that file.

Details

With this technique you create a .wav file using a sine wave. A sine wave is a mathematical curve that is used to create a sound. Essentially, the file would contain a repetitive sound. You insert the covert data throughout this sine wave (thus the term, insertion). In this example, you will let the user pass in a command-line argument to tell us what percent of data should be hidden and where.

Logic Flow

The diagram in Figure 6.22 shows the logic flow that was used for both the encoding and decoding of this technique.

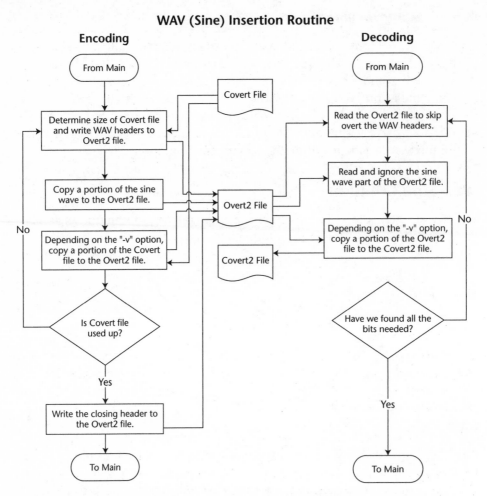

WAV (Sine) Insertion Routine

This algorithm creates a crude sine wave in the data portion of the Overt2 WAV file. Depending on the command line argument "-v <2|4|8>", either half, one-quarter, or one-eighth of the sine wave data is replaced with the covert data.

Figure 6.22   Diagram for wav-sine technique.

Areas for Improvement

This algorithm produces a .wav file that makes a very rudimentary oscillating sound. By producing more robust code, the sound could be tweaked even further to create a file with more harmonics and variation of the pitch. One potential problem is that the amount of insertion is controlled by the user. If the user puts in a varying degree of 2, this means that half of the data in the file is covert and the other half is the sine wave. This much hidden data could degrade the sound of the file. A wav file sounds much better if the ratio between covert and sine data is much lower.

WAV Twiddle

This example adds an improvement to the previous technique by creating a substitution-based stego technique using .wav audio files.

Overview

Type: Substitution

Simplicity: 2

Ease of Detection: 4

Idea

In the first and second examples, you created a technique and modified it to become an insertion technique. Next you will hide data using a substitution technique. First you have to find data that can be modified to encode your information in the file.

Details

This technique hides information in the data portion of a file. The key thing here is to find data that you can overwrite without having a substantial impact on the host file. You could locate a bit that you could twiddle (or change) and then modify only one bit at a time to minimize any impact. You would over-write the least significant bit of each file with a 1 or 0 to match your covert data. The only thing you have to be careful of is that .wav files calculate parity checks on bytes. You may have to tweak the parity a bit so that it still matches up. (A parity check is a simple test to make sure none of the bits in the file has changed.)

Logic Flow

The diagram in Figure 6.23 shows the logic flow that was used for both the encoding and decoding of this technique.

WAV (Twiddling) Substitution Routine

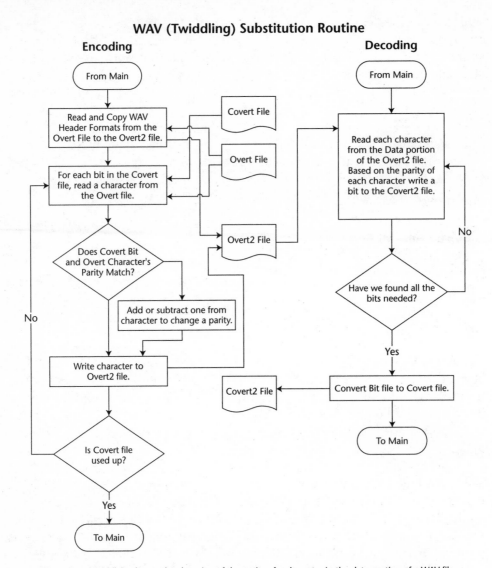

In this routine, "twiddle" refers to the changing of the parity of a character in the data portion of a WAV file.

When encoding each bit of the Covert file determines the needed parity of a character in the Overt2 file. If the current character (acquired from the Overt file) has the correct parity, it is simply written to the Overt2 file. If the parity is not correct, the character is changed (increased by one) to the needed parity and then written to the Overt2 file.

The size of the Covert file are encoded in the first 32 characters in the data portion of the Overt2 file.

When decoding, the process is reversed and a bit is written to the Covert2 file, depending on the parity of the character in the Overt2 file.

Figure 6.23   Logic flow diagram for .wav twiddle technique.

Areas for Improvement

This technique does a very good job of being stealthy, but the amount of data is fairly limited because you are inserting only one bit of data at a time. You could increase the amount of data, but doing so is likely to have an impact on the stealthiness.

Doc Stuffer

In this example, you use a hybrid insertion substitution-based technique for hiding information in Word documents.

Overview

Type: Insertion/substitution

Simplicity: 1

Ease of Detection: 2

Idea

Word or .doc files carry a lot of information that is often not visible to the user or even used by the originating application when displaying the file. You can insert data in one of those areas. This could be achieved by performing either a substitution or an insertion. If there is data in those unused fields, then you would overwrite it. Because these fields are often empty, you could use insertion to place data in those areas.

Details

One area that is ripe for hiding data is the comments field under the properties section of a Word document. This area can contain a lot of data and is often not checked by most people when they view a Word document. Figure 6.24 shows the Properties field for a document that has no data hidden in it.

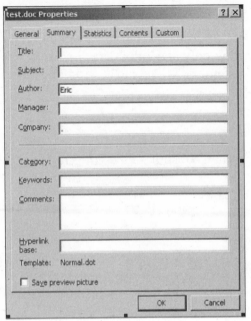

Figure 6.24   Display showing the output from a normal Properties window under Word.

If you put covert data in this field and someone happens to open this dialog box, it would look suspicious. To make this technique more covert, you can insert several blank lines in the comment field and put the data in the last line of the field, as shown in Figure 6.25. Now if someone brings up the comments area it will be blank; however, because there is data not displayed, the scroll bar will be active. Most people would just see a blank field and move on, but if someone looks very closely, he or she will notice something unusual. After data has been hidden in the file, if you bring up the properties field again you will be able to see your information, as shown in Figure 6.25.

Logic Flow

The diagram in Figure 6.26 shows the logic flow that was used for both the encoding and decoding of this technique.

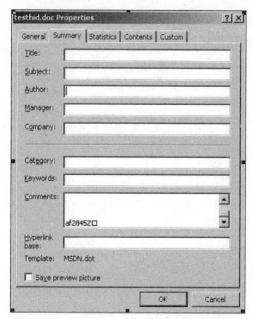

Figure 6.25 Display showing the output from a Properties window under Word that contains hidden information. Notice the active scrollbar.

Areas for Improvement

Because you are rolling your own stego, I've set up this technique to use a marker to determine where the comments field is placed in a Word document. Word does not store the comments field in the same place for each file, but it does follow a set format. I did this to make it easier to hide data, but still show the power of the technique. To improve this technique, you could analyze the structure of the document and locate the comments field so that a marker does not have to be used.

EXE Stuffer

In this example you hide data with an .exe file. This is unique because the space for hiding the data is compiled into the program, but the actual data you hide can be changed.

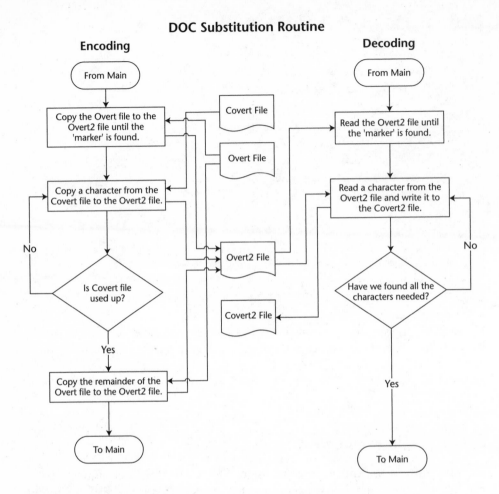

DOC Substitution Routine

The Overt file must be a MS Word document with a special 'marker' typed into the Comment field on the document Properties window.

When encoding, the routine scans until it finds the marker and then puts the covert data after the marker. The covert data may be binary even though the Property Comments field normally takes ASCII input.

On decoding the process is reversed and the routine scans the Overt2 file until the marker is found and then extracts the covert data.

Figure 6.26   Logic flow diagram for the Doc Stuffer technique.

Overview

Type: Insertion/ substitution

Simplicity: 2

Ease of Detection: 4

Idea

There are several existing techniques for hiding data in an .exe. A common insertion technique is to put data after the end-of-file (EOF) marker. The program would still run, but the covert data is ignored because it falls after the end of the file. A common substitution technique used with exe files is to find no operation commands (NOP) and overwrite them with data. The technique used in this example is a little different: Here you put your message into the source code, compile the code into a .exe, and then pull the message out of the .exe itself.

Details

The concern when compiling a message into a .exe is that every time you change your covert message, you have to recompile the code. Not only would this be annoying, but you could end up with many different versions of the same .exe. For that reason, I changed the method of operation of this technique slightly.

With this technique, when you compile the source code into a .exe, a .exe marker is compiled into the program. This program reserves space in the .exe in different areas that can then be overwritten with covert data. This is a technique that compiles the data into the .exe, but it can also be easily modified.

The .exe marker is a module that you link into your source code. When you compile the source code into a .exe, this program reserves space you can use for hidden data. It does this by having the .exe marker use unique strings that are not normally found in a .exe to mark these reserved spaces. This allows the program that actually inserts the covert data to find the space quickly and replace the marked areas with covert data. This technique also turns out to be a hybrid because data is inserted into the .exe at the time you compile it, and then the covert data is substituted when the embedding process is performed.

Logic Flow

The diagram in Figure 6.27 shows the logic flow that was used for both the encoding and decoding of this technique.

Areas for Improvement

Several potential areas can be used in .exe files to hide data. This method is limited to a single location; others could be added.

EXE Substitution Routine

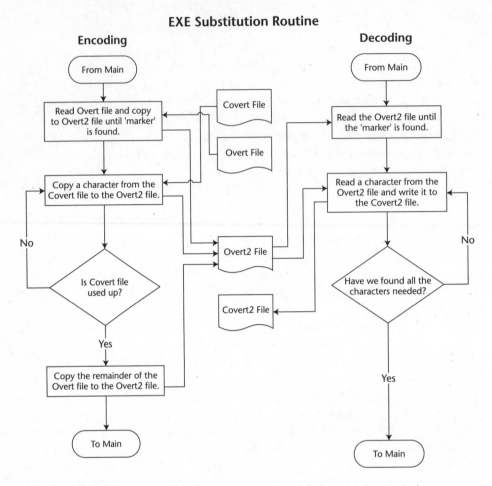

Figure 6.27   Logic flow diagram for the .exe substitution technique.

The Overt executable file must compile in the routine 'exe_marker.c' in order to save the space in the exe file to hide the covert data. When this module is compiled in, there is enough space in the exe file to hold the covert data.

The substitution of the covert data into the compiled exe_marker.c module does not effect the performance of the executable.

HTML White Space

In this example, you embed information in an HTML file by adding white space at the end of each line.

Overview

Type: Insertion

Simplicity: 2

Ease of Detection: 4

Idea

It seems as if everyone in the world uses the Web and has his or her own Web site. There are millions of HTML documents floating around the Internet all the time. It seems only logical to take advantage of that crowded landscape by developing an HTML hiding technique.

From an insertion standpoint you want to find information that the browser ignores. A hidden field is an area that is contained in an HTML document, but is ignored by the browser when it displays the document. E-commerce sites use hidden fields to track state. (Because HTTP is stateless, in order to use the Web for e-commerce, mechanisms have to be built in to track state.) Figure 6.28 shows a very simple Web page viewed in a browser.

When you look at the source code for this document, you see the code shown in Figure 6.29.

Even though the browser did not display it, the message was still there. This technique is very simple, but it is extremely easy for someone to detect the message simply by viewing the document's source. This example creates a somewhat more robust technique.

Details

Today many programs will automatically generate HTML for users. The HTML documents they generate look very nice when displayed in a browser, but when examined from a source-code standpoint, the HTML may be very sloppy. It may not be formatted properly, there may be unneeded spaces, but because what the browser displays looks fine, it usually doesn't matter.

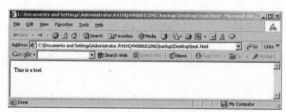

Figure 6.28   Display from a simple Web page.

```
This is a test
<input type="hidden" name="CovertMessage" value="This is a hidden message">
```

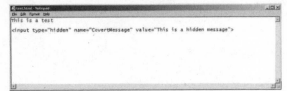

Figure 6.29 Output showing the actual HTML for the page displayed in Figure 6.28.

The HTML source provides an opportunity for stego to be used. Because no one really pays attention to how the HTML looks, you could insert some additional white space and no one would be the wiser. The important thing to remember is that all white space is not created equal. Even though it looks the same to a human, white space could contain spaces or tabs, for example. What if you used a simple encoding scheme, where a 0 bit is a space and a 1 one bit is a tab. Now you insert five white space characters at the end of each line. The resulting file would look the same when displayed with a browser and at the source-code level.

Figure 6.30 shows the source code for an HTML document that has data embedded in the white space at the end of each line.

Figure 6.31 shows part of the HTML code from the original file that does not have data hidden in it. From a visual standpoint it is identical to the HTML source that does not contain any embedded information.

```
    <hr>
    <p align="center"> </p>
    <hr>
    <p align="center"><b><i><font color="#808080" size="4">Security Resources</font></i></b
    <p align="center"><font color="#000000" size="4"><b><a href="tools.html">Tools</a></b><
    <p align="center"><font color="#000000" size="4"><b><a href="web.html">Web Sites</a></b
    <p align="center"><font color="#000000" size="4"><b><a href="mailing.html">Mailing List
    <p align="center"><font color="#000000" size="4"><b><a href="books.html">Books</a></b><
    <p align="center"><font color="#000000" size="4"><b><a href="papers.html">Papers/Articl
    <hr>
    <p align="center"> </p>
    <hr>
    <p align="center"><b><i><font color="#808080" size="4">Security Subject Areas</font></i
    <p align="center"><font color="#000000" size="4"><b><a href="firewalls.html">Firewalls<
    <p align="center"><font color="#000000" size="4"><b><a href="intrusion.html">Intrusion
    Systems</a></b></font></p>
    <p align="center"><font color="#000000" size="4"><b><a href="encryption.html">Encryptio
    <p align="center"><font color="#000000" size="4"><b><a href="stego.html">Steganography<
    <p align="center"> </p>
    <hr>
    <p align="center"> </p>
    <p align="center"> </p>
    <p align="center"> </p>
    <p align="center"> </p>
    <p align="left"> </td>
  <td width="8%"></td>
  <td width="144%">
    <p align="center"><font face="Arial Black" size="6" color="#FFCC00">Hackers
    Beware</font></p>
    <p align="center"><font face="Arial Black" size="4" color="#FFFFFF">Defending
    Your Network From The Wiley Hacker</font></p>
```

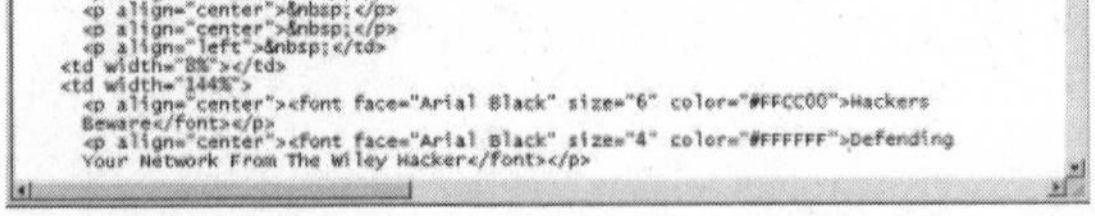

Figure 6.30 HTML source code showing a page that has white space embedded in it.

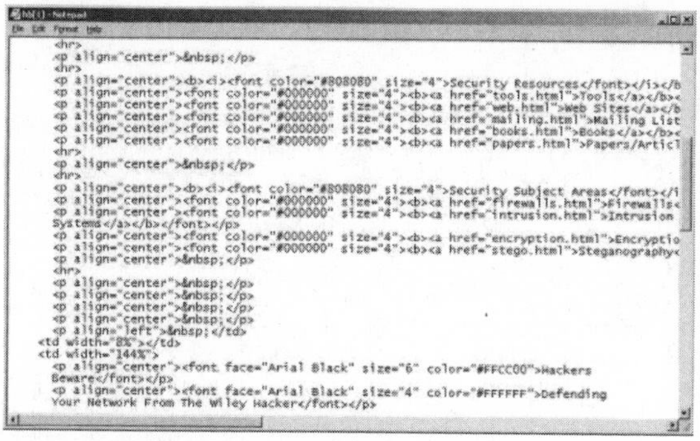

Figure 6.31   Part of the HTML source code for the same Web page shown in Figure 6.30, with no hidden data.

Logic Flow

The diagram in Figure 6.32 shows the logic flow that was used for both the encoding and decoding of this technique.

Areas for Improvement

Even though this technique is very hard to detect by looking at the HTML document in a browser, because it uses a uniform pattern of five white spaces it would be easy for an automated program to detect. Any set patterns that do not normally appear in a file provide a mechanism for detection. One way to fix this is to vary the amount of white space or make it definable by the user (which is what the next technique does).

HTML White Space Variable

In this example, you change the amount of white space that can be embedded on each line.

Overview

Type: Insertion

Simplicity: 2

Ease of Detection: 5

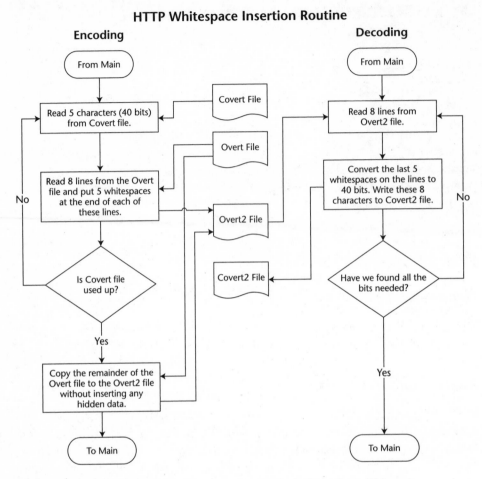

In this routine, bits are encoded as whitespaces at the end of the line in the html code. Whitespaces will not show up when the Overt2 file is viewed in a web browser. A zero is encoded as a space. A '1' bit is encoded as a tab.

Bits are encoded and decoded in groups of 40 so that the Covert and Covert2 files can be read and written as 8 bit characters.

Figure 6.32   Logic flow diagram for HTML white space technique.

Idea

The previous technique embedded five white spaces at the end of every line; this technique creates a detectable pattern across all images that have data embedded this way. An alternative is to have the amount of white space user-defined from the command line.

This technique builds on other techniques in this section and shows you how the stego creation process works. You create a new technique, you use it, you find weaknesses in it, and then you figure out ways to fix those weaknesses to build a stronger technique.

Details

This technique is very similar to the previous technique, except that the user passes a number via the command line that tells the program how many characters of white space to insert at the end of each line.

Logic Flow

The diagram in Figure 6.33 shows the logic flow that was used for both the encoding and the decoding of this technique.

Areas for Improvement

This technique is slightly better because it does not produce a universal pattern across all files that have had data hidden in them using this technique. If a user picks the same variable each time he or she runs the program, though, a pattern would be introduced. One way to fix this problem is to set up the technique to pick the number of characters randomly or embed white space in other areas, such as tables.

RTF Insertion

In this example you explore the diversity of stego by developing an insertion technique for RTF files.

Overview

Type: Insertion

Simplicity: 2

Ease of Detection: 3

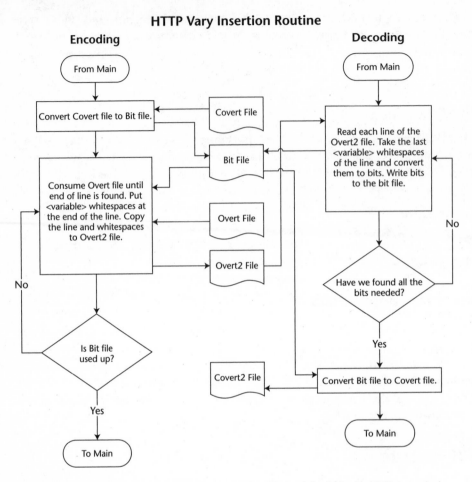

Figure 6.33 Logic flow diagram for variable white space technique.

The <variable> number of whitespaces that are stored at the end of each line in the Overt2 file is acquired from the command line option "-v <1-255>".

A space encodes a bit of '0' and a tab encodes a '1'.

When encoding the HTTP Vary Insertion routine, a line of the Overt file is read and copied to the Overt2 file. At the end of the line, a <variable> number of whitespaces are inserted into the Overt2 file.

The size of the Covert file are encoded in the first 32 whitespaces in the Overt2 file.

When decoding, the process is reversed and a <variable> number of whitespaces are read at the end of each line of the Overt2 file. The Overt2 file is read until the needed number of Covert bits are acquired.

Idea

Rich Text Format (RTF) documents use a similar markup language to HTML. You can find a tag or an area between tags that is ignored and not displayed when the document is shown on the screen. Because it is less common for someone to review the raw input of an RTF file, compared with an HTML document, this would seem to be a more robust technique that should be harder to detect.

Details

When you study the format for RTF files, you'll see that all RTF files start with {\rtf1 and end with a matching }. Any data that exists after the closing bracket is ignored and not displayed on the screen. Also, any place in an RTF file that contains {\nonshppict and ends with a } will also be ignored. Therefore, data can also be inserted in this area. As with most insertion techniques, you can insert as much data as you like. Just remember that too much data will make the file look suspiciously large.

Logic Flow

The diagram in Figure 6.34 shows the logic flow that was used for both the encoding and decoding of this technique.

Areas for Improvement

If all of the data is hidden after the final bracket in an RTF document, it is easy for an automated scanning program to detect. It would be better to spread the data evenly throughout the file.

War

I'll finish up these examples by looking at a creation technique used with the card game called War.

Overview

Type: Creation

Simplicity: 1

Ease of Detection: 2

Idea

The last technique for hiding data is to create a game file. This is essentially a file that shows the moves for playing a game. Because this has been done with chess and checkers, I'll use a card game of War for this stego technique.

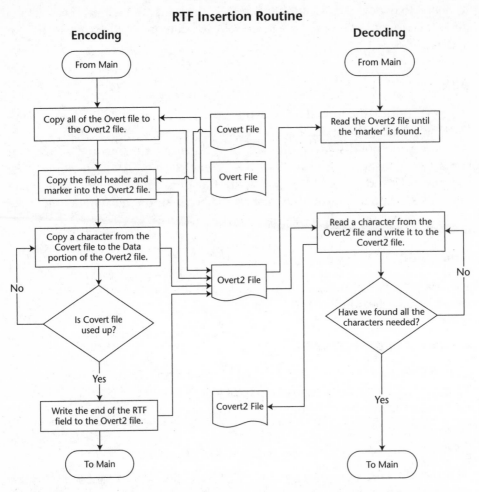

Figure 6.34 Logic flow diagram for RTF insertion technique.

The covert data is stored in a non-printing field of the RTF file. Additionally, the data is put at the end of the RTF file, which may cause it to not display, also.

When the RTF file is opened (in MS Word), the hidden data is not detected.

A unique 'marker' is put in the Overt2 just before the covert data. This is a better, more reliable way to mark the covert data than just relying on the field headers.

Details

This is a creation technique that uses covert data to create a WAR file that simulates the game of War. The algorithm documents a four-person game. The four players are North, South, East, and West. Each plays a card. As with the game of War, each player can play any card in his or her hand; the highest card wins. The hand is scored after all cards are played. The deck is then reshuffled.

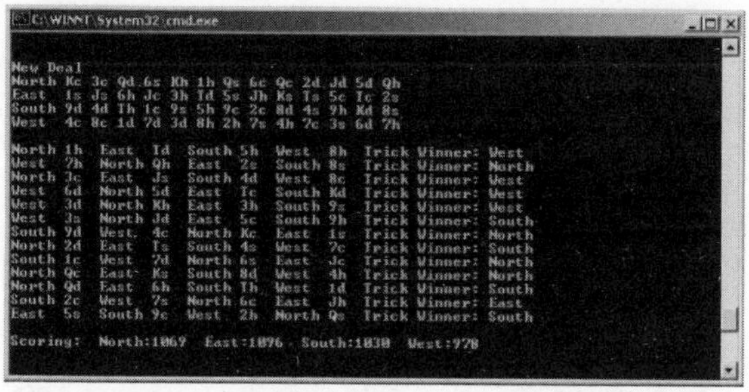

Figure 6.35 Output file from the War technique.

The covert data is embedded in the output file in two ways: (1) how the cards are shuffled and dealt to each player and (2) how the cards are played. Figure 6.35 shows a sample of the file that is generated.

Logic Flow

The diagram in Figure 6.36 shows the logic flow that was used for both the encoding and the decoding of this technique.

Areas for Improvement

With this technique, the algorithm does not play smartly because the cards are played pseudo-randomly. This could be improved, but because WAR is a basic game that someone is sending WAR files might seem a little bizarre. Bridge would make a much better card game because bridge hands and tricks are commonly printed and studied. An intelligent bridge application could be used to evaluate dealt hands and print the results.

Looking Ahead

Stego is an exciting world where a lot is happening. Individual techniques, such as those discussed in this chapter, can be used across your network, intranet, or the Internet to transmit hidden data. Chapter 7 explores the uses of stego on a network.

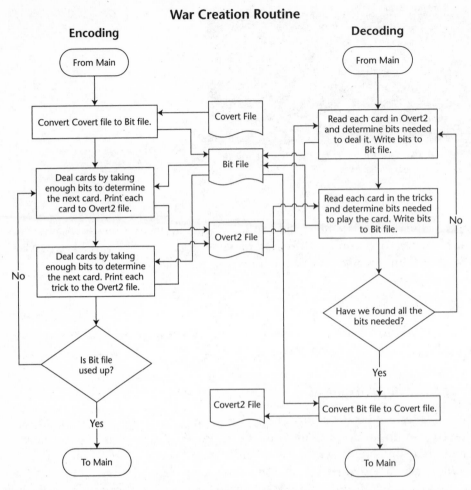

When encoding the War Creation routine, the covert file is converted to bits and put in the bit file. The bit file is then closed and re-opened for reading. The dealing is done by selecting 1 of 52 cards, and so on until only 1 card remains. The choice of the card for the deal is done by splitting the deck into High or Low. Whether the split goes hi or lo depends on the next bit value in the bit file. In this way the maximum number of bits can be used to deal the cards. The same process is used to play the tricks. In the case of the tricks the first card is 1 of 13, then 1 of 12, and so on.

When decoding the overt2 file, the hi/lo process is reversed and the resultant bits are stored in the bit file. The bit file is later converted to the covert2 file.

Figure 6.36   Logic flow diagram for War game technique.

Sending Stego Files
across a Network

When viruses first came out they infected files on a local PC. Because most computers weren't connected via the Internet at that time, viruses spread to other systems by means of floppy disks. When the Internet took off and most computers became connected, spreading viruses via floppy disks was no longer the most efficient way to infect systems. New techniques were developed that allowed viruses to propagate via networks and cause more damage. Today, more advanced viruses even initiate network connections to spread themselves.

A similar evolution has occurred with stego. In the previous chapter, you learned how stego tools are used to hide data in a file. Hiding data in a file is useful, but the whole point of stego is being able to communicate that hidden data to anyone in a networked organization or the world via the super-network of the Internet.

Because digital stego really became popular after the rise of the Internet, the transition from local-file-based stego to network stego has been somewhat rapid. This chapter delves into the various ways that stego can be transmitted over a network.

Uses and Techniques of Network Stego

On a computer network you can use stego techniques to hide files in traffic, transmit viruses, or hide the trail somebody leaves when moving around online.

Hiding in Network Traffic

When stego is used on a file, it covers up the true intent of the communication. A similar technique can be used to hide your message in normal-looking network traffic.

Network administrators have the ability to monitor traffic, looking for anomalies. If you connect to an unused port to transfer information you could attract attention. If an administrator is analyzing network traffic, looking for attacks or anomalies, and if you use a port that is not usually open or used, your activity will be easy to spot. If you make your connection emulate the often-used port 80 traffic (which is HTTP), your message might pass by without raising anyone's suspicions.

Stego Combined with Viruses

When stego is used with other techniques, such as attack tools or viruses, it can help to make an existing technique more effective by making it harder to detect. For example, you could hide a virus on a hard drive or in another file using stego. Traditional viruses exist only in executable content, such as .exe and .com files. Therefore, most virus-detection programs scan only those types of files. If you hid the virus in a .txt file using stego, you could avoid detection, and the virus could pull its payload from the .txt file and infect the system.

Tracking Internet Usage

One of the other possible uses of network stego is to hide information on systems so that Internet access and usage can be tracked.

Many e-commerce stores track your online patterns to make note of your buying habits and sell you more products. Today this tracking is typically done through URL embedding, hidden fields, or cookies. HTTP is stateless, so you have to add state to an application to perform e-commerce functions. Because an attacker can see state information that is being passed when you are online, this information could be used to identify your session ID. If stego was used to track state, because it is hidden, the attacker would not be able to see where the state information is stored. This would make it that much harder for him or her to perform an attack.

Online tracking today is being used by the dark side of our populace to track what people do and where they go. A perfect example of this is online stacking. If I can track your behavior and see all of the sites you go to, I can follow you around the cyberworld and mimic your behavior. Cyberstalking usually leads to more serious crimes, such as identity theft.

Network Stego Techniques

When talking about network stego techniques, I find it useful to break them into different categories. The four categories I use are these:

- Hiding in an attachment
- Hiding in a transmission
- Hiding in network headers
- Hiding in an overt protocol

Each category has a different level of sophistication and takes a different approach to how data is hidden.

Hiding in an Attachment

Hiding data in an attachment is the most basic form of using a network to transmit stego from one person to another. Essentially, you would use a file-based stego technique to hide your covert message in a file. Then you would take the file that contains hidden data and attach it to some other form of network traffic. The three most popular ways to do this are with email, by file transfer such as FTP, or by posting a file on a Web site.

Hiding Data in an Email Attachment

When using email keep in mind that you should have some logical reason for communicating with the person you send the email to so that you can mask your real communication goal. Of course, if you are committing corporate espionage and openly sending an email to the employee of a competitor, this might look suspicious, regardless of what the attachment looks like.

One way to cover up the intended recipient of the hidden data is to send out spam mail to thousands of people with an apparently innocent attachment. This would not look unusual at all—we all receive several spam emails a day that contain attachments or embedded images. The image would contain hidden data that only the intended recipient would think to look for it.

Transmitting Hidden Data with FTP

When you send a file to someone and you don't use a direct connection such as email, you are essentially performing a digital dead drop. In this scenario, you drop a message off somewhere online, and at a later time the intended recipient picks it up. In order to do this successfully you need to make sure that no one else can pick up the message, or if someone can, that he or she cannot read the hidden message by using a technique such as stego or crypto.

FTP is an ideal mechanism for a digital dead drop. In most cases, these repositories are associated with newsgroups, where people with similar interests can post messages. You can connect to an FTP site and upload a file. Say you visit a site where people post messages about UFOs. You could take a picture of a UFO, embed your hidden message in it, and post it to the site. As long as the intended recipient knows the location of the site and how to identify the file, he or she can download the file and retrieve your message.

Posting Stego to a Web Site

The last technique for transferring files is to post a file to a Web site. This is in some ways a hybrid of email and FTP. It is not a true dead drop because you post your image to your own Web site. It is not a true one-to-one connection as with email either because someone is only one among many people visiting your site and is not associated with you as an individual.

If I set up a Web site for stamp collectors and populate it with a lot of information and someone connects to the site and looks at pictures of rare stamps, it would be hard to make the connection between that person and me, especially if I avoid mention of myself on the site. This technique used to be considered beyond the reach of the average person, but today creating and finding a host for a Web site makes this a plausible technique for conveying hidden data.

Hiding in a Transmission

When you hide stego in an attached file you use one program to hide the data and another program to transmit the information. For example, I could use S-Tools to hide a covert message in a file and then use a separate email program to attach the image and send it.

When you hide data in a transmission, you use a single program to hide data in a file and send the image. Two programs you can use to do this are Invisible Secrets and CameraShy. Their built-in transfer feature makes these different from other stego programs such as S-Tools.

Using Invisible Secrets to Hide and Transmit Data

At first glance, Invisible Secrets may seem to have a similar purpose to the programs covered in Chapter 6. You will see, though, that it is a very powerful suite of tools that allow you to both embed hidden data in encrypted files and transmit it. Invisible Secrets can embed information win files in the following formats: JPEG, PNG, .bmp, HTML, and .wav.

Embedding Hidden Data with Invisible Secrets

From the opening screen of Invisible Secrets you can either begin the embedding process or configure how the program works by clicking the Options button. Figure 7.1 shows the Options dialog box and some of the settings available there.

On the general tab of the Options dialog box, you can set the action that occurs when you encrypt information and determine how the Invisible Secrets wizard or shell is displayed to the user.

One of the most critical settings here is for the shredder feature. Remember that if you use stego and someone can obtain a copy of both the original message and the message that has data hidden in it, he or she can do a comparison. When that person does, he or she is likely to notice that, though the files may look the same, they are composed of different bits. Therefore, it is critical to make sure the original message is destroyed using the shredder feature.

The other tabs in the Options dialog box contain settings that enable you to customize the application or enhance it by adding algorithms. These features aren't present in the other tools you explored in Chapter 6, so some are worth a closer look.

The Algorithms tab of the Invisible Secrets Options dialog box is shown in Figure 7.2. The default install of Invisible Secrets comes with a subset of encryption algorithms, but if you want to add others, or even use algorithms you create, the program can easily be customized by clicking the Add Algorithm button.

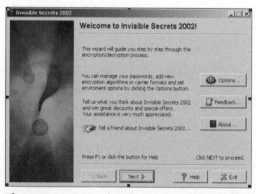

Figure 7.1   General options screen for Invisible Secrets.

Figure 7.2   Algorithms options screen for Invisible Secrets.

NOTE **Some algorithms can be purchased and require you to enter an activation key here to enable you to use them.**

On the Carriers tab of the Options dialog box shown in Figure 7.3, you can designate in what type of files Invisible Secrets can embed data. The default file types that Invisible Secrets can use to hide data are listed; new file types can be added by clicking the Add Carrier button. As with encryption algorithms, additional libraries of stego algorithms can be used to enhance the functionality of the program.

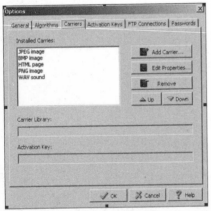

Figure 7.3   Carriers option screen for Invisible Secrets.

Once you've finished setting up options, it's time to use the program to hide some data. When you open Invisible Secrets, from the screen that appears you click Next to display the Select Action settings shown in Figure 7.4. Here you choose what type of action you want the program to take, such as hiding and unhiding data using stego techniques. Because this is an integrated suite, you can also encrypt or decrypt files or securely delete information from a hard drive. You can select any of the first two options to hide and unhide information and to encrypt the data before you hide it and decrypt it after you unhide it. Using encryption with stego provides that extra level of protection; even if someone finds the data, he or she cannot read it.

For the purpose of this example you would choose the Encrypt and Hide File(s) in a Carrier File option. When you click Next to proceed to the next screen, the Select the Files You Want to Hide screen is displayed (see Figure 7.5). As you can see here, Invisible Secrets allows you to add files that already exist or to create a new message to hide.

NOTE The other interesting setting on this screen that you have not seen in any other program is the Fake File feature. Fake files are used to create diversions. Some stego techniques, such as the .wav hiding technique that uses the least significant bits in a graphic file to hide data, are considered fairly weak. If somebody spots such a file, he or she is likely to be able to extract the hidden data. By creating fake files, even if someone can extract the hidden data, some of it will be real and some will be fake, making the attacker's job that much harder. With this feature you can select how many fake files you want the program to create, as well as the size range for the files.

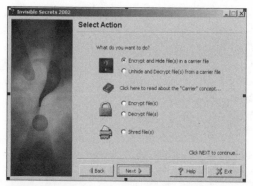

Figure 7.4   Action screen for Invisible Secrets.

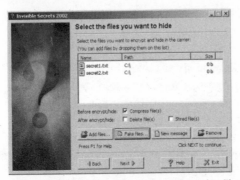

Figure 7.5   Here is where you select the files you want to hide.

After you select the files you want to hide and click Next, the Select a Carrier File screen shown in Figure 7.6 appears. On this screen, you select an overt file or carrier file in which the data will be embedded, as well as the carrier type (the type of stego you want to use).

Selecting the carrier type may not be an obvious setting; you would think that the carrier type is set by the file extension. JPG means it is a JPEG file, and you would use the JPEG hiding technique. Invisible Secrets provides this feature for the sneaky attacker who might want to take a JPEG file and name it as a .txt file to prevent the casual observer from picking up on the fact that stego is being used. If you change the extension type, Invisible Secrets will not be able to determine what technique to use, so you have to select a technique manually here.

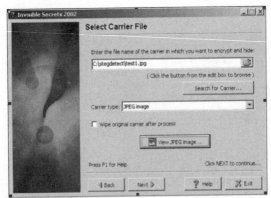

Figure 7.6   Carrier file screen for selecting the overt file.

NOTE If you don't change the file extension, Invisible Secrets will
automatically detect the proper carrier type.

Invisible Secrets also enables you to delete the original carrier file securely
after data has been embedded in it by selecting the Wipe Original Carrier after
Process option. If you want to check the file after you hide data in it, you can
click the View button.

Once you select the carrier file and click Next, you then need to select the
encryption options from the Encryption Settings screen shown in Figure 7.7. To
make sure the information is protected with encryption, you should provide a
strong password here. This password is required to extract and decrypt data.
You can choose Skip Encryption/Hide Only to skip the encryption process and
just hide the data, but for the highest security, this is not recommended.

When you click Next, you will see the screen in Figure 7.8, where you select
the name of the new target file in which Invisible Secrets will save the hidden
data. After you select the target file, a summary of the options you have
selected to this point appears at the bottom of this screen.

Click the Hide button, and the hiding process begins. A screen appears to
show you the progress. Once the data has been hidden you must click the Next
button to proceed to the final step of the wizard. Where other stego tools
would be finished at this point, with Invisible Secrets there is one more step in
the Carrier Transfer wizard that involves making settings for the built-in network component (see Figure 7.9). Here you can review the file, email it, or
transfer the file to an FTP site.

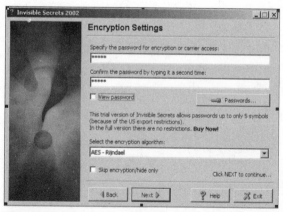

Figure 7.7   Encryption settings for Invisible Secrets.

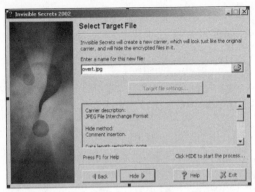

Figure 7.8 The Select Target File screen.

The email option brings up your email client, opens up a new message, and automatically attaches the file.

The FTP wizard brings up an FTP Connection screen where you can select the site to which you want to FTP the file, as shown in Figure 7.10. From the FTP Connection screen you can select an FTP site that allows anonymous access or one on which you have an account.

Once you have either sent an email or transferred an FTP file, you have successfully hidden information and transferred it across the Internet.

Decrypting and Extracting Data with Invisible Secrets

You can now use Invisible Secrets to decrypt information and extract the original message. When you start Invisible Secrets to retrieve data, you see the same opening screen shown in Figure 7.4. This time, however, you would select Unhide and Decrypt Files from a Carrier.

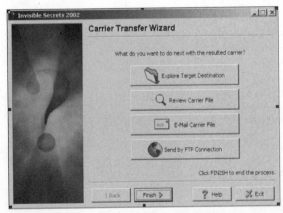

Figure 7.9 Carrier Transfer Wizard screen.

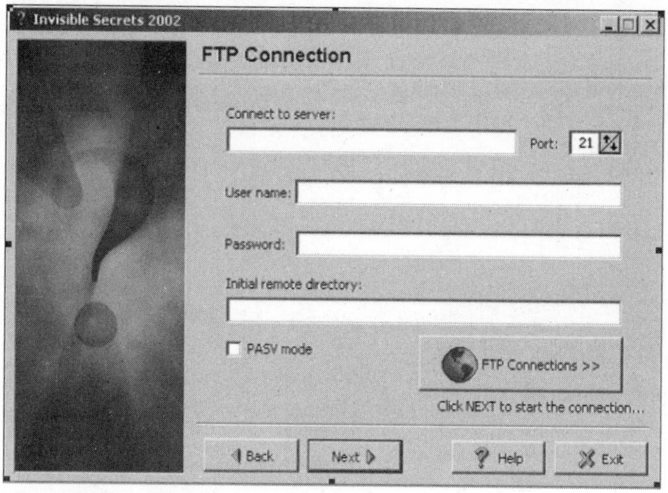

Figure 7.10   FTP Connection screen.

When you click Next, the program then prompts you for the name of the file that has data hidden in it. After you select the file that contains the hidden information and click Next, you have to provide the decryption password and select the decryption algorithm on the screen shown in Figure 7.11. The decryption algorithm is picked by default based on the file type. If you change the file type you also have to tell the program what algorithm was used because the program cannot automatically detect this.

Now the program determines if there are any hidden files in the overt file. Because you can hide many files in a host file, Invisible Secrets displays all of the files it finds, and you can select which ones you want to extract. By default, all of the files are selected for extraction, as shown in Figure 7.12.

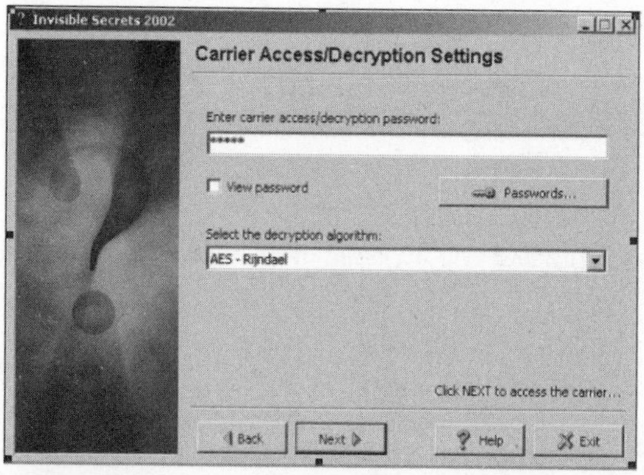

Figure 7.11   Decryption options for Invisible Secret.

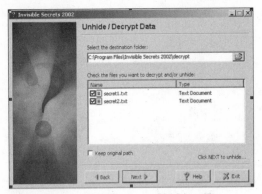

Figure 7.12 Identification of hidden files.

At this point, the program has all of the information it needs to extract the data. When you click Next, the hidden files are extracted; a progress screen appears, and then the files are displayed, as shown in Figure 7.13.

You can see that Invisible Secrets offers several more advanced features than most traditional stego programs you've encountered in this book.

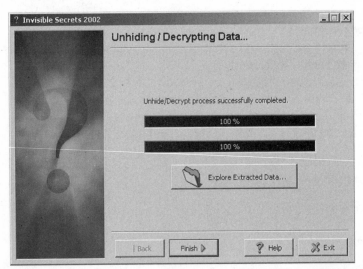

Figure 7.13 Hidden files that have been extracted will be listed in this window.

CameraShy

CameraShy is a program that hides data in the least significant bits of GIF images. What makes this program unique is that its graphical user interface (GUI) makes it a perfect tool for network stego. CameraShy actually looks and acts like a browser that enables you to scan any intranet or the Internet for files containing hidden data.

To hide information with CameraShy you load an image in which you want to hide data. You then type your secret message in the text box provided. As seen in Figure 7.14, the image is on the left side of the screen, and the hidden message appears on the right side. At this point you could embed the image that contains hidden data into a Web site and post it to the Internet for someone to retrieve.

The real power of CameraShy is in how it extracts data. To extract hidden information you run CameraShy as your browser. The icons in the CameraShy program are reminiscent of browser tools you've used in other programs. You can type a URL in the top portion of the CameraShy screen, browse the Web, and select links, just as you would with any browser.

When you load a Web site into Camera Shy, the program scans all images that are loaded to see if there is any data hidden there. CameraShy lists such files on the bottom of the screen, as shown in Figure 7.15. In this example, you can see that the program detected one image that has data hidden in it.

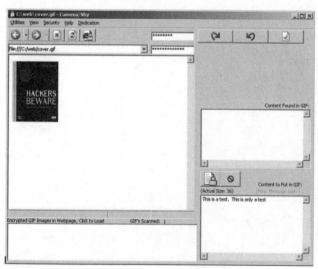

Figure 7.14   The opening screen for CameraShy.

Figure 7.15   CameraShy in action, detecting hidden data on a Web page.

When you click on this filename the file opens in the main CameraShy window, as shown in Figure 7.16.

The way CameraShy is able to detect files on a Web site that contain hidden data and automatically pull out the hidden message makes it an ideal application for network stego. In fact, thanks to the inventors of CameraShy, stego has never been easier.

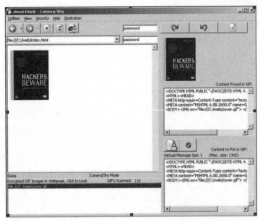

Figure 7.16   Display of an image that has data embedded in it.

Hiding Data in Network Headers

In order to understand this technique, it's important that you have an understanding of networking and the TCP/IP protocol suite. I will briefly describe the basic network terminology you'll need to understand this section. (If you have a networking background, just skip this one.)

Networking and TCP/IP: The Basics

If you want to send someone a letter, you can't just write a letter and drop it in the mailbox because the post office would not know where to deliver it. In order to make sure that the mail gets to its destination you have to put the letter in an envelope and address it. This same concept is used in networks, except that, instead of putting letters into envelopes, data is given protocol headers. The protocol headers act just like an envelope to identify the data's destination.

The protocol that every computer on the Internet uses to communicate with anyone in the world is the TCP/IP protocol suite, which was developed in the 1970s as part of the original research that led to the Internet. The TCP/IP protocol suite actually contains four main communication protocols: IP, TCP, UDP, and ICMP. These protocols run on both the sending computer and the receiving computer to standardize communications. The TCP protocol on the sender's computer communicates with the TCP protocol on the receiver's computer, and the IP protocol on the sender's computer communicates with the IP protocol on the receiver's computer.

Protocol headers were created so that the sender can provide key information about the communication to the receiver. Because these headers were created 30 years ago, some of the information is not needed today or can be modified without having an effect on the traffic. This makes protocol header-based stego possible. Every packet that goes across the Internet must contain these headers, and you can easily embed data in the unneeded portion of them.

Using IP and TCP Headers for Stego

The IP protocol header contains the key information that is needed for packets of data to be routed properly. Figure 7.17 shows the layout of the IP header.

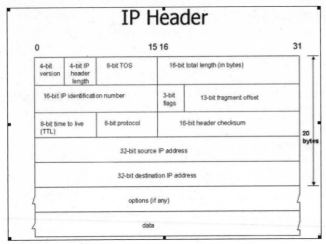

Figure 7.17 The IP header, viewed with a sniffer program.

When using stego you want to find fields that you can overwrite or change that will not have an effect on the host communication. Certain fields in the IP header, such as the version number and the header length, must contain specific values; otherwise, communication will fail. One field in the IP header that you can change without having any effect is the IP identification number. The IP number is used to track packets that have to be fragmented. If a packet is too large, it has to be broken up into smaller pieces as it goes across the Internet. All of the pieces contain the same IP number. The receiving host knows how to put the pieces back together by using the IP number. Usually the IP number is incremented by 1 for each packet that is sent out, but any number can be used and the protocol will still function properly. This ability to make a change and not damage functionality makes this piece of data an ideal candidate for hiding stego.

TCP, or the transmission control protocol, is used for reliable transmission of data. Most Internet applications use TCP. The TCP header is slightly larger than its corresponding protocol, UDP, and that size makes it very useful for network-based stego. Figure 7.18 shows the TCP header.

With TCP headers the sequence and acknowledgment numbers are used to indicate how much data was sent and how much data was received. This is how TCP achieves reliable communication. During the initial handshake the values for the sequence and acknowledgment numbers are picked and randomly generated by the sender and receiver. Therefore, the first packet that is sent can contain data hidden in those fields because the initial values don't

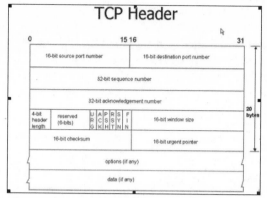

Figure 7.18   TCP header.

have any purpose. During a valid communication, though, those values are critical. For example, if my initial sequence number is 1000 and I send 10 bytes of data, the new value for the sequence will be 1010. If I make it a random value, the communication will not work. Essentially, once communication has been established, these fields can no longer be used to hide data.

UDP and ICMP Headers

There are two other protocols in the TCP/IP protocol suite. UDP, or User Datagram Protocol, is an unreliable transmission protocol. With UDP, the packet is also very small and does not provide a lot of room to hide data.

The last protocol is ICMP, or Internet Control Message Protocol. This is used for troubleshooting networks and sending network error messages. For example, when you ping a host to see if it is alive you use ICMP. Or if you send a message to an invalid host you will most likely receive an ICMP "host unreachable" message.

Because ICMP has a small header size it does not make a good candidate for header stego; however, because there is usually a lot of ICMP traffic occurring on a network, it does make a good candidate for hiding in an overt protocol, which is discussed in the next section.

Covert tcp

It's time for you to see an example of how data can be hidden in protocol headers. Covert tcp is a program that uses IP and TCP headers to hide information in network traffic. Covert tcp was written by Craig Rowland and can be downloaded from www.packetstormsecurity.com.

How Covert tcp Works

In TCP and IP protocols, there are several fields that are logical for hiding data, some of which were discussed in the previous section. Covert tcp hides data in the TCP/IP headers using these fields:

- IP number (IP)
- Sequence number (TCP)
- Acknowledgment number (TCP)

NOTE Most of the programs I have covered run on the Windows platform; however, for the remainder of this chapter, all the tools I cover are Linux-based.

You run Covert tcp on both the sender and receiver systems; the one system will send covert data to the other system by hiding it in the TCP/IP headers, and the other system will retrieve it.

NOTE By default, Covert tcp hides data in the IP number field, but by specifying different options you can hide data in other fields.

Figure 7.19 shows the results of running Covert tcp with no options set. This prints out the standard usage for Covert tcp, along with a list of what each of the command-line options does. This also provides several examples of how to use the program, making it very simple to run.

Figure 7.19   Usage, options, and examples for using Covert tcp.

You can see that although Covert tcp is functionally rich, allowing you to select fields in which to hide data and designate the ports to be used to transfer data, it runs from a command line and has no fancy GUI. Because Covert tcp is Linux based, you even have the source code so you can make additional modifications.

Running Covert tcp

Because Covert tcp is being run from Linux without a GUI, you have to run the program from a command line or a terminal window. To use Covert tcp you first put the receiving computer in listening mode by typing the following:

```
./tcp-dest 10.1.50.200-source 10.1.50.210-dest_port 80-server-file secret.c
```

In this command, tcp is the name of the program; you follow this with the name of the destination system and the source computer. This puts the program into listening mode (see Figure 7.20) on port 80, which is also specified from the command line. The last part of this command tells Covert tcp to take any of the information it receives and write it to a file called secret.c.

The sending computer then runs Covert tcp in active mode. Active mode automatically sends the corresponding file to the server. This is done by typing the following command:

```
./tcp-dest 10.1.50.200-source 10.1.50.210-source_port 1234-dest_port 80 ⤶
-file secret.c
```

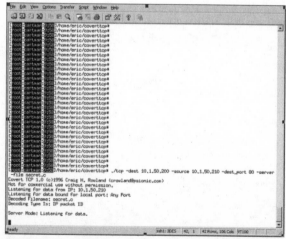

Figure 7.20   System running Covert tcp in listening mode.

The options in this command are similar to the earlier server command, except that, because I did not specify the server option, Covert tcp is going to immediately push the contents of the file secret.c to the destination IP address, which is 10.1.50.200.

As you can see in Figure 7.21, the sending computer is going to send the receiving computer whatever ASCII text is contained in the file secret.c. In this case the file contains the word "test".

Figure 7.22 shows the screen of the receiving computer, where you can see the letters "t e s t" being received on the listening host. All of the sending and receiving is done automatically, with no user intervention required.

I sent data from the sender to the receiver, embedding the data in the IP packets. In order to prove that network stego was used, I included the tcp dump output of the session where you can see the data being sent. The important thing to remember is that the letters "t e s t" are encoded in ASCII before they are sent across the wire and the tcp dump output displays the header information in HEX. By looking up ASCII numbers at www.asciitable.com/ you see that "t" encoded into HEX is 74, "e" is 65, "s" is 73, and "t" is 74.

Remember that the IP number is contained in the fourth and fifth bytes of the IP header. (When counting bytes in an IP header you always start counting with 0, and then every two hex characters are equal to one byte). Look at the first IP header; to help you out I have highlighted the fourth and fifth bytes corresponding to the IP number:

```
00    01    02    03    04    05    06
45    00    00    28   74 00   0000 4006 8d34 0a01 32d2
```

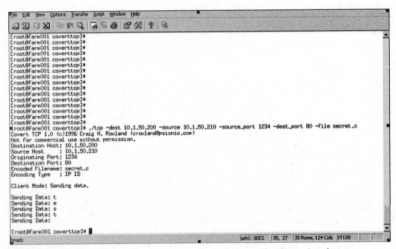

Figure 7.21　Sending computer sending data to the listening host.

Figure 7.22   Data being received by the listening host.

Notice that 74 corresponds to the HEX representation of the letter "t". The following shows the full tcp dump for the entire session: I highlighted the four letters of the word "test" so that you can see where they are in the transmission.

```
10:06:48.976736 10.1.50.210.1234 > 10.1.50.200.http: S 822411264:822411264(0)
win 512
        4500 0028 7400 0000 4006 8d34 0a01 32d2
        0a01 32c8 04d2 0050 3105 0000 0000 0000
        5002 0200 fe1f 0000 0000 0000 0000
10:06:48.976800 10.1.50.200.http > 10.1.50.210.1234: R 0:0(0) ack 822411265 win
0 (DF)
        4500 0028 0000 4000 ff06 0234 0a01 32c8
        0a01 32d2 0050 04d2 0000 0000 3105 0001
        5014 0000 000d 0000
10:06:49.986707 10.1.50.210.1234 > 10.1.50.200.http: S 2502033408:2502033408(0)
win 512
        4500 0028 6500 0000 4006 9c34 0a01 32d2
        0a01 32c8 04d2 0050 9522 0000 0000 0000
  5002 0200 9a02 0000 0000 0000 0000
10:06:49.986770 10.1.50.200.http > 10.1.50.210.1234: R 0:0(0) ack 1679622145 win
0 (DF)
        4500 0028 0000 4000 ff06 0234 0a01 32c8
        0a01 32d2 0050 04d2 0000 0000 9522 0001
        5014 0000 9bef 0000
10:06:50.996735 10.1.50.210.1234 > 10.1.50.200.http: S 1696792576:1696792576(0)
win 512
        4500 0028 7300 0000 4006 8e34 0a01 32d2
        0a01 32c8 04d2 0050 6523 0000 0000 0000
        5002 0200 ca01 0000 0000 0000 0000
10:06:50.996798 10.1.50.200.http > 10.1.50.210.1234: R 0:0(0) ack 874381313 win
0 (DF)
```

```
         4500 0028 0000 4000 ff06 0234 0a01 32c8
         0a01 32d2 0050 04d2 0000 0000 6523 0001
         5014 0000 cbee 0000
10:06:52.006754 10.1.50.210.1234 > 10.1.50.200.http: S 3523739648:3523739648(0)
win 512
         4500 0028 7400 0000 4006 8d34 0a01 32d2
         0a01 32c8 04d2 0050 d208 0000 0000 0000
         5002 0200 5d1c 0000 0000 0000 0000
10:06:52.006817 10.1.50.200.http > 10.1.50.210.1234: R 0:0(0) ack 2701328385 win
0 (DF)
         4500 0028 0000 4000 ff06 0234 0a01 32c8
         0a01 32d2 0050 04d2 0000 0000 d208 0001
         5014 0000 5f09 0000
10:06:53.016764 10.1.50.210.1234 > 10.1.50.200.http: S 3540647936:3540647936(0)
win 512
         4500 0028 0a00 0000 4006 f734 0a01 32d2
         0a01 32c8 04d2 0050 d30a 0000 0000 0000
         5002 0200 5c1a 0000 0000 0000 0000
10:06:53.016824 10.1.50.200.http > 10.1.50.210.1234: R 0:0(0) ack 2718236673 win
0 (DF)
         4500 0028 0000 4000 ff06 0234 0a01 32c8
         0a01 32d2 0050 04d2 0000 0000 d30a 0001
         5014 0000 5e07 0000
10:06:53.974820 arp who-has 10.1.50.210 tell 10.1.50.200
         0001 0800 0604 0001 00a0 c9e1 bd5b 0a01
         32c8 0000 0000 0000 0a01 32d2
10:06:53.975037 arp reply 10.1.50.210 is-at 0:6:5b:69:f4:79
         0001 0800 0604 0002 0006 5b69 f479 0a01
         32d2 00a0 c9e1 bd5b 0a01 32c8 0000 0000
         0000 0000 0000 0000 0000 0000 0000
```

Someone looking at the network traffic would not see the message, which is hidden right in the packet. By using additional command-line options you can also hide information in the sequence field of the TCP header. Figure 7.23 shows the same data being sent, but now the covert message is embedded in the TCP header rather than the IP header.

Just as with the IP header example, the receiver is receiving the data, as shown in Figure 7.24.

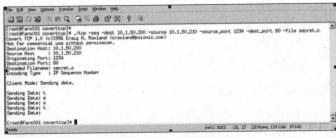

Figure 7.23   Sending data in the TCP header.

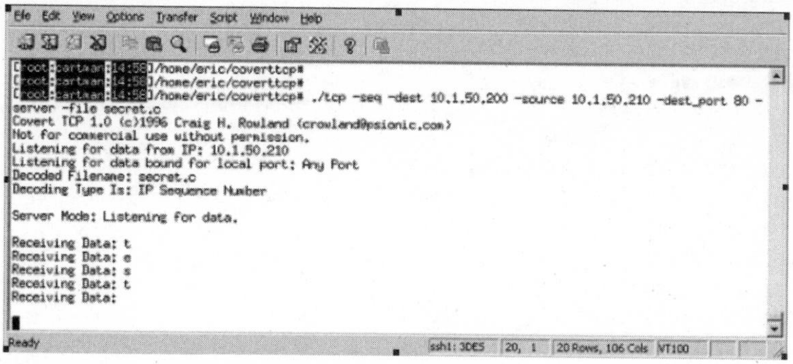

Figure 7.24 System receiving data that is hidden in the TCP header.

Once again, I've provided the tcp dump output so that you can see where the data is being hidden. Because I am using TCP and every TCP packet is embedded in an IP packet and the standard size of the IP packet is 20 bytes, you have to count 20 bytes to get to the beginning of the TCP header. Then, starting at 0, you count to the fourth and fifth byte, which contain the sequence number and our data, which I've highlighted in the tcp dump.

```
14:59:35.911325 10.1.50.210.1234 > 10.1.50.200.http: S 1946157056:1946157056(0)
win 512
        4500 0028 9b00 0000 4006 6634 0a01 32d2
        0a01 32c8 04d2 0050 7400 0000 0000 0000
        5002 0200 bb24 0000 0000 0000 0000
14:59:35.911410 10.1.50.200.http > 10.1.50.210.1234: R 0:0(0) ack 1946157057 win
0 (DF)
        4500 0028 0000 4000 ff06 0234 0a01 32c8
        0a01 32d2 0050 04d2 0000 0000 7400 0001
        5014 0000 bd11 0000
14:59:36.921308 10.1.50.210.1234 > 10.1.50.200.http: S 1694498816:1694498816(0)
win 512
        4500 0028 8800 0000 4006 7934 0a01 32d2
        0a01 32c8 04d2 0050 6500 0000 0000 0000
        5002 0200 ca24 0000 0000 0000 0000
14:59:36.921374 10.1.50.200.http > 10.1.50.210.1234: R 0:0(0) ack 4043309057 win
0 (DF)
        4500 0028 0000 4000 ff06 0234 0a01 32c8
        0a01 32d2 0050 04d2 0000 0000 6500 0001
        5014 0000 cc11 0000
14:59:37.931326 10.1.50.210.1234 > 10.1.50.200.http: S 1929379840:1929379840(0)
win 512
        4500 0028 ab00 0000 4006 5634 0a01 32d2
        0a01 32c8 04d2 0050 7300 0000 0000 0000
        5002 0200 bc24 0000 0000 0000 0000
14:59:37.931388 10.1.50.200.http > 10.1.50.210.1234: R 0:0(0) ack 4278190081 win
0 (DF)
```

```
            4500 0028 0000 4000 ff06 0234 0a01 32c8
            0a01 32d2 0050 04d2 0000 0000 7300 0001
            5014 0000 be11 0000
14:59:38.941330 10.1.50.210.1234 > 10.1.50.200.http: S 1946157056:1946157056(0)
win 512
            4500 0028 4e00 0000 4006 b334 0a01 32d2
            0a01 32c8 04d2 0050 7400 0000 0000 0000
            5002 0200 bb24 0000 0000 0000
14:59:38.941391 10.1.50.200.http > 10.1.50.210.1234: R 0:0(0) ack 1 win 0 (DF)
            4500 0028 0000 4000 ff06 0234 0a01 32c8
            0a01 32d2 0050 04d2 0000 0000 7400 0001
            5014 0000 bd11 0000
14:59:39.951357 10.1.50.210.1234 > 10.1.50.200.http: S 167772160:167772160(0)
win 512
            4500 0028 0e00 0000 4006 f334 0a01 32d2
            0a01 32c8 04d2 0050 0a00 0000 0000 0000
            5002 0200 2525 0000 0000 0000
14:59:39.951419 10.1.50.200.http > 10.1.50.210.1234: R 0:0(0) ack 2516582401 win
0 (DF)
            4500 0028 0000 4000 ff06 0234 0a01 32c8
            0a01 32d2 0050 04d2 0000 0000 0a00 0001
            5014 0000 2712 0000
14:59:40.904822 arp who-has 10.1.50.210 tell 10.1.50.200
            0001 0800 0604 0001 00a0 c9e1 bd5b 0a01
            32c8 0000 0000 0000 0a01 32d2
14:59:40.905047 arp reply 10.1.50.210 is-at 0:6:5b:69:f4:79
            0001 0800 0604 0002 0006 5b69 f479 0a01
            32d2 00a0 c9e1 bd5b 0a01 32c8 0000 0000
            0000 0000 0000 0000 0000 0000 0000
```

It is important to make sure that the sender and the receiver are both in the same mode. For example, if the sender is sending data in the IP number but the receiver is looking for the data in the sequence number, what the receiver will read will be garbage. For example, as shown in Figure 7.25, the receiver is listening for the data in the sequence number, but the sender hid the data in the IP number.

Figure 7.25 Data hidden in a different area.

As you can see, Covert tcp is a very powerful program and can easily be enhanced to enable it to hide data in other fields of the TCP/IP header.

Hiding in an Overt Protocol

The last category of network stego involves hiding data in an overt protocol. Essentially, this is what is called *data camouflaging*, where you make data look like something else. With this technique you take data, put it in normal network traffic, and modify the data in such a way that it looks like the overt protocol.

For example, most networks carry large amounts of HTTP or Web traffic. You could send data over port 80, and it would look like Web traffic. The problem is that if someone examined the payload, it would not look like normal Web traffic, which usually contains HTML. What if you added symbols such as < > </> to the data? Because these are the types of characters that HTML contains, the traffic would look like Web traffic and probably would slip by the casual observer.

This is exactly the process used by the program Reverse WWW Shell. Reverse WWW Shell not only masks data to look like Web traffic, it does it in a way that can get around most firewalls. Instead of the attacker trying to connect to a client, which in most cases is protected by a firewall, Reverse WWW Shell is installed on a client system behind a firewall. Then, at set intervals, it connects on port 80. Now the firewall thinks this is a client computer surfing the Web and allows the traffic out. In reality, the client initiates a connection outbound to an attacker and then pushes a command prompt to him or her. Now the attacker can type whatever commands he or she wants to on the client. Meanwhile, all of the commands and data are being hidden in HTML traffic. Figure 7.26 shows the main screen for Reverse WWW Shell.

In this example, the attacker system is listening for the client to open up a connection. At a set time interval, the client system will send data to the listening attack box, as shown in Figure 7.27.

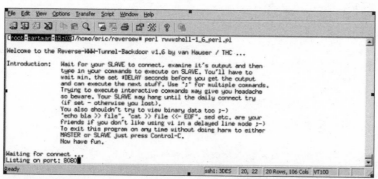

Figure 7.26 Main screen for Reverse WWW Shell.

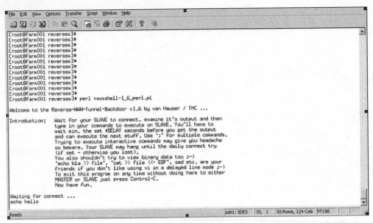

Figure 7.27   Data being sent to the attacker.

Figure 7.28 shows the ethereal output of the message "hello" being sent across the wire.

The highlighted line in Figure 7.28 contains the hidden data. If you look at the packet it looks just like an HTTP GET request, but within the packet lies the covert message.

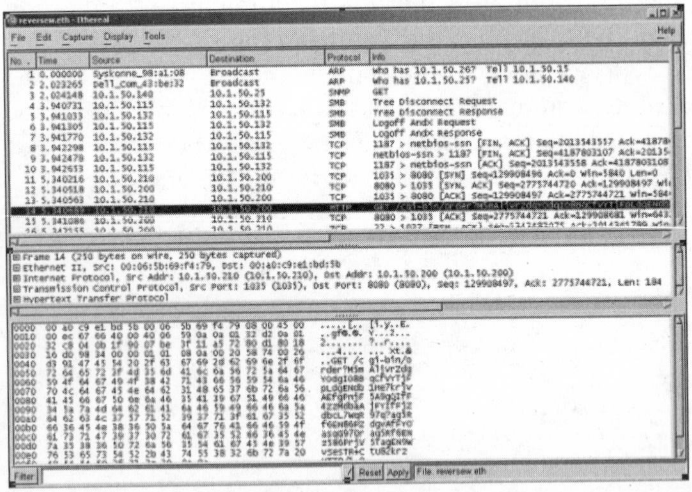

Figure 7.28   Sniffer output of the packets.

Detecting Reverse WWW Shell is very hard because it looks like normal Web traffic. The only way to detect this program is by observing trends across the traffic. For example, with normal Web traffic the client sends small amounts of information out and receives large amounts of data back. This makes sense because when you download a Web page the client issues a simple GET request outbound and the Web site sends back all of the contents of the page to the browser. With Reverse WWW Shell, the client sends large amounts of data out and only small amounts of data are received back. The attacker is sending commands that are fairly small to the client and receiving fairly large replies back. Even though this program can be detected in this manner, most sites are not equipped to do so.

NOTE Another program that operates in a similar fashion to Reverse WWW Shell is LOKI. The only difference is that, instead of using HTTP traffic, LOKI hides the data in ICMP traffic and DNS requests. Most networks contain large amounts of both ICMP and DNS traffic, so a little extra traffic would be very hard to detect.

Looking Ahead

You've seen various tools for creating stego in Chapters 6 and 7. In Chapter 8, look at the flip side of this coin: techniques you can use to crack steganography and cryptography.

Making Your Own
Communications Secure

Cracking Stego and Crypto

As you've read elsewhere in this book, the only way to test the strength of an algorithm is to have smart people try to crack it. Understanding how you go about cracking a given algorithm will help you grasp the strengths and weaknesses of different approaches to building one.

Building crypto or stego that is strong and will stand the test of time takes a special skill set. It is not the ingredients of an algorithm but the unique way that somebody combines them that differentiates an expert from a mere amateur. A chef can tell you the ingredients that go into a gourmet pastry, but you can use the same ingredients and the results just won't be the same. Secret communication requires a similar specialized expertise.

Just as building strong algorithms is a skill, knowing how to test them or break them also requires a special talent. In this chapter, I'll examine some of the unique techniques that make this a profession where only a few succeed.

FAX FACTS

Cracking can come in many forms. Now, I'm sure everyone has received a fax where the top of the printout appears to have a set of lines that are elongated and distorted running off the edge, like a product bar code from a box of cereal. Most of us assume it's some automatic fax information with the sender's fax number and name. But did you ever think those wavy lines could contain hidden data?

(continued)

FAX FACTS *(continued)*

Ahmed was a Middle Eastern businessman in France on a supposedly routine trip. In reality, he was gathering information on foreign power plants for his government. When Ellen Mendez, an information specialist with the U.S. Army, was asked to look at copies of faxes Ahmed had been sending back to his office in Saudi Arabia, she figured out that he had encrypted data with a binary code using 0s and 1s and put lines representing the code at the top of the faxed page. To the unsuspicious, the lines looked like a fax glitch—just garbage. But on closer examination she realized they were really a code he was using to transmit data.

Ellen also noticed the way Ahmed would adjust the spacing between letters and words. The code was in the variations of the spacing. She ran a software program used to shift letters in a document to hide data this way, and she discovered hidden data.

Who's Cracking What?

Cracking by the criminal, hacker, or spy elements is done for a variety of purposes, but whatever their motivation, they are out to get information that simply doesn't belong to them.

Cracking by the cryptanalyst community is critical in order to understand whether a given algorithm is strong. By knowing how a technique can be broken, a developer can fix the weakness and, in doing so, make the technique more robust.

Making strong crypto is an iterative approach. When somebody finds a chink in the armor of a particular algorithm, the developer fixes the weakness and makes the crypto more robust. This may happen several times, helping the developer to strengthen the algorithm over time.

> **NOTE** The general rule of thumb is that you can never rely solely on testing code that you built. That's because you know too much. Because you wrote the code, you might overlook something obvious simply because you are too familiar with the code.

So, the fact that someone is able to crack a technique is not a sign that the technique is no good; it is just a sign that something was missed in the original development. The real question is this: Can the weakness be fixed in a timely manner, in a way that introduces no other weaknesses and that makes the resulting technique more robust?

NOTE When DES was released there were some weaknesses in how the data was broken up before it was encrypted. The developers were able to fix this problem, and the resulting technique was very robust. On the other hand, Double-DES had a weakness that could not be fixed without significantly impairing the algorithm. That's why you don't hear of anyone using Double-DES. Everyone today uses Triple-DES because Triple-DES was able to overcome the weaknesses of Double-DES. This was an example of the meet-in-the-middle attack, described later in this chapter.

Cracking Analysis

Even though most developers of crypto and stego techniques test their algorithms and try to break them, the skill set required to break algorithms is a different skill set than the one used to develop the algorithms or techniques. Cracking algorithms is actually a separate discipline that could take years, if not a lifetime, to master. In this section, I'll briefly introduce the roles people play in this highly specialized industry.

Cryptanalysts

Cryptanalysts are people who analyze encryption techniques, looking for weaknesses and ways to break the technique. By deciphering a plaintext message encoded with a cryptography technique, the cryptanalyst has essentially broken the code.

A good cryptanalyst knows so much about the inner working of crypto that he or she can usually tell which part of the code needs to be fixed and whether the weakness is a major or minor one.

The cryptanalyst's job is only to find the weakness, not to fix it. Once the cryptanalyst has discovered the flaw, it is the job of the developer of the technique to figure out how to strengthen it.

There are various approaches to breaking a crypto technique. A cryptanalyst might look for a general weakness in the algorithm that impacts all implementations or for a weakness in a specific implementation, though the general algorithm is still robust.

The most common way to break a technique is to find a unique situation in which the technique does not work as intended. For example, let's say an algorithm breaks text into blocks of data and then encrypts each block with the same key. If the block is too short or if the cryptanalyst feeds it large amounts of repeated text, two blocks of data might encrypt to the same value. This could be considered a weakness because any patterns that can be inferred from the encrypted text can help a cryptanalyst break the technique.

Other specific attacks that a cryptanalyst performs are detailed later in this chapter in the section titled *Cracking Cryptography*.

Steganalysts

"Steganalyst" is a relatively new term that was developed to refer to someone who tries to break stego techniques. Even though the terms "cryptanalyst" and "steganalyst" are similar, their roles are quite different.

The difference becomes obvious when you look at the goals of the two techniques. A cryptanalyst tries to break an encrypted message to read it. The goal of a steganalyst is to detect *whether* a message has data hidden in it.

Once a steganalyst has determined that a file has a message hidden in it and the message has been extracted, if it is encrypted it then becomes the job of a cryptanalyst to try to break the ciphertext and figure out what the plaintext message is.

The Role of Detection

With steganography, detecting that a message is hidden is the goal. With cryptography, even though the mere fact that something is encrypted could call attention to it, the main focus is usually not on whether people can detect that data is encrypted; what's important is that no one can crack the encryption and read the plaintext masked by it.

Of course, sometimes the lines do blur and detection of crypto becomes important. In certain countries where the mere use of encryption is illegal or deemed highly suspicious, just the fact that a message or file is encrypted could raise enough suspicion to get those involved in sending and receiving it into trouble.

Detecting Encryption

Encryption takes a plaintext message and converts it to ciphertext, which is unreadable. In general, weak encryption has patterns, and strong encryption does not because any patterns that can be found in the ciphertext make it easier to crack.

Another characteristic of strong encryption is that there should be no relationship between the plaintext and the ciphertext. Any relationship between the two makes it easy to crack because that establishes a pattern that can be used to map out the plaintext.

OUT OF PLACE ENCRYPTION

I often work with companies that wish to protect their intellectual property. In one particular case it turned out that a competitor was releasing similar products and beating them to market. After this happened several times the management finally realized that something was seriously wrong.

In looking at this company's situation I noted that it was part of its corporate culture that encryption was not used on any of the servers or for any communication. I was able to use that information to find the person who was committing corporate espionage.

I knew that there were no supported company-wide encryption programs and no policies stating that encryption be used. That suggested to me that there should not be any encrypted traffic on the network. Therefore, I set up a system that would pull data off the network and run it through a program that could detect whether data had been encrypted.

I began to see a pattern: Two accounts were being used to send large amounts of encrypted data to anonymous email addresses. This became even more suspicious when I realized that both accounts belonged to the same person. I was able to use the fact that encryption had been detected to focus in on this individual and help the company take legal action, even though I had no idea what the encrypted material said.

For example, the word "the" appears frequently in the English language. With weak encryption, the word "the" would appear the same way in the ciphertext each time it occurs. Now if I study the ciphertext and notice that three letters are repeated through the message, I can guess that those three letters refer to a commonly used word such as "the."

If strong encryption does not have any patterns in the cipher text, it may be hard to crack, but the very randomness of the text can help you to detect that encryption is being used.

One final method used to detect encryption involves headers. Encryption applications need some way to identify the files that they encrypted. If you look at a traditional Windows program such as Microsoft Word, it includes some sort of header on a file that tells the application what to do with it. Most encryption programs do the same thing.

PGP or PEM (two popular encryption applications) will actually put their own unique headers at the top of a file to make it easier to find and process the data that they encrypt. Therefore, you could write a program that looks for these unique headers and not only discerns that the data is encrypted, but also determines what application created the encrypted file.

Looking for headers will work in some cases, but this approach turns out to be less reliable than looking for randomness, which you'll look at next.

Randomness and Compression

Is the mere fact of random data a foolproof way of detecting that data has been encrypted? No. It turns out that some other file formats contain random data. Any file that contains compressed data or utilizes compression randomizes that data.

A compression program takes a large file and produces a smaller file that contains the same information. These programs find redundancy in the files and remove it.

Say that in a particular file the pattern of 11010110000101101010010011010 appears 40 times. I can go into that file and every place that pattern appears, replace it with a smaller value, such as 011. By doing this I would greatly reduce the size of the file, but also remove the patterns and create random-looking data.

Most compression programs contain a header and a lookup table to store the values. By performing a quick scan of the header you can tell whether the file has the header for a compression program. Of course, a clever person could put a compression file type of header on encrypted data to fool us. In those cases, you would have to perform a quick analysis of the lookup table to detect this.

Detection and Image Files

One other popular file format that contains random-looking data is JPEG images. Take a look at the following two images, Figure 8.1 and Figure 8.2.

The images may look exactly the same, but the first is a .bmp and the second is a JPEG. The .bmp file is 347KB, and the JPEG is 48KB. That means that the .bmp file is almost 10 times larger than the JPEG file. That's because JPEG files use a compressed format. This characteristic becomes extremely important with Web sites where larger image files take longer to download.

Figure 8.1 Even though the image looks the same as Figure 8.2 the format and bit composition of the files are very different.

Figure 8.2   A JPEG image uses compression to make the size much smaller.

Because they are compressed, the output of JPEG files appears random. Also, JPEG images contain headers identifying which version of the JPEG standard is being used.

Building a Program for Detection

If you assume that someone does not know that you are monitoring traffic looking for encrypted data, you can use header information to distinguish between encrypted files, compressed files, and JPEG images. You can build a simple program to do that.

Finding random data is at the heart of this problem. After you do that you can then use the header in the file to determine whether it is encrypted or in some other format, such as a compressed file.

The easiest way to find random data is to plot a histogram of the bytes across a file. With most files that do not contain random data you would get a histogram that has peaks and valleys where certain characters appear often and others appear only infrequently.

Figure 8.3 is a histogram for unencrypted data. You can see that certain values appear much more often than others.

On the other hand, with encrypted data, because it is random, you acquire a much flatter histogram, as you can see in Figure 8.4.

You can see that, compared to Figure 8.3, Figure 8.4 looks extremely flat. Every character appears with equal frequency. The program we're building will calculate randomness; if a file has a flat histogram it will be flagged. The program then checks the header and determines whether the file is encrypted, compressed, or a JPEG image.

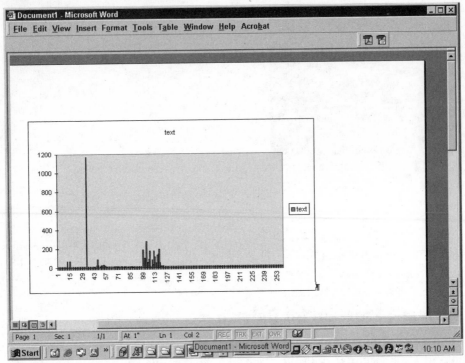

Figure 8.3 The histogram of an unencrypted file.

The following is the high-level algorithm (or pseudo-code) for such a program:

1. Find random data.

   a. Calculate the histogram across the files.

   b. Determine the high and low points.

   c. Determine the relative frequency of each byte.

2. If file contains a flat histogram, continue; otherwise, move on to next file and do the following:

   a. Check whether file contains header for compressed data.

   b. Check whether file contains header for JPEG images.

   c. If both a and b fail, then the file contains encrypted data.

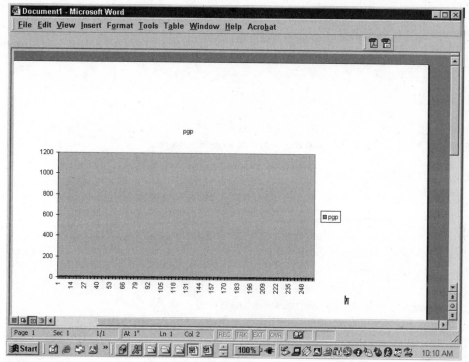

Figure 8.4   A histogram showing encrypted data.

The full code for implementing this is contained in Appendix A, but the following shows the output from running the program:

```
c:\encrypttest\testpgp.pgp may contain encrypted data.
c:\encrypttest\testpgp.exe may contain encrypted data.

Tested  8 files in  1 directories
 Encrypted files:    2
 Small files:      1
 Compressed files:   2
 Image files:     2
 Warnings:       0
```

In order to help you to understand this output, Figure 8.5 shows the files contained in the directory that this program was run against. (You can run the program against an entire hard drive or against a single directory.)

Figure 8.5 A listing of files that the program was run against.

In this example, the filename reveals the type of file, not the extension. Notice that there are two .zip files, one named testzip.zip and one named textzip.txt. There are also two encrypted files, two .zip files, and two .exe files. I changed the extension on the files to show you that this program is smart enough to figure out what type of files these are, regardless of whether the files have the correct extension. Most programs don't have that capability.

When this program runs all output is displayed on the screen. You can pipe this output to a file to save it for later analysis. The program prints only the name of the encrypted files on the screen. This is done to conserve space. This program could easily be expanded to print the names of the compressed and image files.

Cracking Cryptography

Chapter 2 covered various encryption techniques that can be used to keep your information secure. But how do you know that the encryption techniques are robust and really doing what they say they are doing? How do we know that there are no hidden back doors in the program that someone can use to extract your information?

The simple answer is that you cannot know how robust a given technique is when it is initially developed. That's where the process of cracking encryption comes in.

In most cases, reading encrypted data involves having the key that was used to encrypt the data. Once you know the key, you can decrypt the data and read the encrypted message. The secrecy of the encrypted text is based not on the secrecy of the algorithm, but on the secrecy of the key. Even if someone knows the algorithm, without the key he or she cannot crack the encrypted text.

In this section, you'll learn about some of the methods cryptanalysts use to crack encryption.

General Attacks

A general attack is a high-level attack that works against any type of encryption algorithm. There are four general attacks that can be performed against encrypted information:

- Ciphertext only
- Known plaintext
- Chosen plaintext
- Chosen ciphertext

These attacks are usually used independently of each other. The attack that you use depends on what information is available to you. For example, if you intercept an encrypted message, then you can perform only a ciphertext-only attack. If you compromise a system and have access to the encryption scheme, then you can perform all four attacks.

As you move down the list the attacks require access to more information. In most cases, the chances of being able to perform a ciphertext-only attack are high, but the chances of having enough information to perform a chosen ciphertext attack are very low.

In contrast, as you move down the list, the chances of being able to break the encryption become much higher. The more information you have, the higher the chances that you can acquire the plaintext message.

We will look at all of these in detail; however, in most cases, you are given only the ciphertext. The other attacks are more appropriate if you also compromise someone's computer.

Ciphertext-Only Attack (COA)

With a ciphertext-only attack, the only thing the cryptanalyst has available is encrypted text. This is the traditional attack, and it is very difficult to determine the plaintext message when strong encryption algorithms have been used.

With ciphertext-only attacks, sometimes the amount of data can help you. The more encrypted data you have, the higher the chances that there will be patterns in the text. For example, if you have 15 pages of encrypted information, you can perform character frequency calculations and look for patterns. If you only have three 3 of encrypted text, that analysis is much less likely to yield useful information.

You also have to determine whether data has been encrypted with the same key or different keys. If each page of the encrypted document was encrypted with a different key, you have to find the unique key for each page. If the entire document was encrypted with the same key, then you have to figure out only one key to read the entire document. Therefore, how you go about attacking this problem can vary depending on the information available to you.

NOTE If the goal is to crack the algorithm, rather than a specific piece of encrypted data, then having data that has been encrypted with different keys might be very helpful.

A critical point to remember is that all encryption is breakable. How will you know when you have successfully cracked the encryption? With binary data, gibberish and the actual data could look very similar. If you know that you are trying to decrypt a text message it may be easy for a human to tell when he or she has cracked the scheme, but it might be hard for a computer to do so.

Sometimes the hardest is part is figuring out how to determine when you can declare success. If you are trying to crack a .exe program, the real .exe code and the output of unsuccessful cracks will look the same.

NOTE In the case of .exe programs, you could create an automated script that tries to run each output; when the program runs you know you successfully cracked it.

Known Plaintext Attack (KPA)

Known plaintext attacks can occur when the cryptanalyst is somehow able to find the original plaintext message that was used to generate the cipher text. For example, let's say two parties are using the same key and algorithms for several messages. The text of one message is known along with its ciphertext, and the goal is to find the key based on that.

This attack depends on whether there are patterns between the plaintext and ciphertext and the overall strength of the algorithm. If there are no discernable patterns, having the plaintext may not help at all. Also, the overall length of the message would dictate how valuable or successful this attack will be.

For example, imagine that somebody is using a basic substitution algorithm. Each letter in the alphabet is substituted for another letter. In this case, there is a one-to-one mapping. A known plaintext attack would tell you the mapping for every letter that appears in the message. If the message is short, it might reveal only 20 percent of the key, but if the message is long it might reveal 90 percent. Once you have that much of the key, obtaining the rest of the key is easy.

Having part of the key is like playing the Wheel of Fortune game, minus Vanna White. When you have part of the key, part of the message is revealed; then, you simply have to guess the rest of it.

Chosen Plaintext Attack (CTA)

In some cases, access to the device that generates the encryption can be obtained without having the key. In this case, you could feed in plaintext and you will receive the corresponding ciphertext. This is one step easier than the known plaintext method because you can pick whatever plaintext you want to use. The chosen plaintext could contain every single letter in the alphabet, which would provide the key in the form of mapping for every character. This will work best with simple encryption, where there is a one-to-one mapping.

NOTE In launching a chosen plaintext attack the phrase that is often used is "The quick brown fox jumped over the lazy dogs." Notice anything unusual about this phrase? It contains every letter in the alphabet.

Chosen Ciphertext Attack (CCA)

The last general attack is a very sophisticated one. In this attack you can pick the ciphertext and the system will give you the corresponding plaintext. As you can imagine, by using this method you can obtain a lot of critical information that makes it easier to crack a given algorithm. This attack, though, is considered theoretical; in most cases, it is possible only in a lab. In the real world the chances of performing such an attack are practically nil.

You have to acquire the algorithm as a black box for this attack to work. A black box algorithm is one in which the algorithm and key are put together in such a way that you can encrypt and decrypt information, but you cannot see the key. (If you could see the key and acquire it, then there would be no need to break the algorithm.) If you have the algorithm in a black box format you could take your cipher text and have it decrypted. In most cases, the resulting plaintext will have little value, although it could be used for analysis.

Specific Attacks

Specific attacks are attacks that can be launched only against certain types of algorithms or encryption. Where general attacks will work against any algorithm, these attacks would work only in certain situations.

In this section, I'll examine specific attacks that can be launched against encryption systems.

Brute-Force Attack

All encryption can be cracked eventually from a brute-force attack that tries every possible combination to determine the key. If the key was composed of letters you would try every possible combination of letters. The beginning of such an attack would look like this: A, AA, AB, AC, and so on. It could take 500 years to find the key with this method, but finding it is inevitable.

Therefore, when you pick a key length you have to figure out the time it would take to brute-force that key and make sure the value of the content expires before the technique can be brute-forced.

NOTE It is also important to remember that computers become faster in an exponential manner. Encryption that would take 100 years to crack if you started today might take 5 years to crack 10 years from now because of advances in computer technology.

From a brute-force perspective, the two things that are critical are the length of the key and the characters included in the key. For example, if a technique used a binary key of two characters, I could crack that in less than 10 seconds with all possible combinations:

00

01

10

11

It would take longer to crack this if I increased the length or increased the character spaces. Increasing the length would involve, for example, using 4 or 8 characters instead of 2. Increasing the character space means that instead of just using 0 or 1 for the possible value of each character I could use A through Z, or 26 possible characters.

Replay Attack

A replay attack involves taking encrypted information and playing it back at a later time. For example, to gain access to a network a user would enter a password that is sent in encrypted form to the server. You cannot read the password because it has been encrypted with a large key; however, you could sniff the encrypted password. Then, when you want to impersonate a given user, you would just reply or send the server the encrypted information you gathered from the network.

The best way to defeat replay attacks is to put something else, such as time, in the equation. In this case, if you try to replay information 10 minutes from now it would not work because the time factor would change what's required to replay the data.

Man-in-the-Middle Attack

In Chapter 2, you learned about symmetric and asymmetric encryption. There I mentioned that symmetric keys should be sent over a secure channel, but asymmetric keys can be sent over a trusted channel. A trusted channel prevents an attacker from inserting himself or herself in the middle of a communication channel and impersonating either side.

For example, say that Alice and Bob want to communicate using asymmetric encryption, so they exchange keys on a nontrusted communication medium. Evil Eve controls the access point that all of the traffic flows through, so she has inserted herself in the middle of the communication. Now Eve could generate a false public-private key pair for Alice and Bob. When Alice and Bob try to exchange keys, Eve intercepts the real keys and sends the fake keys to them. Alice and Bob think they have valid keys because they did not bother to send them through a trusted source or channel. Now, because Eve controls the keys, she can decrypt, modify, and reencrypt all information sent between the two parties.

Meet-in-the-Middle Attack

Meet-in-the-middle is a specific attack against Double-DES. This is the attack that broke Double-DES, and this is why today people use DES and Triple-DES, but never Double-DES to encrypt data.

To perform the meet-in-the-middle attack you need to have both the plaintext message and the ciphertext. Starting with the plaintext, you try all possible keys to attempt to yield C1 with the formula E(M,K1) = C1. This formula states that if you encrypt (E) your message (M) with your key (K1) the output yields your ciphertext (C1). Then you start from the other end with your ciphertext and try to decrypt C2 with all possible keys to yield C1 with the formula D(C2,K2) = C1.

> **IT'S A THEORY...**
>
> This attack requires both the ciphertext and the plaintext message. Because of this unlikely scenario, some people consider this attack theoretical. After all, if you have both pieces, why bother to crack the algorithm at all?
>
> Those who are devoted to it take crypto very seriously. The mere fact that this attack is possible caused them to stop using Double DES. Theoretical or not, the fact that there is a successful attack is reason enough not to use the algorithm.

The total number of possible keys for K1 is 2^{56} because DES uses a 56-bit key. The total number of possible keys for K2 is also 2^{56}. If you add $2^{56} + 2^{56}$ you get 2^{57}. Because of this weakness Double-DES gives an effective key length of only 57 bits, which is only one more than DES, rather than the key length of 122 bits (56 + 56) you might think it would provide. Because of this weakness, people use Triple-DES instead of Double-DES.

Figure 8.6 shows a graphical view of the meet-in-the-middle attack.

Birthday Attack

A hash function is a one-way function. Therefore, it is critical that there is little chance that two random messages will hash to the same value, which would make it easy for someone to defeat the algorithm.

This becomes clearer when you consider that passwords are usually protected with a hash. When you enter your password, the value is hashed and compared with the output of the encrypted password that your system stores. If the values match, you are allowed access. To obtain your password I just have to guess a value that hashes to the same encrypted value.

Meet-in-the-middle Attack

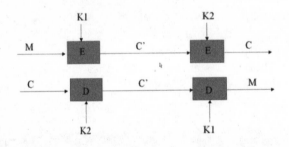

Figure 8.6 You can see that even though this act requires both ciphertext and plaintext it is still a powerful attack.

It should be difficult, if not impossible, when using a hash to figure out what the input text was based solely on the output text. If there is any relationship at all between the encrypted text and the original message, then there will be patterns that can be used to try to break the encryption. For example, if the word "test" always hashes to the same output value, whenever I see that value I immediately know part of the plaintext message.

When you use a birthday attack against hash functions you attempt to find two different messages that hash to the same value. If you can, you can infer certain information and discover potential weaknesses.

NOTE The name of the attack derives from taking a room full of people and figuring out the chance, expressed as a percentage, that 2 people in the room have the same birthday. You might think that because there are 366 possible birthdays, with a group of fewer than 100 people the chances of 2 people having the same birthday would be extremely low. In reality, the number is quite high, actually greater than 50 percent.

Cracking Steganography

Because the goal of stego is different from that of crypto, the techniques for cracking it are also quite different. I'll start by looking at ways to crack stego created using several of the common stego tools available today. Then I'll cover some general stego cracking techniques that work no matter which stego program has been used.

Specific Techniques

One of the most important attributes of good steganography is how well the technique hides data. If one can tell that there is data hidden in a file, then the steganography technique is essentially useless.

In this section, I'll review some methods used to detect data hidden in a file. I'll focus on five popular tools: S-Tools, Hide and Seek, J-Steg, EZ Stego, and StegDetect.

NOTE Before reading this section it's a good idea to have read Chapter 6 so that you understand how the various techniques and image files work.

S-Tools Version 4.0

There are specific ways to detect whether data has been hidden with S-Tools based on how that program works.

Naturally occurring 8-bit color files have few duplicated colors. Files that have data hidden with S-Tools have many duplicated colors. That happens because S-Tools hides date by reducing the number of total colors and creating duplicates. These are not exact duplicates, but rather colors that are very close to each other; so close that the difference can't be discerned by the human eye.

I have written a program that I call sdetect (included in Appendix A) that examines the color table of .bmp images for near duplicates and reports a measurement of duplication. When run on images without hidden data, it reports a small number, usually around zero. When run on images with data hidden using S-Tools, it reports a number in the thousands. Using this program, you can detect the presence of hidden data for 8-bit color images with almost complete accuracy.

Here are some examples from the program. First here is the output from a normal image:

D:\DH\Data\BMP>bmpmap forest.bmp

File Name: forest.bmp

actual size: 66146 Reported: 66146

Duplicate colors: 2

File header: Bytes 0–13

Bitmap header: Bytes 14–53

Color map: Bytes 54–609

Image data: Bytes 610–66145

Next, here is the output from the same image after data has been hidden in it:

D:\DH\Data\BMP\STools>bmpmap forest_h.bmp

File Name: forest_h.bmp

actual size: 66614 Reported: 66614

Duplicate colors: 1046

File header: Bytes 0–13

Bitmap header: Bytes 14–53

Color map: Bytes 54–1077

Image data: Bytes 1078–66613

Note that there is a small change in the size of the file because S-Tools increased the size of the color palette from 139 colors to 256 colors. While this is different from the original, it would not look unusual in and of itself. If you look at the number of duplicated colors reported, you see a large discrepancy. In the original image, there were only 2 duplicates. In the image with embedded data, the number of duplicates is 1046. If the reported number is over 200, there is a good chance that there is hidden data present.

The program that looks for duplicate entries in the color table currently works only with .bmp files, but the exact same concept would be equally successful for GIF images. Accessing the color table with a program such as this one is not difficult. Like other image file formats, .bmp files follow published specifications that control the layout of data within the file.

> **NOTE** The .bmp specification has gone through multiple revisions. This is important to know when processing image files because you have to detect which revision of the specification is being used. Usually headers include information about the version. For example, in .bmp files the header has a field that indicates the size of the header. This information can also be used to determine the version. The more recent versions of .bmps have a flag in the header that indicates whether there is a color table and a variable that indicates its size. When this flag is present, the color table is immediately after the header. Thus, to access the color table, one reads the header to determine the size of the header, the size of the color table, and if a color table is used. If there is a color table, you can look at the end of the header and note an amount of data equal to the size of the color table.

8-bit grayscale images do commonly have near duplicates in the color table, so this test fails on them. 8-bit grayscale is far less common than 8-bit color, but it is hardly a rarity. Use of 8-bit grayscale would not by itself be an indicator of hidden data; however, you can try this to determine whether data has been hidden in a grayscale image. In normal images, each pixel has a strong correlation with its neighboring pixels. The bit changes that S-Tools uses to embed data break up this correlation. Therefore, a program that measures the average correlation of a pixel with its neighbors will detect data hidden in grayscale images.

> **NOTE** This test will not work on 24-bit color images, because S-Tools hides the secret message a different way. However, with 24-bit images, a program is not required because these images are so rare their use would itself be suspicious.

Figure 8.7   An image with no data hidden in it.

It is critical when data is embedded that any degradation of the image can't be discerned by the human eye. Figure 8.7 shows a clean image, and Figure 8.8 shows the same image with data hidden in it using S-Tools. On first glance at the images, your eye perceives little degradation. But if you look very closely at the images, you'll see several white dots in the image that has data hidden in it that are not in the original image. You would be able to perceive the slight degradation only if you had both images to compare them. In most cases, though, you don't have both images.

Figure 8.8   An image after data has been hidden with S-Tools.

Hide and Seek

Hide and Seek is vulnerable to the same detection technique as S-Tools because the method of hiding data is fundamentally the same as the 8-bit method used by S-Tools. Hide and Seek actually includes two programs: one to hide the information (called Hide) and one to extract the information (called Seek).

Hide and Seek disperses data in a pseudo-random way, meaning that the data is dispersed in an unpredictable fashion. Also, the header information is encrypted. This randomness and encryption are important because without them, if you reverse-engineered the code (where you produce the original source code given only the .exe), you could determine where the data is hidden and pull it out.

Figure 8.9 shows a clean image, and Figure 8.10 shows the same file with data hidden in it. By studying the before and after images, you can identify degradation of the image. In addition, the file size changed from 32,814 bytes to 37,674 bytes. Again, without the two images to compare, the presence of hidden data would be hard to determine.

J-Steg

J-Steg works by embedding messages in the DCT coefficients. DCT stands for discrete cosine transformation; it is the calculation that is performed to compress information in the file. Because of this, messages hidden in this way are quite difficult to detect. An artifact of the embedding can be exploited to detect that data has been hidden with J-Steg. In ordinary JPEGs without embedded messages, the DCT coefficients have a nearly symmetric distribution, smoothly falling away from a central value. In images that have messages embedded by J-Steg, the smoothness and symmetry are interrupted. Statistical testing can detect this difference.

Figure 8.9   An image with no data hidden in it.

Figure 8.10 An image after data has been hidden in it with Hide and Seek.

This test will yield only a good probability of the presence of hidden data, and it is not nearly as certain as the tests included in S-Tools. That's because there is some overlap with images that have a smooth and symmetric distribution and ones where the smoothness and symmetry are interrupted. In a file that has no data hidden in it the curve is smooth. When you start to hide data in the file, the smooth curve starts to display a staircase effect. The more data that is hidden, the more pronounced the effect. With a small amount of data hidden, there will still be portions of the file that are smooth and that overlap with the jagged portions. In these areas of overlap, it is hard to determine whether data is hidden in the file.

Figure 8.11 shows a clean image, and Figure 8.12 shows the same file with data hidden in it using J-Steg. There is no degradation visible, and the two images appear to be identical.

Figure 8.11 An image with no data hidden in it.

Figure 8.12   An image after data has been hidden in it with J-Steg.

EZ Stego

Because EZ Stego sorts the existing colors in the image's palette rather than reducing the colors in the image and making duplicate color entries, the correlation test described for S-Tools and Hide and Seek will be ineffective here. Most color images will have noticeable image degradation when hidden using EZ Stego.

Because there is no linear sorting for three-dimensional color data, there will be adjacent colors that are not good matches. Also, because most images write the most important colors first in the color table, most color tables are not sorted with corresponding colors close to each other. You can look at the color table and see how it is arranged, which will typically indicate whether data has been hidden with EZ Stego.

Figure 8.13 shows a clean image. Figure 8.14 shows the same file with data hidden using EZ Stego. The image that has data embedded in it has some parts that are badly degraded. Even if you didn't have the original image for comparison, you can see that the image is degraded enough to raise suspicion.

Figure 8.13   An image with no data hidden in it.

Figure 8.14 An image after data has been hidden in it with EZ-Stego.

StegDetect

StegDetect is a program that detects data hidden with a variety of Stego programs. This well-designed program was written by Niels Provos. StegDetect can be downloaded from OutGuess at www.outguess.org/detection.php.

StegDetect performs tests for use of specific stego programs, as well as some statistical tests against JPEG images. You can download the source code for StegDetect and add other techniques if you have developed algorithms of your own.

StegDetect currently detects the following programs:

- J-Steg
- JPHide (Unix and Windows)
- Invisible Secrets
- OutGuess 01.3b
- F5 (header analysis)
- appendX and Camouflage

NOTE In order to run StegDetect you need to download the software from the OutGuess Web site. You can download a .zip file that contains the Windows binaries, or you can download the source code and compile it yourself. For more information on the program and the specific command-line options, go to the program Web site at www.outguess.org.

StegDetect runs on the command line and produces a listing of files that might have data hidden in them.

The following is the general format for running StegDetect from the command line:

```
stegdetect [ -qnV][-s float][-d num][-t tests][file ...]
```

Type the program name, followed by any options, followed by the names of the files you want to scan.

Options can include a specific technique for which you want to search, as well as other refinements to how the program operates. The following list includes the various options you can use to configure StegDetect:

-q   Reports only images that are likely to have steganographic content.

-n   Enables checking of JPEG header information to suppress false positives. This is similar to, but a little more robust than, checking the file extension. For example, JPEG images should always have an extension of .jpg and a certain header. If you change this information you can make it harder to detect by programs such as StegDetect. If you do try to detect these modified files you will generate a large number of false positives. If this option is enabled, all JPEG images that contain comment fields will be treated as negatives.

V   Displays the version number of the software.

-s *float*   Changes the sensitivity of the detection algorithms. The results are multiplied by the specified number: The higher the number, the more sensitive the test becomes. The default is 1. It is important to be careful when using this option because you can increase your false alarms by making these numbers too high or too low. If you set the sensitivity very high, you increase false negatives (the results show a file has nothing hidden in it when it does); if you set the sensitivity too low, you increase false positives (the result shows a file has hidden data in it when it doesn't).

-d *num*   Prints debug information.

-t *tests*   Sets the tests that are being run on the image. If you suspect a specific type of program was used to hide data, you can run a specific test. If you have no idea what type of technique might have been used you run the program using all of the options (jopi). The letters you can use for this option are as follows:

- j—Tests if information has been embedded with J-Steg.
- o—Tests if information has been embedded with OutGuess.
- p—Tests if information has been embedded with JPHide.
- i—Tests if information has been hidden with Invisible Secrets.

When you run StegDetect, the program indicates the accuracy of the test by placing an asterisk after each file. The more asterisks, the more accurate the result. This indicates to the user the chance that there is a false alarm. For example, if I type the following:

```
Stegdetect-t jopi test1.jpg
```

and receive the following response:

```
test3.jpg : negative
```

this means that the program did not detect any hidden data. If I run the same command against a file that contains hidden data, I receive the following response:

```
test3.jpg : J-Steg (***)
```

This works well when running the program against a single file, but what if I wanted to run the program against a large number of files? Because the program reads the file list from standard input I have several options. One option is to put all of the files I want to scan into a file called filelist.txt and pass that into the program. Now to run the program against several files I type the following command:

```
Stegdetect-t jopi <filelist.txt
```

and receive the following response:

```
test1.jpg : negative
test2.jpg : J-Steg (***)
test3.jpg : outguess (**)
test4.jpg : jphide (***)
test5.jpg : J-Steg (***)
```

Running a command line is fine for automated scripts, but some people prefer a tool with a more Windows-like GUI. StegDetect comes with a program called xsteg, which provides a GUI interface for the program (see Figure 8.15).

In this dialog box, you use the checkboxes to select your options and pick the files you want to scan from the File menu. The Filename list shows you the output, and the Message window shows you what commands are being issued and any errors that might have occurred.

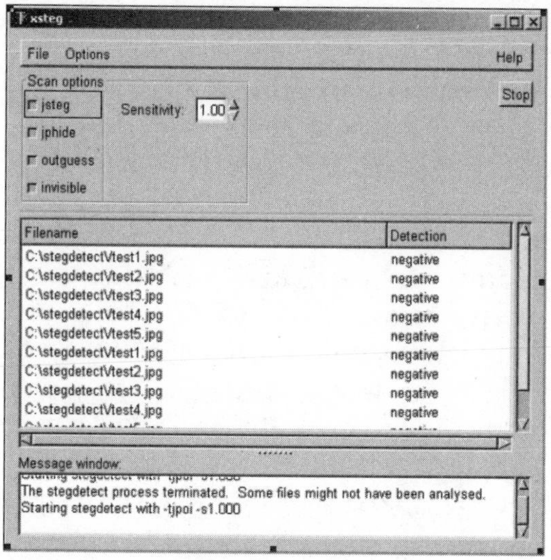

Figure 8.15   The xsteg interface sports a more user-friendly GUI.

There is one other tool included with Stegdetect, called stegbreak. Remember that the goal of a steganalyst is to determine whether data is hidden in a file, not to actually extract the data. In some cases, it is useful to try to identify what the actual data is. To prevent this, most stego programs provide a utility so that the person hiding the data can enter a password to protect the information. Once you know that data is hidden in a file you can use stegbreak to perform a brute-force attack to determine the password so that it can extract the data.

The following output from stegbreak shows the password in parentheses:

```
stegbreak -tj test1.jpg
Loaded 1 files...
dscf0002.jpg : J-Steg(simplepass)
Processed 1 files, found 1 embeddings.
Time: 36 seconds: Cracks: 324123,  8915 c/s
```

General Techniques for Detecting Stego

Being able to detect a specific technique is a good start, but it is very time-consuming. Also, this approach is victim to the same problem that other fields, such as virus detection, suffer: You are able to detect only known techniques.

For this reason, it would be useful to have universal detection measures that would detect any type of stego. At a very basic level, a simple universal technique is to take the original image and compare it to a copy. If the two images look exactly the same but are composed of different binary bits, then most likely one of the files has data hidden in it. Because comparison with the original can unmask hidden data, it is considered best practice to destroy the original image once you have created a new image with hidden data.

Another general technique is to perform statistical analysis against a file and determine the normal properties of the image. The assumption is that steganography would modify these normal properties such that there would be deviations across the statistics.

I have included a program in Appendix A called stats that will allow you to run statistics against a single file and to run statistics against a group of files so that you can spot any similarities or differences. Six statistical tests can be performed:

- Average bytes
- Variations of the bytes
- Skew
- Kurtosis
- Average deviation
- Differential values

Figures 8.16 through 8.21 show the mapping of the values for clean and dirty files. Clean files have no data embedded in them; dirty files have data hidden in them.

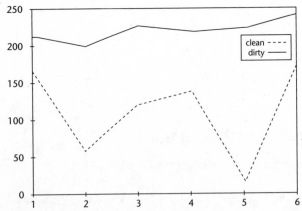

Figure 8.16   Graph showing the average bytes across both clean and dirty files.

Variations

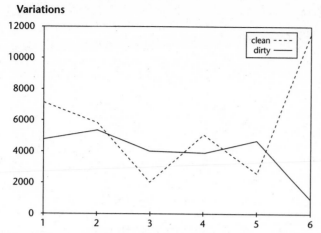

Figure 8.17 Graph showing the variation of bytes across both clean and dirty files.

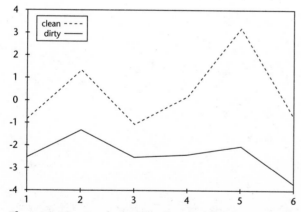

Figure 8.18 Graph showing the skew bytes across both clean and dirty files.

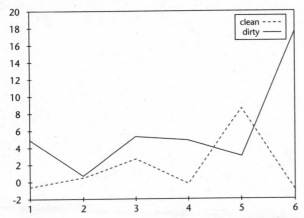

Figure 8.19 Graph showing the kurtosis across both clean and dirty files.

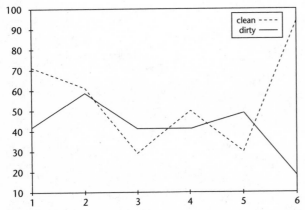

Figure 8.20 Graph showing the average deviation across both clean and dirty files.

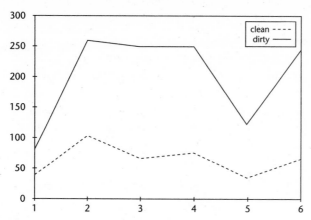

Figure 8.21   Graph showing the differential values across both clean and dirty files.

For this technique to work there has to be a clear division between the clean files and the dirty files; if both types occupy the same space you would not be able to distinguish between them. For example, if a clean file is in the range of 0 to 50 and a dirty file is in the range of 100 to 150, then they occupy different space and it is easy to detect them. If both clean and dirty files have values in the range of 0 to 50, then they occupy the same space and hidden data is hard to detect.

By analyzing the graph in Figure 8.16 you can see that when you calculate the average there is a clear division between clean and dirty files. Any value above 175 indicates that a file has data embedded in it, and any value below that indicates a clean file.

Looking at the skew graph in Figure 8.18 and the differential values graph in Figure 8.21 you will notice some overlap, but you cannot determine with 100 percent accuracy whether a given file has data embedded in it. With Figure 8.21 if a value is above 150, then you know the file is dirty or contains hidden information. If a file has a value below 50, then you know it is clean and it does not contain hidden information.

With variation, kurtosis, and average deviation graphs, there is no distinct break point, so these are not good tests for universal stego detection.

Looking Ahead

In Chapter 9 it's time to take what you've learned about crypto and stego and see how these technologies fit into your strategies to protect your company's data and to detect use of steganography against your organization.

Chapter 9 provides a decision tree to help you decide which technologies you should use in your communication plan and identify common problems to avoid.

Developing Your Secure Communications Strategy

One of the biggest problems that most companies have regarding security technology is that they don't develop a strategy for implementation. Many companies seem to have the attitude that implementing a single technology, such as firewalls, will make them secure. In reality, just putting a firewall in place is not enough: That firewall has to be designed and configured properly for it to do its job successfully, and it must be used in concert with other security measures. And all these security measures must be properly integrated with the current network.

Secure communication is no different from information security: You have to pick the right tools, implement them properly, and train users to use them in their daily work.

This chapter will look at the kind of assessment involved in developing a secure communications strategy that might include stego and crypto.

HONG KONG CONNECTION

Chen Yu-tang was a small man, unremarkable, but with a keen intelligence in his eyes, which looked out from behind wire-rimmed spectacles. Mr. Chen wasn't high up in the Chinese Mafia, but the most powerful people in the hierarchy usually knew his name. That's because quiet, polite Mr. Chen had masterminded quite a few successful money laundering schemes for the

(continues)

organization. Without his services, several people would be living out their lives behind bars at the end of a paper trail followed assiduously by Chinese law enforcement. But Mr. Chen's specialty was erasing that paper trail with his unique stego and crypto skills.

Using those skills was a particular challenge in Hong Kong, where use of encryption and steganography is illegal. For that reason, it was important to distract law enforcement not only from deciphering hidden messages, but from discovering the existence of the messages themselves.

Mr. Chen's current assignment was to convey the details about where to transmit the proceeds of a large drug deal to a member of the Mafia based in Tokyo. Both Mr. Chen and the drug dealer were being watched carefully, so he'd have to figure out a strategy that would at least slow the police down, if not stop them from uncovering the message.

What he figured out took advantage of the old adage that there's safety in numbers. He took a few days to gather image files off the Internet. Then, within a few hours, he used a program he'd written to flood a couple of Web sites the Mafia often used to drop off and pick up encrypted files with more than 20,000 images. Only two photos—one of the Eiffel Tower and one of the Statue of Liberty—actually had hidden messages in them, and the drug dealer knew by prearrangement where to look. By the time the cops worked their way through several thousand images, the information would have been picked up, the money transmitted and broken up into small, almost-impossible-to-detect deposits in banks all around the world.

Secure versus Secret

You may not have a master of secure communications on your payroll, but you need to develop internal expertise to make important communications secure in your working world.

As you begin developing a secure communications plan it is important to remember the distinction between secure and secret. Making something secure involves ensuring that no one can read or gain access to a piece of information. When you go to bed at night you may first lock the house and set the alarm. You have made the house secure. In most cases, when we talk about secure communications we are referring to cryptography, which keeps people from being able to read information.

Secret or covert communication involves hiding the fact that anything sensitive exists at all. Generally, when people talk about secret or covert communication, they are referring to stego.

What is important to remember is that, at some level, if something is secret it is also secure to a degree. The degree of security rests in how well the secret item has been hidden.

The difference between secure and secret communications reinforces the concept of defense in depth. Only by putting many different technologies together, creating a layered approach, will you be secure. In the area of secure communication, this approach would suggest the wisdom of using both crypto and stego in concert.

NOTE Another reason why you should use both crypto and stego is because crypto is more evolved, with very robust and highly secure techniques in place, such as Triple-DES and RSA. Stego, on the other hand, is still developing into a formal science and does not yet provide techniques that have stood the test of time.

Setting Communication Goals

There is a saying that if you define your target after you shoot an arrow, you will hit your target every time. Many companies approach secure communication this way. Let's put something together, and whatever protection we build will define our security goal. In the long run, this is not an effective approach. You have to define your communication goals before you can plan your secure communication strategy.

What follows is a list of the goals an organization might want to achieve when using secret communication. For each goal I have noted whether it is achieved through using crypto, stego, or both.

Communication goes to the intended party (crypto). If you send a message it is important that it goes to the person for whom it is intended. At a basic level this is done by specifying the proper destination, such as an IP address or email address. At a more sophisticated level, guaranteeing the identity of the recipient can be ensured by crypto and the use of private key encryption.

Communication is not modified in transit (crypto). Validating the integrity of a message is critical to ensuring that a person-in-the-middle attack, where data is modified in transit, was not performed. Performing a digital signature with crypto is critical to making sure that data has not been modified.

Communication does not go through a hostile person (crypto/stego). In a situation where you cannot control where packets of data actually go as they travel to the intended recipient, if the data is hidden and protected the impact of a hostile entity accessing the data is minimized.

Communication is not read by unauthorized people (crypto).   If someone can intercept data, the concern is whether they can read or access information that they should not have access to. By encrypting the information nobody will be able to read or make changes to it.

The fact of the communication is hidden from unauthorized people (stego/digital dead drop).   In some situations, even if someone cannot read the information that is being communicated, the mere fact that information is being communicated or that encrypted information is being transmitted can raise suspicion. By using stego with a digital dead drop the relationship between the two parties is hidden, in addition to the existence of the communication.

The true intent of the communication is not discovered (stego).   In some cases, the fact that there is communication between two parties may not be a concern, but the intent of that communication may be. This situation is ideal for stego because the two parties can communicate, but the true intention (message) of the communication is hidden.

The organization can prove in a court of law that communication was sent from a given person (crypto).   Non-repudiation (being able to prove in a court of law that a specific person sent a communication) is at the heart of e-commerce. Why would anyone use digital contracts or electronic signatures if they were not binding? Using crypto with digital signatures provides the means for non-repudiation.

The Roles of Crypto and Stego in Business

Though these technologies are more in use by the criminal element of our world, the growing interest in them in the corporate sector suggests that they will become an everyday part of information security as time goes by. How will they fit into your organization? Read on.

Why You Need Both Stego and Crypto

Whenever you consider two or more technologies to be used in your communications security strategy, you should determine whether they are complementary or competing. If they are competing, that means they both do the same thing and the technologies are redundant. If they are complementary, they provide different services; by putting them together, you obtain a more robust result.

Stego and crypto are definitely complementary technologies. They provide two different services to the data they are protecting. Stego hides the existence of the data, while crypto makes the contents of the data difficult to read.

Crypto and Stego in Business Today

I know of several organizations that have gone to great lengths to roll out encryption across their enterprise, only to use the same key for all their data. To add insult to injury, they then make that key available to everyone in the organization. I have seen organizations put their key on a public server with no protection whatsoever. Organizations may use crypto during the transmission of data but then store the data in unencrypted form on a Web server that is accessible from the Internet. In short, not many businesses are using crypto, and those that are often use it incorrectly.

If the crypto side of the coin does not look so good, the stego side is even worse. Since September 11, 2001, the corporate security landscape is changing, but a large percentage of people still do not even know what steganography is. In fact, I do not know of any companies that are actually using stego as part of their corporate communication scheme. (But I do know of criminal organizations that are using stego against those corporations.) Unfortunately, this is a common technology trend: The bad guys will use a technology, and only later will legitimate uses be discovered to protect the victims.

> **NOTE** Heck, Microsoft Word spell-check still does not even include steganography as a word in its spelling dictionary, though it is a term that has been around for hundreds of years. As an indication of the growing awareness of stego today, however, I understand that the new version of Office will have the word "steganography" in its dictionary.

How Crypto and Stego Make You More Secure

In my opinion, a lot of the issues relating to secure communication on the Internet (email, Web page contents, and file transfer, to name a few) would go away if all data was stored in an encrypted format and hidden in files on hard drives on workstations or servers. Attackers would face the challenge of first locating the information, then breaking the crypto to read it. Certain types of attacks, such as denial of service, would still occur, but corporate espionage methods that modify or access proprietary information could be foiled to a great extent.

Remember that there is no silver bullet when it comes to security, but crypto and stego used together provide a high grade of protection against the most serious attacks that occur when data is placed on a network or transmitted via the Internet.

Developing a Strategy

The first step in developing a secure communications strategy is to analyze the communication patterns in your organization, detailing what type of information is communicated and by whom.

Based on that information you can establish a data security ranking system with categories such as these:

- Highly confidential data, such as product plans.

- Private data, such as employee salaries.

- Internal data, such as product code names and release dates.

- Public data, such as product brochures.

With these categories of data in place, instruct each employee on how to use the ranking and to respect how each type of data is to be used, stored, shared, and communicated.

Your next task is to go through a decision process about which form of secure communications tools might be used with each type of data.

Don't forget to train your employees and management in the use of the data-ranking system and secure communication tools. Let them know the seriousness of the need for security by instituting certain actions if the guidelines are not followed.

Set up a reporting process for breaches of information security so these can be reported and acted on to stop an attack in progress, minimize damage, or prevent future security breaches.

To determine whether your organization should use crypto, stego, or both in certain situations, use the decision process flowchart shown in Figure 9.1.

Using this chart you consider the key goals of your communication and pick the technology or technologies that correspond to those goals.

Common Problems with Secure Technologies

In the spirit of David Letterman, I thought it was appropriate to put together a Top 10 list of common questions you should ask before deploying secure technologies. This list can also be thought of as a checklist for a secure communication strategy.

1. **Did you determine which technology is a higher priority and deploy that technology first?** It is usually considered good practice to deploy one technology, make sure it works, and then deploy the next technology. If you deploy two technologies at the same time and there is a

problem, troubleshooting the problem becomes harder. On the other hand, even though you are only deploying one technology at a time, if you are planning on eventually implementing multiple technologies, it is highly recommended that you test them together for compatibility before deploying them. Also, if your company is planning to use these technologies with business partners, it is usually a good idea to make sure that those partners use the same technologies or compatible technologies.

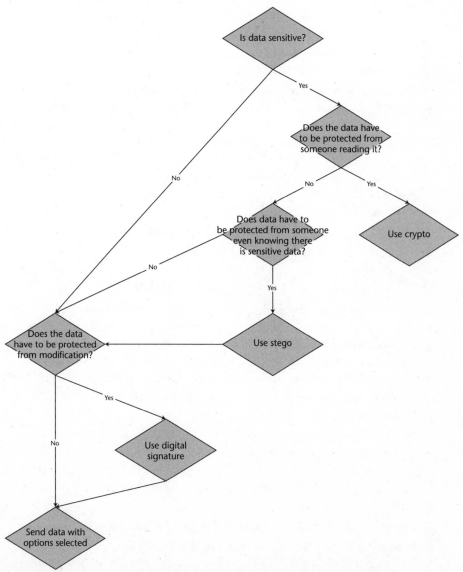

Figure 9.1   Flow chart for the secure communication decision process.

2. **Did you integrate the technology at the lowest level possible?** For example, it is usually better to implement encryption between layers 3 and 4 in a VPN rather than at the application layer. If you implement the technology at a higher level you have to deploy a version for every single application you use. If you integrate it at a lower level, all corresponding applications will also be able to take advantage of the same encryption.

3. **Did you use the techniques in the proper order?** When using crypto and stego together, it is recommended that you encrypt the information first and then hide it in a file. Because crypto has a signature and is detectable, performing crypto last will leave a signature someone can use to track down suspicious files. By using crypto and then stego, and then hiding the encryption in a file or network stream, you make it much harder for someone to detect it.

4. **Are your keys and passwords for encryption and stego properly protected?** Remember one of the golden rules of secure communication: The strength of a communication technology is based on the secrecy of the key, not the secrecy of the algorithm. If someone can find your keys or the password/pass phrase that you used to protect your information, you have just defeated the whole purpose of using such a technique. It is critical that keys and passwords be very hard to guess, and even harder to find.

5. **Are your stego tools properly protected from detection or tampering?** The goal of stego is to avoid detection, so if you are not supposed to be using stego but you leave stego tools on your system where someone can find them, he or she can figure out what you're up to.

6. **Are your users properly trained, and do they understand the technologies?** This is a challenging process to institute at some companies. On one hand, you should not expect your users to have a thorough understanding of stego or crypto in order to use them; on the other hand, they should have an understanding of the value of decryption and encryption and appreciate that a private key must be kept secure.

7. **Are the technologies as transparent to the user as possible?** Even though users should have an appreciation of the need for secure communication, you should make the technologies as transparent as possible to them. The less they have to learn and remember, the less chance of error.

8. **Is your IT and administrative staff trained on the potential implications of stego and crypto?** When you encrypt information or hide data in files or network traffic, it should be made known to the people that

manage the servers and networks. Surprises are not a good thing when it comes to healthy networks. Make sure your technical staff is well trained and understands any potential implications these technologies might have—for example, as they use traffic analysis or intrusion detection systems. Because the data portion of encrypted files might look unusual, these systems may flag them. Also, because stego uses image files in many cases, if you want to generate a lot of stego, you may be saving a great many large graphics files that eat up server space.

9. **Did you test the tools before deploying them?** The golden rule of technology is that you should always test before you deploy. After you test it, test it again. If you roll out a technology to 2000 computers and then find a problem, it can be very hard to rectify that problem. I recommend doing incremental rollouts. Once a technology is tested, roll it out to 10 people and make sure there are no problems, then roll out to 30 more people, then to 100, and so on. In this way, you minimize the chances of introducing errors to a large number of systems at once.

10. **Do you understand the inherent weaknesses in the tools and take measures to protect against them?** No tool is perfect, and you need to understand the shortcomings of any techniques that you deploy. Deploying a technique and thinking it is going to make you completely secure is naïve at best. Understanding the limitations and taking action to minimize the impact those limitations can have on your organization are the smart things to do.

Looking Ahead

In the final chapter of this book, Chapter 10, I want you to think about what the future landscape for covert communication might look like. Knowing what you now know about cryptography and steganography and their uses, take a moment to consider how they may evolve as we move through the twenty-first century.

The Future of Steganography

The future is a place we can visit only in our imaginations. Still, the current characteristics and trends in steganography point us to possible futures. By understanding trends in technology you can sometimes make accurate predictions about what will happen in the future. In some scenarios, stego is used to help maintain our personal and professional privacy. In others, it could be used against us by terrorists, criminals, and even by our own governments.

Which future will come to pass? This chapter looks at a few possibilities.

MARCH 3, 2025

Jake puts his coffee cup in the sonic dishwasher and walks over to his wall computer to begin his workday at his company, Digital Rights Management, International. His personal Net comes up with all the contacts and Web sites he communicates with assembled there on his modular home page. He signs on to his company intranet, which scans his retina for identification and opens the virtual door to his digital office. Jake's virtual assistant Brad welcomes him and displays videophone messages from the day before. Jake views the videos and returns a couple of calls, jotting notes right on his digital pad, which instantly encrypts the notes and stores them in corresponding client folders for later retrieval.

(continued)

MARCH 3, 2025 *(continued)*

Having completed a report on the progress of a new product development project, he pops a thin, stamp-sized disk into his computer's stego drive. The entire report is instantly placed into a streaming video file in encrypted form, which he z-mails to his boss. He knows the file won't even seem to exist to anybody but his boss, who has a private key embedded in his head that only he can use to detect and read the message.

He replicates another cup of coffee and clicks on an icon on his computer screen to hear a report on the day's news. The holographic newscaster reports of a terrorist skirmish on the Ohio/Pennsylvania border with 200 dead. An investigator into the incident reports that advance knowledge of the act could have been retrieved if the government had thought to look for hidden communications in the classified section of the digital *New York Times* of a few weeks earlier. Jake searches his digital mailbox for his copy of the newspaper in question, runs the stego detection program built into his Web browser, and immediately spots three messages embedded in ads.

That's followed by a story on piracy of television programs and a huge digital swap meet that occurs every month to trade pirated content freely. There's also a story about a new technology being used by the criminal element to replicate biometric signatures, so that a crook could emulate your retina scan results or voice print. Jake shakes his head, wondering what the world is coming to. A commercial comes on his computer for Time Warner AOL eBay, and Jake absorbs the subliminal audio messages hidden in the video without realizing he's doing so. Suddenly he considers going to eBay to buy things.

His thoughts are interrupted by an audio transmission from a colleague in Paris. Jacqueline wants to show Jake a new video watermarking technology, and her message directs him to the Web site of a popular video-on-demand company. He assembles a personal movie with clips from several blockbuster hits of the day, then places his order for a review copy using voice money—a method of using a voiceprint to identify a buyer by his or her vocal characteristics and charging the corresponding credit bank for the purchase.

With the personal movie review copy downloaded, he studies it for signs of video watermarking technology. After the 15-minute review cycle is over, a digital time stamp appears on the video, instructing him to click on the stamp to extend his review copy time or purchase the movie. When he does neither, after 3 minutes the video self-destructs. He sends off an encrypted voice memo to his boss, suggesting the company research the technology for possible acquisition.

Having finished his half-day-long work week, Jake heads out to the Transporter Center to beam to Paris and have lunch with Jacqueline.

Improving the Techniques

One thing that you can certainly say about the future of technology: Change and the introduction of new approaches will continue to occur on a frequent basis. The first area where we can anticipate stego making strides is in the technology used to produce and break it.

Improved Resistance to Analysis

As stego gets more sophisticated, its resistance to being analyzed, or even recognized, will improve. In the current state of stego technology, if you suspect stego is being used, it is relatively easy to detect it. Once you detect it, you can probably retrieve the contents, which would then be protected only by the strength of the encryption applied to it, if any.

In the future, efforts will be made to make stego undetectable and irretrievable except by those for whom it is intended. The actual form that this takes may be dependent on the types of carriers and communication types available—for example, if large video files can be easily sent via a personal wireless network with some form of wireless protocol that successfully protects the data from detection. Because the world is becoming completely digital, you will see techniques developed for new media formats such as video, electronic books, holograms, and even data hiding with digital watermarks.

The ability to manipulate data (for example, by hiding it in digital format), then printing out a hard copy, rescanning it, and again being able to retrieve the hidden data would be an intriguing scenario.

NOTE The ability to recover distorted images and underlying messages is being researched today. Bennet Haselton, the coordinator of Peacefire.org, which seeks to end censorship, has described his anticipation of a stego protocol that is "undetectable to censors."

How Much Can You Hide?

The ability to hide huge amounts of data with stego is another logical area for improvement. Currently stego can use only a certain amount of data bits in a host file without degrading the file to the point where it's obvious that stego is being used. As stego is used in crimes such as corporate espionage, there will be more demand to hide larger amounts of data. Large-scale stego, where you can perform compression on huge amounts of data on the fly and store it in small files, is one possible future.

> **NOTE** Currently a program called DRIVECRYPT can hide a whole volume of music files using stego techniques.

One of the limitations of steganography today that may be overcome in the future is the one-to-one relationship between a covert and an overt file. To hide one byte of covert data requires one byte of overt data. This relationship will eventually be overcome with a new technology that will enable a large covert file to be hidden in a smaller overt file.

Improved Attack Tools

In the field of cryptography, a great deal of effort has been expended to break various techniques; however, though there are hundreds of tools for performing stego, little has been done to determine the overall strength of the various methods. The same methods of systematic attack used with cryptography must be developed to make stego algorithms more secure and improve the various techniques. Techniques for combining stego and crypto to make data more secure may be one outcome of this effort.

New and Improved Ways to Use Stego

As people learn more about stego, it will simply be used more. When people use a technology they demand new features and applications. Various elements of our society will demand different improvements for their own purposes.

Law Enforcement

Since September 11, 2001, law enforcement has become aware of stego and its use by terrorists and criminals, such as child pornographers and drug dealers. The future for law enforcement and stego largely involves playing catchup, as federal and state agencies educate workers about the technology, its uses, and its techniques.

Once the law enforcement community understands the uses of stego, they should be a part of the movement to build more robust tools for detecting it. Intelligence agencies will also increase their use of the technology to keep their own secrets secret.

Corporate Uses

In light of the Enron and WorldCom scandals, executives are likely to be more paranoid about how their communications and data can be tracked. I believe there will be a huge increase in the legitimate uses of stego in the business world. One key to the increased use of stego will be more automation of the process of transporting a file to the end user. The technology is here today, but it is very difficult to use.

Companies will also continue to explore technologies that protect their digital assets, yet keep their products user-friendly for consumers.

NOTE Hiding data in holograms may be in the cards. Currently the technology to produce holograms is expensive, but if that technology develops so that the average user or company can access it, hiding images in holograms may become popular for uses such as ID or credit cards.

Illegal Uses

On a less productive note, stego's use to enable the spread of computer viruses could increase. An HTML-based email could hold a photo attachment—once opened, a stego-embedded virus could deliver its payload to an unsuspecting recipient.

Most television stations will have to broadcast digital signals in the near future, making piracy of television content the next big wave. A technology that used self-executing embedded messages in video or audio tracks could provide protection of digital content. This could also be used for timed rentals of digital content. This will mean that consumer devices receiving digital broadcasts would have to be able to recognize video watermarks that indicate whether certain content can be copied or shared.

Corporate espionage will increase as business gets more globally competitive. Identity theft will allow people to go where they shouldn't, and stego will allow them to get data they shouldn't have from the corporate network.

Where Will Stego Tools Reside?

One vision of the future is something called the Personal Net. In this scenario, we will all manage our own data, communications, and security. No longer will we trust our information and identities to a public Internet, which we already know to be dangerous and lax about security. We will all have greater power over our own security, and stego is likely to be a part of that.

Hand in hand with a Personal Net is a personal computing experience. You may build your own operating system and assemble your software tools in modules, rather than buying office suites. And what kind of security tools will you have to choose from in your personal computing environment? Consider this: Operating systems that now have encryption built in (five years ago few would have imagined this) will in the future have stego programs built in. You may have a Hide Data button right next to the Save button on the software toolbars of the future.

Browser technology will include filtering and permissions features to locate and open embedded messages. Finally, attack tools to break stego and crypto will become commonplace security measures in corporations, and perhaps even on the personal desktop as telecommuting increases and workers must stay secure in their home computing environment.

Steganography Source Code

Throughout this book I have talked about various programs that can be used in the realm of secret communication. To help make this book more valuable to you I have included all of the source code in this appendix, including the techniques described in Chapters 6 and 8. To make your life easier, I have also included the source code and .exe files on the accompanying CD ROM included with this book.

Chapter 6 Code Examples

The sample code discussed in Chapter 6 demonstrates three different steganography techniques: insertion, substitution, and creation. Six file formats are used in these examples: Word .doc, WAV, RTF, .exe, HTML, and .txt. See Chapter 6 for more discussion about how to use these techniques.

Term Definitions

In these code examples the following terms are used:

Covert file or covert data.   The file containing the data to be hidden by the algorithm. The covert file can be ASCII or binary.

Covert2 file. The file created by the decoding function of the algorithm. The covert file and the covert2 file will be exactly the same as verified by a CRC check.

Overt file. The file into which the covert data will be hidden before any data is hidden in it. Not all routines need an overt file. In general, a creation routine should not need an overt file.

Overt2 file. The file in which the covert data has been hidden. The file should operate normally with no apparent irregularities as a result of the data hidden in it.

All of the modules (*.c) should be compiled into objects (*.o). All of the objects should be linked together into the executable, stego.exe.

Command-Line Arguments

All of the algorithms are run from a single executable, stego.exe. The choice of the algorithm is made with command-line arguments. The following is the usage function in the stego.exe application.

```
Usage:
        File names must be less than 32 characters
        -C <covert file name>
        -c <decoded file name>
        -O <overt file name>
        -o <final overt file name>
        -r <1-?? hidding routine>
        -v <1-255 variable>
        -?      Display this message\n

Insertion - Additional data added to the overt file.  File size grows.
Stuffing - Bytes in overt file are replaced.  File size is the same.
Twidle - Bytes in overt file are changed slightly.  File size is the same.
Creation - A new file is made based on covert data.  There is no overt
file.

Routines:
1 HTTP Insertion encode
2 HTTP Insertion decode
3 EXE Stuffer encode
4 EXE Stuffer decode
5 RTF Insertion encode
6 RTF Insertion decode
7 WAV Creation encode
8 WAV Creation decode
9 WAV Twidle encode
10 WAV Twidle decode
11 WAR Create encode
12 WAR Create decode
```

```
13 DOC Stuffer encode
14 DOC Stuffer decode
15 HTTP_VARY Insertion encode
16 HTTP_VARY Insertion decode
17 WAV_SINE Creation encode
18 WAV_SINE Creation decode

Example, to HTTP_WS encode:
stego.exe -r 1 -C covertSmall.txt -O overtBig.html -o out.html

Example, to HTTP_WS decode:
stego.exe -r 2 -c covert2.txt -o out.html

Example, to exeStuffer encode:
stego.exe -r 4 -C covertMedium.bin -c covertMedium2.bin -O stego.exe-o ↩
stego1.exe

Example, to exeStuffer decode:
stego.exe -r 5 -C covertMedium.bin -c covertMedium2.bin -O stego.exe-o ↩
stego1.exe
```

Config

This code is responsible for processing the command-line arguments that are entered by the user.

```
/**************************************************
 * config.c
 *
 * Default values
 * Command line Arguments
 * Logging related processes
 *
 * Code Designed and Written by Eric Cole and Jim Conley
 **************************************************
 */


#include "stegoGlobal.h"

// Prototypes
//
void myUsage(void);
void ProcessArgs (int argc, char *argv[]);

//############# ProcessArgs() ##################

void ProcessArgs (int argc, char *argv[]) {
    int i;
    int x;
```

```
        char * val;

        // Set some defaults...
        vary = 0;
        routine = 0;
        strcpy(covertFile, "covertFile.txt");
        strcpy(overtFile,  "overtFile.txt");
        strcpy(overt2File, "overt2File.txt");
        strcpy(logFile,    "logFile.txt");
        strcpy(bitFile,    "bitFile.txt");

        dbmask = 0x0000001010100000;
//dbmask = 0x0000 0010 1010 0000;
//              |||| |||| |||| ||||
//              |||| |||| |||| ||||- TBD0
//              |||| |||| |||| |||-- TBD1
//              |||| |||| |||| ||— TBD2
//              |||| |||| |||| |— TBD3
//              |||| |||| ||||
//              |||| |||| ||||—- TBD4
//              |||| |||| |||—— CON_ERRS        // send error info to
the  console
//              |||| |||| ||——- CON_ARGS        // send arg info to
the console
//              |||| |||| |—— CON_VERB          // send verbose info
to the console
//              |||| ||||
//              |||| ||||—— INTERACTIVE       // get keyboard hit at
certain times
//              |||| |||—— LOG_ERRS            // send error info to
log file
//              |||| ||—— TBDa
//              |||| |——- TBDb
//              ||||
//              ||||—— TBDc
//              |||—— TBDd
//              ||——- TBDe
//              |—— TBDf


// Defaults provided in each server's main() code
// Go through command-line options that must start with "-", be a single
// character, and take a value
        for (i=1; i<argc; i++) {
              if (argv[i][0] == '-' && argc > i) {
                    x = argv[i][1];
                    val = argv[++i];

//We are incrementing the index!

                    switch (x) {
                    case 'C':

// Input file - data to be hidden
                          if(strlen(val) > FILENAMESIZ) {
```

```
                            myUsage();
                            break;
                    } //if strlen
                    strcpy (covertFile, val);
                    break;
            case 'c':

// decoded file - data extracted
                    if(strlen(val) > FILENAMESIZ) {
                            myUsage();
                            break;
                    } //if strlen
                    strcpy (covert2File, val);
                    break;
            case 'O':

// Target file - place to hide data
                    if(strlen(val) > FILENAMESIZ) {
                            myUsage();
                            break;
                    } //if strlen
                    strcpy (overtFile, val);
                    break;
            case 'o':

// Output file - after data is hidden
                    if(strlen(val) > FILENAMESIZ) {
                            myUsage();
                            break;
                    } //if strlen
                    strcpy (overt2File, val);
                    break;
            case 'r':

// which hiding routine is to be used
                    routine = atoi(val);
                    if(routine < 1) {
                        printf("Error, Invalid Routine\n");
                        myUsage();
                        exit(0);
                    }
                    break;
            case 'v':

// which hidding routine is to be used
                    vary = atoi(val);
                    if(vary < 1  ||  vary > 255) {
                        printf("Error, Invalid amount for Vary\n");
                        printf("Value must be 1 - 255\n");
                        myUsage();
                        exit(0);
                    }
                    break;
            case '?':
```

```
        // Help
                        myUsage();
                        printf("Last Build %s %s\n",
                                        __DATE__, __TIME__);
                        exit(0);
                        break;
                } // switch
        } else {
            printf ("Invalid arguments!  run %s -?", argv[0]);
            myUsage();
            exit(0);
        } // if '-'
    }


    // Check for some mandatory args...
    if( routine == 0 ) {
        printf("A routine must be provided!\n\n");
        myUsage();
        exit(0);
    }


    if(dbmask & CON_ARGS)
        myUsage();
}


void myUsage(void) {
    printf("Usage:\n");
    printf("     File names must be less than than %d characters\n",
FILENAMESIZ);
    printf("     -C <covert file name>       Current: %s\n", covertFile);
    printf("     -c <decoded file name>      Current: %s\n", covert2File);
    printf("     -O <overt file name>        Current: %s\n", overtFile);
    printf("     -o <final overt file name>  Current: %s\n", overt2File);
    printf("     -r <1-?? hidding routine>   Current: %d   \n", routine);
    printf("     -v <1-255 variable>         Current: %d   \n", vary);
    printf("     -?       Display this message\n\n");
    printf("        \n");
    printf("  Definitions: \n");
    printf("  Insertion - Additional data added\n");
    printf("    to the overt file.  File size\n");
    printf("    grows.\n");
    printf("  Stuffing - Bytes in overt file\n");
    printf("    are replaced.  File size is\n");
    printf("    the same.\n");
    printf("  Twidle - Bytes in overt file\n");
    printf("    are changed slightly.  File size\n");
    printf("    is the same.\n");
    printf("  Creation - A new file is made based\n");
    printf("    based on covert data.  There is\n");
    printf("    no overt file.\n");
    printf("        \n");
    printf("  Routines:\n");
    printf(" 1 HTTP Insertion encode \n");
    printf(" 2 HTTP Insertion decode \n");
```

```
            printf(" 3 EXE Stuffer encode    \n");
            printf(" 4 EXE Stuffer decode    \n");
            printf(" 5 RTF Insertion encode  \n");
            printf(" 6 RTF Insertion decode  \n");
            printf(" 7 WAV Creation encode   \n");
            printf(" 8 WAV Creation decode   \n");
            printf(" 9 WAV Twidle encode     \n");
            printf("10 WAV Twidle decode     \n");
            printf("11 WAR Create decode     \n");
            printf("12 WAR Create decode     \n");
            printf("13 DOC Stuffer encode    \n");
            printf("14 DOC Stuffer decode    \n");
            printf("15 HTTP_VARY Insertion encode \n");
            printf("16 HTTP_VARY Insertion decode \n");
            printf("17 WAV_SINE Creation encode   \n");
            printf("18 WAV_SINE Creation decode   \n");
            printf("          \n");
            printf("Example, to HTTP_WS encode:\n");
            printf("stego.exe -r 1 -C covertSmall.txt");
            printf(" -O overtBig.html -o out.html\n\n");
            printf("          \n");
            printf("Example, to HTTP_WS decode:\n");
            printf("stego.exe -r 2 -c covert2.txt");
            printf(" -o out.html\n\n");
            printf("          \n");
            printf("Example, to exeStuffer encode:\n");
            printf("stego.exe -r 4 -C covertMedium.bin ");
            printf(" -c covertMedium2.bin -O stego.exe");
            printf(" -o stego1.exe\n\n");
            printf("          \n");
            printf("Example, to exeStuffer decode:\n");
            printf("stego.exe -r 5 -C covertMedium.bin ");
            printf(" -c covertMedium2.bin -O stego.exe");
            printf(" -o stego1.exe\n\n");
    }
```

Docstuffer

This algorithm puts the covert data in the "Properties: Comments" field of a Microsoft Word document file. The algorithm looks for a specific marker that is already in the Comments field. Therefore, the Word document must be prepared for use as an overt file by manually placing the marker in the Comments field. The covert data is put into the comment field in binary format (if the covert file is binary). The first null character (0x00) encountered will cause the remaining data to not be visible in the Comments field.

```
/*************************************************
 * doc_stuffer.c
 * Place Data into a DOC file.  The file should
 * still operate normally.
 *
```

```
 *
 * Code Designed and Written by Eric Cole and Jim Conley
 **************************************************
 */


//############ Load Headers ####################

#include "stegoGlobal.h"              // everyone adds
#include "doc_stuffer.h"              // define DOC_MARKER

// Prototypes
unsigned __int32 count_covert(void);
int copyRemainingOvert(void);


//############ doc_stuffer_encode ##########
int doc_stuffer_encode(void) {
    int i;
    int done;
    int read_cnt, write_cnt;
    unsigned __int32 covert_siz, tmp;
    char ch;
    char marker[DOC_MARKER_SIZ+1];
    char match[DOC_MARKER_SIZ+1];

    // Initialize variables...
    strcpy(marker, DOC_MARKER);

    // Search overt file until marker found...
    fread( match, sizeof(char), DOC_MARKER_SIZ-1,
                overtStream );

    // Copy overt file to overt2 file...
    fwrite( match, sizeof(char), DOC_MARKER_SIZ-1,
                overt2Stream );

    done = FALSE;
    while(done == FALSE) {
        read_cnt = fread( &ch, sizeof(char), 1, overtStream );
        if(read_cnt > 0) {
            match[DOC_MARKER_SIZ-1] = ch;
            match[DOC_MARKER_SIZ] = 0;                // null terminate
            if(strcmp(match, marker) == 0) {
                done = TRUE;
            } else {
                for(i=0; i<(DOC_MARKER_SIZ-1); i++) {
                    match[i] = match[i+1];
                }
            }

            // Copy overt file to overt2 file...
            fwrite( &ch, sizeof(char), 1, overt2Stream );
        } else {
```

```
                printf("Error, overt file missing marker\n");
                printf("Did not find %s\n", DOC_MARKER);
                exit(0);
            }
        }


        // Get size of covert file and rewind...
        covert_siz = count_covert();
        if(covert_siz > MAX_DOC_COVERT) {
            printf("Error, covert file to large\n");
            printf("Limit file to %d bytes\n", MAX_DOC_COVERT);
            exit(0);
        }


        // Put covert file size in overt file...
        fwrite( &covert_siz, sizeof(__int32), 1, overt2Stream );
        fread( &tmp, sizeof(__int32), 1, overtStream );


        // Read a covert char and put in overt2 file,
        // until covert file exhausted (normal ending)
        // or overt file exhausted (error)
        done = FALSE;
        while(done == FALSE) {
            read_cnt = fread( &ch, sizeof(char), 1, covertStream );
            if(read_cnt > 0) {
                write_cnt = fwrite( &ch, sizeof(char), 1, overt2Stream );
                if(write_cnt < 1) {
                    printf("Error, overt2 file too small\n");
                    exit(0);
                }

                // Move the pointer into the overt file
                // forward one character, so that docs
                // have the same size.
                read_cnt = fread( &ch, sizeof(char), 1, overtStream );
            } else {
                done = TRUE;
            }
        }

        // Write remaining overt file to overt2...
        copyRemainingOvert();

        return SUCCESS;
    } //doc_stuffer_encode();



//############# doc_stuffer_decode ##########
int doc_stuffer_decode(void) {
    unsigned __int32 i;
```

```
int done;
int read_cnt;
unsigned __int32 covert_siz;
char ch;
char marker[DOC_MARKER_SIZ];
char match[DOC_MARKER_SIZ+1];

// Initialize variables...
strcpy(marker, DOC_MARKER);

// Search overt file until marker found...
fread( match, sizeof(char), DOC_MARKER_SIZ-1, overt2Stream );

done = FALSE;
while(done == FALSE) {
    read_cnt = fread( &ch, sizeof(char), 1, overt2Stream );
    if(read_cnt > 0) {
        match[DOC_MARKER_SIZ-1] = ch;
        match[DOC_MARKER_SIZ] = 0;                    // null term
        if(strcmp(match, marker) == 0) {
            done = TRUE;
        } else {
            for(i=0; i<(DOC_MARKER_SIZ-1); i++) {
                match[i] = match[i+1];
            }
        }
    } else {
        printf("Error, overt2 file missing marker\n");
        printf("Did not find %s\n", DOC_MARKER);
        exit(0);
    }
}

// Read an __int32 to find the size of the
// covert file....
fread( &covert_siz, sizeof(__int32), 1, overt2Stream );
if(covert_siz > MAX_DOC_COVERT) {
    printf("Error, in covert data size.\n");
    printf("Limit data to %d bytes.\n", MAX_DOC_COVERT);
    exit(0);
}


// Read a covert_siz overt2 characters and put
// them into the covert2 file,
for(i=0; i<covert_siz; i++) {
    read_cnt = fread( &ch, sizeof(char), 1, overt2Stream );
    if(read_cnt > 0) {
        fwrite( &ch, sizeof(char), 1,
                covert2Stream );
    } else {
        printf("Error, overt2 file too small\n");
        exit(0);
    }
```

```
        }

        return SUCCESS;
} //doc_stuffer_decode();
```

Exemarker

This routine reserves space for the substitution .exe algorithm by defining some strings in a module that is never called. Using this method it is safe to clobber the space used by the strings.

```
/****************************************************
 * exeMarker.c
 *
 * This is a useless module that saves space in an
 * exe for later stuffing covert data.

 * If changes are made in this module, delete all
 * intermediate build files ('clean') and do a
 * complete rebuild (rebuild all) of the project.
 *
 * Code Designed and Written by Eric Cole and Jim Conley
 ****************************************************
 */


//############ Load Headers ###################
// Global headers that everyone adds...
#include "stegoGlobal.h"

#include "exe_marker.h"

//############ exeMarker #########
int exe_marker(void) {
    char t[50];

    //       123456789-123456789-123456789-12
    strcpy(t, "0 00000000000000000000000000000000");
    strcpy(t, "1 11111111111111111111111111111111");
    strcpy(t, "2 22222222222222222222222222222222");
    strcpy(t, "3 33333333333333333333333333333333");
    strcpy(t, "4 44444444444444444444444444444444");
    strcpy(t, "5 55555555555555555555555555555555");
    strcpy(t, "6 66666666666666666666666666666666");
    strcpy(t, "7 77777777777777777777777777777777");
    strcpy(t, "8 88888888888888888888888888888888");
    strcpy(t, "9 99999999999999999999999999999999");
    strcpy(t, "00 00000000000000000000000000000000");
    strcpy(t, "11 11111111111111111111111111111111");
    strcpy(t, "22 22222222222222222222222222222222");
    strcpy(t, "33 33333333333333333333333333333333");
    strcpy(t, "44 44444444444444444444444444444444");
```

```
strcpy(t, "55 5555555555555555555555555555");
strcpy(t, "66 6666666666666666666666666666");
strcpy(t, "77 7777777777777777777777777777");
strcpy(t, "88 8888888888888888888888888888");
strcpy(t, "99 9999999999999999999999999999");
strcpy(t, "000 0000000000000000000000000000");
strcpy(t, "111 1111111111111111111111111111");
strcpy(t, "222 2222222222222222222222222222");
strcpy(t, "333 3333333333333333333333333333");
strcpy(t, "444 4444444444444444444444444444");
strcpy(t, "555 5555555555555555555555555555");
strcpy(t, "666 6666666666666666666666666666");
strcpy(t, "777 7777777777777777777777777777");
strcpy(t, "888 8888888888888888888888888888");
strcpy(t, "999 9999999999999999999999999999");
strcpy(t, "0000 0000000000000000000000000000");
strcpy(t, "1111 1111111111111111111111111111");
strcpy(t, "2222 2222222222222222222222222222");
strcpy(t, "3333 3333333333333333333333333333");
strcpy(t, "4444 4444444444444444444444444444");
strcpy(t, "5555 5555555555555555555555555555");
strcpy(t, "6666 6666666666666666666666666666");
strcpy(t, "7777 7777777777777777777777777777");
strcpy(t, "8888 8888888888888888888888888888");
strcpy(t, "9999 9999999999999999999999999999");
strcpy(t, "00000 0000000000000000000000000000");
strcpy(t, "11111 1111111111111111111111111111");
strcpy(t, "22222 2222222222222222222222222222");
strcpy(t, "33333 3333333333333333333333333333");
strcpy(t, "44444 4444444444444444444444444444");
strcpy(t, "55555 5555555555555555555555555555");
strcpy(t, "66666 6666666666666666666666666666");
strcpy(t, "77777 7777777777777777777777777777");
strcpy(t, "88888 8888888888888888888888888888");
strcpy(t, "99999 9999999999999999999999999999");
strcpy(t, "000000 0000000000000000000000000000");
strcpy(t, "111111 1111111111111111111111111111");
strcpy(t, "222222 2222222222222222222222222222");
strcpy(t, "333333 3333333333333333333333333333");
strcpy(t, "444444 4444444444444444444444444444");
strcpy(t, "555555 5555555555555555555555555555");
strcpy(t, "666666 6666666666666666666666666666");
strcpy(t, "777777 7777777777777777777777777777");
strcpy(t, "888888 8888888888888888888888888888");
strcpy(t, "999999 9999999999999999999999999999");
strcpy(t, "0000000 0000000000000000000000000000");
strcpy(t, "1111111 1111111111111111111111111111");
strcpy(t, "2222222 2222222222222222222222222222");
strcpy(t, "3333333 3333333333333333333333333333");
strcpy(t, "4444444 4444444444444444444444444444");
strcpy(t, "5555555 5555555555555555555555555555");
strcpy(t, "6666666 6666666666666666666666666666");
strcpy(t, "7777777 7777777777777777777777777777");
```

```
strcpy(t, "8888888 8888888888888888888888");
strcpy(t, "9999999 9999999999999999999999");
strcpy(t, "00000000 0000000000000000000000");
strcpy(t, "11111111 1111111111111111111111");
strcpy(t, "22222222 2222222222222222222222");
strcpy(t, "33333333 3333333333333333333333");
strcpy(t, "44444444 4444444444444444444444");
strcpy(t, "55555555 5555555555555555555555");
strcpy(t, "66666666 6666666666666666666666");
strcpy(t, "77777777 7777777777777777777777");
strcpy(t, "88888888 8888888888888888888888");
strcpy(t, "99999999 9999999999999999999999");
strcpy(t, "000000000 0000000000000000000000");
strcpy(t, "111111111 1111111111111111111111");
strcpy(t, "222222222 2222222222222222222222");
strcpy(t, "333333333 3333333333333333333333");
strcpy(t, "444444444 4444444444444444444444");
strcpy(t, "555555555 5555555555555555555555");
strcpy(t, "666666666 6666666666666666666666");
strcpy(t, "777777777 7777777777777777777777");
strcpy(t, "888888888 8888888888888888888888");
strcpy(t, "999999999 9999999999999999999999");
strcpy(t, "0000000000 0000000000000000000000");
strcpy(t, "1111111111 1111111111111111111111");
strcpy(t, "2222222222 2222222222222222222222");
strcpy(t, "3333333333 3333333333333333333333");
strcpy(t, "4444444444 4444444444444444444444");
strcpy(t, "5555555555 5555555555555555555555");
strcpy(t, "6666666666 6666666666666666666666");
strcpy(t, "7777777777 7777777777777777777777");
strcpy(t, "8888888888 8888888888888888888888");
strcpy(t, "9999999999 9999999999999999999999");
strcpy(t, "00000000000 0000000000000000000000");
strcpy(t, "11111111111 1111111111111111111111");
strcpy(t, "22222222222 2222222222222222222222");
strcpy(t, "33333333333 3333333333333333333333");
strcpy(t, "44444444444 4444444444444444444444");
strcpy(t, "55555555555 5555555555555555555555");
strcpy(t, "66666666666 6666666666666666666666");
strcpy(t, "77777777777 7777777777777777777777");
strcpy(t, "88888888888 8888888888888888888888");
strcpy(t, "99999999999 9999999999999999999999");
strcpy(t, "000000000000 0000000000000000000000");
strcpy(t, "111111111111 1111111111111111111111");
strcpy(t, "222222222222 2222222222222222222222");
strcpy(t, "333333333333 3333333333333333333333");
strcpy(t, "444444444444 4444444444444444444444");
strcpy(t, "555555555555 5555555555555555555555");
strcpy(t, "666666666666 6666666666666666666666");
strcpy(t, "777777777777 7777777777777777777777");
strcpy(t, "888888888888 8888888888888888888888");
strcpy(t, "999999999999 9999999999999999999999");
strcpy(t, "0000000000000 0000000000000000000000");
```

```
strcpy(t, "1111111111111 111111111111111111");
strcpy(t, "2222222222222 222222222222222222");
strcpy(t, "3333333333333 333333333333333333");
strcpy(t, "4444444444444 444444444444444444");
strcpy(t, "5555555555555 555555555555555555");
strcpy(t, "6666666666666 666666666666666666");
strcpy(t, "7777777777777 777777777777777777");
strcpy(t, "8888888888888 888888888888888888");
strcpy(t, "9999999999999 999999999999999999");
strcpy(t, "0000000000000 000000000000000000");
strcpy(t, "11111111111111 11111111111111111");
strcpy(t, "22222222222222 22222222222222222");
strcpy(t, "33333333333333 33333333333333333");
strcpy(t, "44444444444444 44444444444444444");
strcpy(t, "55555555555555 55555555555555555");
strcpy(t, "66666666666666 66666666666666666");
strcpy(t, "77777777777777 77777777777777777");
strcpy(t, "88888888888888 88888888888888888");
strcpy(t, "99999999999999 99999999999999999");
strcpy(t, "00000000000000 00000000000000000");
strcpy(t, "111111111111111 1111111111111111");
strcpy(t, "222222222222222 2222222222222222");
strcpy(t, "333333333333333 3333333333333333");
strcpy(t, "444444444444444 4444444444444444");
strcpy(t, "555555555555555 5555555555555555");
strcpy(t, "666666666666666 6666666666666666");
strcpy(t, "777777777777777 7777777777777777");
strcpy(t, "888888888888888 8888888888888888");
strcpy(t, "999999999999999 9999999999999999");
strcpy(t, "000000000000000 0000000000000000");
strcpy(t, "1111111111111111 111111111111111");
strcpy(t, "2222222222222222 222222222222222");
strcpy(t, "3333333333333333 333333333333333");
strcpy(t, "4444444444444444 444444444444444");
strcpy(t, "5555555555555555 555555555555555");
strcpy(t, "6666666666666666 666666666666666");
strcpy(t, "7777777777777777 777777777777777");
strcpy(t, "8888888888888888 888888888888888");
strcpy(t, "9999999999999999 999999999999999");
strcpy(t, "0000000000000000 000000000000000");
strcpy(t, "11111111111111111 11111111111111");
strcpy(t, "22222222222222222 22222222222222");
strcpy(t, "33333333333333333 33333333333333");
strcpy(t, "44444444444444444 44444444444444");
strcpy(t, "55555555555555555 55555555555555");
strcpy(t, "66666666666666666 66666666666666");
strcpy(t, "77777777777777777 77777777777777");
strcpy(t, "88888888888888888 88888888888888");
strcpy(t, "99999999999999999 99999999999999");
strcpy(t, "00000000000000000 00000000000000");
strcpy(t, "111111111111111111 1111111111111");
strcpy(t, "222222222222222222 2222222222222");
strcpy(t, "333333333333333333 3333333333333");
```

```
        strcpy(t, "444444444444444444 4444444444444");
        strcpy(t, "555555555555555555 5555555555555");
        strcpy(t, "666666666666666666 6666666666666");
        strcpy(t, "777777777777777777 7777777777777");
        strcpy(t, "888888888888888888 8888888888888");
        strcpy(t, "999999999999999999 9999999999999");
        //         123456789-123456789-123456789-12
        strcpy(t, EXE_MARKER);

        return SUCCESS;                                    // success
} //exeMarker()
```

Exestuffer

This algorithm puts the covert data in a compiled-in, but unused, portion of
the executable file. The file exe_Marker.c reserves space for the algorithm by
defining some strings in a module that is never called. In this way, it is safe to
clobber the space used by the strings.

The overt file for this algorithm is an executable with the exe_marker.c module compiled in. In the code examples, this executable is the stego.exe program
itself. Once the covert data is hidden in the executable, the new overt2 executable will function normally in every respect.

```
/**************************************************
 * exeStuffer.c
 *
 * Place data into an exe file.  The exe should
 * still operate normally.
 *
 *
 * Code Designed and Written by Eric Cole and Jim Conley
 **************************************************
 */


//########### Load Headers ###################

#include "stegoGlobal.h"              // everyone adds
#include "exe_marker.h"               // define EXE_MARKER



// Prototypes
unsigned __int32 count_covert(void);
int copyRemainingOvert(void);


//########### exe_stuffer_encode #########
int exe_stuffer_encode(void) {
```

```
int i;
int done;
int read_cnt, write_cnt;
unsigned __int32 covert_siz, tmp;
char ch;
char marker[EXE_MARKER_SIZ+1];
char match[EXE_MARKER_SIZ+1];

// Initialize variables...
strcpy(marker, EXE_MARKER);

// Search overt file until marker found...
fread( match, sizeof(char), EXE_MARKER_SIZ-1,
            overtStream );
// Copy overt file to overt2 file...
fwrite( match, sizeof(char), EXE_MARKER_SIZ-1,
            overt2Stream );

done = FALSE;
while(done == FALSE) {
    read_cnt = fread( &ch, sizeof(char), 1, overtStream );
    if(read_cnt > 0) {
        match[EXE_MARKER_SIZ-1] = ch;
        match[EXE_MARKER_SIZ] = 0;                  // null terminate
        if(strcmp(match, marker) == 0) {
            done = TRUE;
        } else {
            for(i=0; i<(EXE_MARKER_SIZ-1); i++) {
                match[i] = match[i+1];
            } //for
        } //if

        // Copy overt file to overt2 file...
        fwrite( &ch, sizeof(char), 1, overt2Stream );
    } else {
        printf("Error, overt file missing marker\n");
        exit(0);
    } //if
} //while


// Get size of covert file and rewind...
covert_siz = count_covert();
if(covert_siz > MAX_EM_COVERT) {
    printf("Error, covert file to large\n");
    printf("Limit file to %d bytes\n", MAX_EM_COVERT);
    exit(0);
} //if


// Put convert file size in overt file...
fwrite( &covert_siz, sizeof(__int32), 1, overt2Stream );
```

```
            fread( &tmp, sizeof(__int32), 1, overtStream );


            // Read a covert char and put in overt2 file,
            // until covert file exhausted (normal ending)
            // or overt file exhausted (error)
            done = FALSE;
            while(done == FALSE) {
                read_cnt = fread( &ch, sizeof(char), 1, covertStream );
                if(read_cnt > 0) {
                    write_cnt = fwrite( &ch, sizeof(char), 1,
                                overt2Stream );
                    if(write_cnt < 1) {
                        printf("Error, overt2 file too small\n");
                        exit(0);
                    } //if

                    // Move the pointer into the overt file
                    // forward one character, so that exe's
                    // have the same size.
                    read_cnt = fread( &ch, sizeof(char), 1, overtStream );
                } else {
                    done = TRUE;
                } //if
            } //while

            // Write remaining overt file to overt2...
            copyRemainingOvert();

            return SUCCESS;
} //exe_stuffer_encode();



//############ exe_stuffer_decode ##########
int exe_stuffer_decode(void) {
    unsigned __int32 i;
    int done;
    int read_cnt;
    unsigned __int32 covert_siz;
    char ch;
    char marker[EXE_MARKER_SIZ];
    char match[EXE_MARKER_SIZ+1];

    // Initialize variables...
    strcpy(marker, EXE_MARKER);

    // Search overt file until marker found...
    fread( match, sizeof(char), EXE_MARKER_SIZ-1, overt2Stream );

    done = FALSE;
    while(done == FALSE) {
        read_cnt = fread( &ch, sizeof(char), 1, overt2Stream );
```

```
            if(read_cnt > 0) {
                match[EXE_MARKER_SIZ-1] = ch;
                match[EXE_MARKER_SIZ] = 0;                  // null terminate
                if(strcmp(match, marker) == 0) {
                    done = TRUE;
                } else {
                    for(i=0; i<(EXE_MARKER_SIZ-1); i++) {
                        match[i] = match[i+1];
                    } //for
                } //if
            } else {
                printf("Error, overt2 file missing marker\n");
                exit(0);
            } //if
        } //while

        // Read an __int32 to find the size of the
        // covert file....
        fread( &covert_siz, sizeof(__int32), 1, overt2Stream );
        if(covert_siz > MAX_EM_COVERT) {
            printf("Error, in covert data size.\n");
            printf("Limit data to %d bytes.\n", MAX_EM_COVERT);
            exit(0);
        } //if


        // Read a covert_siz overt2 characters and put
        // them into the covert2 file,
        for(i=0; i<covert_siz; i++) {
            read_cnt = fread( &ch, sizeof(char), 1, overt2Stream );
            if(read_cnt > 0) {
                fwrite( &ch, sizeof(char), 1,
                            covert2Stream );
            } else {
                printf("Error, overt2 file too small\n");
                exit(0);
            } //if
        } //for

    return SUCCESS;
} //exe_stuffer_decode();
```

File

This code involves input and output functions with files to include opening and closing of files, count size of covert data, and so on.

```
/*************************************************
 * file.c
 *
 * Miscellaneous routines that are shared by
```

```
 * different algorithms.
 *
 * Code Designed and Written by Eric Cole and Jim Conley
 ***************************************************
 */

#include <time.h>
#include "stegoGlobal.h"

#define BIGBUF          1024

FILE *myfopen(char *file, char *options) {
    if( (anyStream  = fopen( file, options )) == NULL ) {
        if(dbmask & CON_ERRS) {
            printf("###############\n");
            printf("%s ERROR opening %s\n", getTime(), file);
            printf("###############\n");
        } //dbmask
        if(dbmask & LOG_ERRS) {
            if(logStream) {
            fprintf(logStream, "%s ERROR opening %s\n", tTime(), file);
                    fflush(logStream);
            } //if logStream
        } //dbmask
        if(dbmask & INTERACTIVE) {
            while( !_kbhit() ) {Sleep(500);}
        } //dbmask
        exit(FAILURE);
    } else {
        if(dbmask & CON_VERB) {
            printf("%s Opening %s for %s\n", getTime(), file, options);
        } //dbmask
    } //if-else fopen
    return anyStream;
} //myfopen()


//############# covertFile2BitFile() ############
// Return characters in covert file
//
unsigned __int32 covertFile2BitFile(unsigned __int32 siz) {
    int i, done;
    unsigned __int32 read_cnt;
    unsigned __int32 read_cnt_sum;
    unsigned __int32 mask=1;
    char ch, bit;

    // Put the size of the covert file in bit file...
    for(i=0; i<32; i++) {
        if(siz & (mask<<i)) {
            bit = '1';
        } else {
            bit = '0';
```

```
            } //if
            fwrite( &bit, sizeof(char), 1, bitStream );
    } //for

    done = FALSE;
    read_cnt = 0;
    read_cnt_sum = 0;
    while(done==FALSE) {
        read_cnt = fread( &ch, sizeof(char), 1, covertStream );
        if( read_cnt < 1 ) {
            done = TRUE;
        } else {
            read_cnt_sum += read_cnt;
            if( read_cnt_sum == 0xFFFFFFFF ) {
                printf("Error - Covert file too large.\n");
                printf("Limit file to 0xFFFFFFFF.\n");
                exit(0);
            } //if

            for(i=0; i<8; i++) {
                if(ch & (mask<<i)) {
                    bit = '1';
                } else {
                    bit = '0';
                } //if
                fwrite( &bit, sizeof(char), 1, bitStream );
            } //for
        } //if
    } //while

    rewind( covertStream );

    fflush( bitStream );
    fclose( bitStream );
    bitStream = myfopen(bitFile, "r");

    return read_cnt_sum;
} //covertFile2BitFile()




//############ bitFile2covertFile() ##################
void bitFile2covertFile(void) {
    int i;
    unsigned __int32 siz;
    unsigned __int32 written;
    unsigned __int32 read_cnt;
    unsigned __int32 imask=1;
    char cmask=1;
    char ch, bit;

    // Close bitFile for writing, reopen for reading,
```

```
        fflush( bitStream );
        fclose( bitStream );
        bitStream = myfopen(bitFile, "r");

        // The first 32 bits contain the covert2File
        // size...
        siz = 0;
        for(i=0; i<32; i++) {
            read_cnt = fread( &bit, sizeof(char), 1, bitStream );

            if( read_cnt < 1) {
                printf("Error - bitFile file too small.\n");
                exit(0);
            } //if

            if(bit == '1') {
                        siz = siz | (imask<<i);
            } //if bit
        } //for

        // We've gotten the first 32 bits, now write
        // remaining bits to covert2Stream...
        written = 0;
        while(written < siz) {
            ch = 0;
            for(i=0; i<8; i++) {
                read_cnt = fread( &bit, sizeof(char), 1, bitStream );

                if( read_cnt < 1) {
                    printf("Error - bitFile file too small.\n");
                    exit(0);
                } //if

                if(bit == '1') {
                        ch = ch | (cmask<<i);
                } //if bit
            } //for

            fwrite( &ch, sizeof(char), 1, covert2Stream );
            written++;
        } //while
} //bitFile2covertFile()


//############ count_covert() ##################
unsigned __int32 count_covert(void) {
    int done;
    unsigned __int32 read_cnt;
    unsigned __int32 read_cnt_sum;
    char buffer[BIGBUF];            // read line into buffer

    done = FALSE;
    read_cnt = 0;
```

```
          read_cnt_sum = 0;
          while(done==FALSE) {
               read_cnt = fread( buffer, sizeof(char), BIGBUF, covertStream );
               read_cnt_sum += read_cnt;
               if( read_cnt < BIGBUF ) {
                    done = TRUE;
               } //if
               if( read_cnt_sum == 0xFFFFFFFF ) {
                    printf("Error - Covert file too large.\n");
                    printf("Limit file to 0xFFFFFFFF.\n");
                    exit(0);
               } //if
          } //while

          rewind( covertStream );
          return read_cnt_sum;
} //covert_count()

//############ copyRemainingOvert() #############
int copyRemainingOvert(void) {
     int done;
     int read_cnt;
     char buffer[BIGBUF];
     char *pbuffer;
// pointer to buffer

     pbuffer = buffer;
     done = FALSE;
     while(done==FALSE) {
          read_cnt = fread( pbuffer, sizeof(char), BIGBUF, overtStream );
          fwrite( pbuffer, sizeof(char), read_cnt, overt2Stream );
          if(read_cnt < BIGBUF)
               done = TRUE;
     } //while

     return SUCCESS;
// success
} //copyRemainingOvert()


// ************************************************

/* getTime( string )
 * This program places the system time
 * in the long integer aclock, translates it into
 * the structure newtime, and then converts it to
 * string form for return, using the asctime
 * function.
 */

char * getTime( void ) {
     static char str[40];

     _strtime(str);
```

```
        return str;
    }



// *************** xtoc() ***********************
// Convert string "5A" to char 'Z'
char xtoc(char *hex) {
    int i;
    char val;

    val = 0;
    for(i=0; i<2; i++) {
        if(hex[i] >= '0' && hex[i] <='9') {
            val += (hex[i] - '0') * (i?1:16);
        } else if(hex[i] >= 'A' && hex[0] <='F') {
            val += (hex[i] - 'A' + 10) * (i?1:16);
        } else {
            val += (hex[i] - 'a' + 10) * (i?1:16);
        } //if
    } //for

    return val;
} //xtoc()



// *************** otox() ***********************
void ctox(char ch, char *hex) {
    unsigned char ord;
    char tmp[5];
// 0xFF format

    ord = ch;

    // convert char 'Z' to string "5A"
    if(ord == 0) {
        hex[0]='0'; hex[1]='0'; hex[2]=0;
    } else {
        sprintf(tmp, "%#X", ord);
        if(ord < 16) {
            hex[0] = '0';
            strcpy(hex+1, tmp+2);
        } else {
            strcpy(hex, tmp+2);
        } //if
    } //if
} //otox()

// *************** int32_to_hex() ***********************
// Return string in little endian "lo hi"
// For example, 11590 would be "462D" which is
//    0x2D46
void int32_to_hex(unsigned __int32 val, char *hex) {
```

```
        unsigned __int32 ord;

        strcpy(hex, "xxxx");   // always ends in 0000

        ord = (val & 0xFF00);
        ord = ((val & 0xFF00) << 8);
        ord = ((val & 0xFF00) > 8);

        ord = (val << 8);
        ord = (val > 8);


        ord = (val & 0xFF00) > 8;


    } //int32_to_hex()
```

HTML_WS

This algorithm puts five white spaces at the end of every HTML line. One bit from the covert file is encoded in every white space. The white spaces do not show up when the HTML is viewed in a Web browser. A "zero" bit is encoded as a space. A "one" bit is encoded as a tab. The first 32 bits or white space encode the size of the covert data. This is needed because white spaces might naturally occur at the end of an HTML line, and you can't be sure that the covert data ends when the white spaces end.

```
/**************************************************
 * http_ws.c
 *
 * Hide white space within an html file by adding 5 white space characters
 * to the end of each line
 *
 *
 * Code Designed and Written by Eric Cole and Jim Conley
 **************************************************
 */


//########### Load Headers ###################
// Global headers that everyone adds...
#include "stegoGlobal.h"

// Defines
// space... dec-32 hex-20 oct-040
// tab....dec-09 hex-09 oct-??
#define ZERO          32
#define ONE            9
```

```
#define NEWLINE          13

// Prototypes
unsigned __int32 count_covert(void);
int copyRemainingOvert(void);
int int32_to_ws(unsigned __int32 val, char *str);
int array2ws(char *arr, char *str);
int get5chars(char *arr);
int hide5ws(char *str);
int decode5ws(char *pstr);
unsigned __int32 ws2int32(char *pstr);
int ws2char5(unsigned __int32 limit, char *pstr);

//############# http_ws_encode ##########
int http_ws_encode(void) {
    int rtn;
    int done;
    int hidden_cnt=0;


    char str[45];                      // Hold at least 40 char
    char *str_ptr;
    unsigned __int32 covet_siz;        // characters to hide
    char char_array[5];
    char *char_array_ptr;

    str_ptr = str;
    char_array_ptr = char_array;


    // Get # of covert characters and put it in
    // overt2 file...
    covet_siz = count_covert();

fprintf(logStream, "covert_siz %d encode\n",covet_siz);      fflush(logStream);

    // convert 32 bits to 32 WS's...
    int32_to_ws(covet_siz, str_ptr);

    // put zero's in unused spaces - 33, 34, 35
    str_ptr[32] = ONE;
    str_ptr[33] = ONE;
    str_ptr[34] = ONE;

    // put the 35 white spaces in to overt2...
    hide5ws( str_ptr );

// first 5 WS
    hide5ws( str_ptr+5 );

// next 5 WS
    hide5ws( str_ptr+10 );
```

```
            hide5ws( str_ptr+15 );
            hide5ws( str_ptr+20 );
            hide5ws( str_ptr+25 );
            hide5ws( str_ptr+30 );
// last 5 WS

        // Hide covert data until overt file is used
        // up...
        done = FALSE;
        while(done==FALSE) {
            // get 5 covert characters...
            rtn = get5chars(char_array_ptr);
            if( rtn == SUCCESS ) {
                array2ws(char_array_ptr, str_ptr);
// convert 5*8 bits to WS's

// hide 5 white spaces at a time...
                hide5ws( str_ptr+0 );
                hide5ws( str_ptr+5 );
                hide5ws( str_ptr+10 );
                hide5ws( str_ptr+15 );
                hide5ws( str_ptr+20 );
                hide5ws( str_ptr+25 );
                hide5ws( str_ptr+30 );
                hide5ws( str_ptr+35 );
            } else {
                copyRemainingOvert();
                done = TRUE;
            } //if
        } //while

        return SUCCESS;
// success
} //http_ws_encode()




//#################### http_ws_decode ############################
int http_ws_decode(void) {
    unsigned __int32 i;
    int to_go;                              // chars to decode
    char achar;                         // one character buffer
    char *achar_ptr;                        // pointer to achar
    char str[45];                       // hold tmp characters
    char *pstr;                         // pointer to str
    unsigned __int32 covet_siz;     // chars hidden

    pstr = str;
    achar_ptr = &achar;

    // Get first 32 bits from overt2 file, this is
```

```
            // size of covert data...
        decode5ws(pstr);
        decode5ws(pstr+5);
        decode5ws(pstr+10);
        decode5ws(pstr+15);
        decode5ws(pstr+20);
        decode5ws(pstr+25);
        decode5ws(pstr+30);

            // Convert 32 white spaces to a 32-bit integer
        covet_siz = ws2int32(pstr);

    fprintf(logStream, "covert_siz %d decode\n",covet_siz);        fflush(logStream);

            // Decode remaining white spaces in overt2, 40 @@@
            // at a time.  40 ws ==> 5 characters
        for(i=0; i<(covet_siz*8); i+=40) {
            decode5ws(pstr);
            decode5ws(pstr+5);
            decode5ws(pstr+10);
            decode5ws(pstr+15);
            decode5ws(pstr+20);
            decode5ws(pstr+25);
            decode5ws(pstr+30);
            decode5ws(pstr+35);

                // Determine chars to decode, yet...
            to_go = covet_siz - i/8;

                // Convert 40 ws to 5 chars and put into
                // covert2File...
            ws2char5(to_go, pstr);
        } //for

        return SUCCESS;                                            // success
} //http_ws_decode()




//########### decode5ws #########################
int decode5ws(char *pstr) {
    int i;
    int done;
    int read_cnt;
    int str_index;                                 // index into strtmp[]
    char achar;                                  // one character buffer
    char *achar_ptr;                                // pointer to achar
    char strtmp[45];                                // hold tmp characters

    achar_ptr = &achar;
    str_index = 0;
```

```
        done = FALSE;
        while(done==FALSE) {
            read_cnt = fread( achar_ptr, sizeof(char), 1, overt2Stream );

            if( read_cnt < 1 ) {
                done = TRUE;
            } else {
                if( achar != NEWLINE ) {
                    strtmp[str_index%5] = achar;
                    str_index++;
                } else {
                    if( str_index < 5 ) {
                        printf("Error - Invalid Overt2 file.\n");
                        exit(0);
                    } //if

                    str_index -= 5;
                    for(i=0; i<5; i++) {
                        pstr[i] = strtmp[(i+str_index)%5];
                    } //for
                    done = TRUE;
                } //if
            } //if
        } //while

        return SUCCESS;                                      // success
} //decode5ws()




//########### int32_to_ws() #####################
int int32_to_ws(unsigned __int32 val, char *pstr) {
    unsigned __int32 i;
    unsigned __int32 mask;                          // must be 32 bits

    mask = 1;
    for(i=0; i<32; i++) {                               // 32 bits in val
        if( val & (mask<<i) ) {
            pstr[i] = ONE;
        } else {
            pstr[i] = ZERO;
        } //if
    } //for
    pstr[32] = 0;                                       // null terminate
    return SUCCESS;
} //int32_to_ws()




//############### array2ws() ###################
```

```
int array2ws(char *arr, char *pstr) {
    int i, a;
    char mask;

    for(a=0; a<5; a++) {
        mask = 1;
        for(i=0; i<8; i++) {                    // 8 bits in a char
            if( arr[a] & mask ) {
                pstr[(a*8)+i] = ONE;
            } else {
                pstr[(a*8)+i] = ZERO;
            } //if

            mask = mask << 1;
        } //for i
    } //for a
    pstr[5*8] = 0;
    return SUCCESS;
} //array2ws()


    //############# get5chars() ##################
int get5chars(char *arr) {
    int read_cnt;

    read_cnt = fread( arr, sizeof(char), 5, covertStream );
    if( read_cnt == 0 ) {
        return FAILURE;
    } else {
        return SUCCESS;
    } //if
} //get5chars()


//############# hide5ws() #####################
int hide5ws(char *pstr) {
    int i;
    int done;
    int read_cnt;
    int str_index;
    char achar;                 // one character buffer
    char *achar_ptr;               // pointer to achar

    achar_ptr = &achar;
    str_index = 0;
    done = FALSE;
    read_cnt = 0;
    while(done==FALSE) {
        read_cnt = fread( achar_ptr, sizeof(char), 1, overtStream );

        if( read_cnt < 1 ) {
            printf("Error - Overt file too small.\n");
```

```
                exit(0);
            } //if

            if( achar != NEWLINE ) {
                fwrite( achar_ptr, sizeof(char), 1, overt2Stream );
            } else {
                for(i=0; i<5; i++) {
                    fwrite( pstr+str_index, sizeof(char), 1, overt2Stream );
                        str_index++;
                } //for
                fwrite( achar_ptr, sizeof(char), 1, overt2Stream );
                done = TRUE;
            } //if
        } //while

        return SUCCESS;                                    // success
} //hide5ws()




//############### ws2int32 #####################
unsigned __int32 ws2int32(char *pstr) {
        int i;
        unsigned __int32 mask;
        unsigned __int32 rtn;                           // decoded value


        rtn = 0;
        mask = 1;
        for(i=0; i<32; i++) {
            if(pstr[i] == ONE) {
                rtn = (rtn | mask);
            } //if
            mask = mask << 1;
        } //for
        return rtn;                              // success
} //ws2int32()



//############### ws2char5 #####################
int ws2char5(unsigned __int32 limit, char *pstr) {
        int i;
        unsigned __int32 a;
        char achar;                              // decoded value
        char mask=1;


        // decode 5 characters...
        for(a=0; a<5; a++) {
            // decode one character...
```

```
            achar = 0;
            for(i=0; i<8; i++) {
                if(pstr[(a*8)+i] == ONE) {
                    achar = (achar | (mask<<i));
                } //if
            } //for i
            if(a < limit) {
                fwrite( &achar, sizeof(char), 1, covert2Stream );
            } //if
    } //for a
    return SUCCESS;                              // success
} //ws2char5()
```

HTML_WS_Vary

This algorithm puts a variable number of white spaces at the end of each line
in the HTML file. The number of white spaces used is supplied by the user on
the command line using the "-v ??" option.

```
/**************************************************
 * http_ws_vary.c
 *
 * Hides data within the white space but varies the number of characters
 * to insert on each line.  Number is controlled by user input.
 *
 * Code Designed and Written by Eric Cole and Jim Conley
 **************************************************
 */


//############ Load Headers ###################
// Global headers that everyone adds...
#include "stegoGlobal.h"
#include "http_ws_vary.h"

// Defines
// space... dec-32 hex-20 oct-040
// tab....dec-09 hex-09 oct-??
#define ZERO            32
#define ONE             9
#define NEWLINE         13
#define CRETURN         10

// Prototypes
unsigned __int32 covertFile2BitFile(unsigned __int32 siz);
unsigned __int32 count_covert(void);
void move2lineEnd(void);
void copyRemainingOvert(void);
```

```
void bitFile2covertFile(void);

//############# http_ws_vary_encode ##########
int http_ws_vary_encode(void) {
    int i;
    int read_cnt;
    int wsPerLine;                              //get from cmd line
    char ch, bit;
    char mask=1;
    unsigned __int32 bwritten=0;          // bits written
    unsigned __int32 covert_siz;          // chars to hide

    // We limit wsPerLine to 1 - 255 (8 bits)
    // Check range of wsPerLine...
    wsPerLine = vary;                     // in config.c
    if(wsPerLine < 1 || wsPerLine > 255) {
        printf("Error - ws per line out of range!\n");
        printf("Range is 1 - 255\n");
        printf("Set with -v <1-255>\n");
        exit(0);
    } //if

    // Get size of covert file and rewind file...
    covert_siz = count_covert();
    if(covert_siz > MAX_HTTP_COVERT) {
        printf("Error - Covert file too large!\n");
        printf("Limit file to %d bytes.\n", MAX_HTTP_COVERT);
        exit(0);
    } //if

    // Populate bit file, put size in first...
    covertFile2BitFile(covert_siz);

    // Hide covert data until overt file is used
    // up...
    while(bwritten < (covert_siz*8+32)) {
        move2lineEnd();                   // copy overt to overt2
        for(i=0; i<wsPerLine; i++) {
            read_cnt = fread( &bit, sizeof(char), 1, bitStream );
            if( read_cnt<1 && i==0 ) {
                // read_cnt can be zero if bitFile is
                // exhausted before wsPerLine is written
        printf("Error - Bit file too small.\n");
        printf("bwritten:%d covert_siz:%d\n",      bwritten, covert_siz);
                exit(0);
            } //if

            if(bit == '1') {
                ch = ONE;
            } else {
                ch = ZERO;
            } //if
            fwrite( &ch, sizeof(char), 1, overt2Stream );
```

```
                    bwritten++;
            } //for i


        ch = NEWLINE;
        fwrite( &ch, sizeof(char), 1, overt2Stream );
    } //while


    copyRemainingOvert();

    return SUCCESS;                                    // success
} //http_ws_vary_encode()




//#################### http_ws_vary_decode ##########################
int http_ws_vary_decode(void) {
    int i, ii;
    int read_cnt;
    int str_index;                              // index into strtmp[]
    int wsPerLine;
    char ch;                                     // one character buffer
    char strtmp[257];                            // hold tmp characters
    char covert_siz_bits[33]; // hold 1's and 0's
    unsigned __int32 mask = 1;
    unsigned __int32 covert_siz = 0;
    unsigned __int32 bwritten = 0;      // to bit file

    wsPerLine = vary;                            // from cmd line
    str_index = 0;
    while(bwritten < (covert_siz*8+32)) {
        read_cnt = fread( &ch, sizeof(char), 1, overt2Stream );

        if( read_cnt < 1 ) {
            printf("Error - Overt2 file too small\n");
            exit(0);
        } else {
            if(ch != NEWLINE) {
                strtmp[str_index%wsPerLine] = ch;
            } else {
                if( str_index < wsPerLine ) {
                    printf("Error - Invalid Overt2 file\n");
                    exit(0);
                } //if

                for(i=str_index-wsPerLine; i<str_index; i++) {

                    if(strtmp[i%wsPerLine] == ONE) {
                        ch = '1';
                    } else if(strtmp[i%wsPerLine] == ZERO) {
```

```
                                      ch = '0';
                            } else {
                                printf("Error - Invalid bit\n");
                                fclose(bitStream);
                                exit(0);
                            } //if '1'

                            if(bwritten < 32) {
                            covert_siz_bits[bwritten] = ch;
                            fwrite( &ch, sizeof(char), 1, bitStream );
                                if(bwritten == (32-1)) {
                                    // Get covert_siz from the 1st 32 bits...
                                    for(ii=0; ii<32; ii++) {
                                        if(covert_siz_bits[ii] == '1') {
                                            covert_siz = (covert_siz |
(mask<<ii));
                                        } //if
                                    } //for ii
                                } //if 32-1
                            } else {
                                fwrite( &ch, sizeof(char), 1, bitStream);
                            } //if bwritten

                            bwritten++;
                        } //for i
                    } //if NEWLINE
                    str_index++;
                } //if read_cnt
        } //while

    bitFile2covertFile();
    return SUCCESS;                                    // success
} //http_ws_vary_decode()



//############# move2lineEnd() #####################
void move2lineEnd(void) {
    int read_cnt;
    char ch;                            // one character buffer

    while(1) {
        read_cnt = fread( &ch, sizeof(char), 1, overtStream );

        if( read_cnt < 1 ) {
            printf("Error - Overt file too small.\n");
            exit(0);
        } //if

        if( ch == NEWLINE ) {
            return;
        } //if

        fwrite( &ch, sizeof(char), 1, overt2Stream );
```

```
        } //while

    } //move2lineEnd()
```

Main

This is the main program that calls all of the other modules.

```
/**************************************************
 * main.c
 *
 * Get command-line options (config.c)
 *   - debug level
 *   - stego routine to use
 *   - filenames
 * Open all files here
 * Call the specific stego routine
 *     (such as http_ws.c)
 * Check return code for an error
 * Close all files
 *
 * Code Designed and Written by Eric Cole and Jim Conley
 **************************************************
 */


//############## Load Headers ###################
// Global headers that everyone adds...
#include "stegoGlobal.h"

// Prototypes
void ProcessArgs (int argc, char *argv[]);
void myUsage(void);
FILE *myfopen(char *file, char *options);

// Hiding Routine Prototypes
int http_ws_encode(void);              // http_ws.c
int http_ws_decode(void);              // http_ws.c
int exe_marker(void);                   // exe_marker.c
int exe_stuffer_encode(void);         // exe_stuffer.c
int exe_stuffer_decode(void);         // exe_stuffer.c
int rtf_insertion_encode(void);        // rtf_insertion.c
int rtf_insertion_decode(void);        // rtf_insertion.c
int wav_creation_encode(void);         // wav_creation.c
int wav_creation_decode(void);         // wav_creation.c
int wav_twidle_encode(void);          // wav_twidle.c
int wav_twidle_decode(void);          // wav_twidle.c
int war_creation_encode(void);         // wav_creation.c
int war_creation_decode(void);         // wav_creation.c
int doc_stuffer_encode(void);          // doc_tuffer.c
int doc_stuffer_decode(void);          // doc_stuffer.c
```

```
int http_ws_vary_encode(void);       // http_ws_vary.c
int http_ws_vary_decode(void);       // http_ws_vary.c
int wav_sine_creation_encode(void);     // wav_sine_creation.c
int wav_sine_creation_decode(void);     // wav_sine_creation.c


//################ main() #####################
int main(int argc, char **argv){
    int status;                 // Was routine successful?

    // Get command-line args and set defaults
    ProcessArgs(argc, argv);

    logStream = myfopen(logFile, "a+");
    fflush(logStream);

    // The bit file is the covert file converted to
    // ones '1' and zeros '0'. This simplifies
    // a lot of stego routines.
    // This will be closed in covertFile2BitFile
    // and will be reopened as "r".
    bitStream = myfopen(bitFile, "w");
    fflush(bitStream);


    // Switch on the Stego Routine...
    switch(routine) {
    case HTTP_WS_ENCODE:
        // Store covert file as spaces and tabs in an html file
        covertStream = myfopen(covertFile, "rb");

// covert file - data to be hidden
        overtStream = myfopen(overtFile, "rb");

// overt file - place to hide data
        overt2Stream = myfopen(overt2File, "wb");

// final overt file - after data is hidden
        status = http_ws_encode();
        break;

    case HTTP_WS_DECODE:
        // Store covert file as spaces and tabs in an html file
        covert2Stream = myfopen(covert2File, "wb");

// final covert file - after data decoded
        overt2Stream = myfopen(overt2File, "rb");

// final overt file - after data is hidden
        status = http_ws_decode();
        break;

    case EXE_STUFFER_MARKER:
```

```
        // exe stuffing algorithm
        // Don't call this option... it is just for
        // getting the exeMarker.c module to link in
        exe_marker();
        break;

case EXE_STUFFER_ENCODE:
        // exe stuffing algorithm
        covertStream = myfopen(covertFile, "rb");

// covert file - data to be hidden
        overtStream = myfopen(overtFile, "rb");

// overt file - place to hide data
        overt2Stream = myfopen(overt2File, "wb");

// final overt file - after data is hidden
        status = exe_stuffer_encode();
        break;

case EXE_STUFFER_DECODE:
        // exe stuffing algorithm
        covert2Stream = myfopen(covert2File, "wb");

// final covert file - after data decoded
        overt2Stream = myfopen(overt2File, "rb");

// final overt file - after data is hidden
        status = exe_stuffer_decode();
        break;

case RTF_INSERT_ENCODE:
        // rtf insertion algorithm
        covertStream = myfopen(covertFile, "rb");

// covert file - data to be hidden
        overtStream = myfopen(overtFile, "rb");

// overt file - place to hide data
        overt2Stream = myfopen(overt2File, "wb");

// final overt file - after data is hidden
        status = rtf_insertion_encode();
        break;

case RTF_INSERT_DECODE:
        // rtf insertion algorithm
        covert2Stream = myfopen(covert2File, "wb");

// final covert file - after data is decoded
        overt2Stream = myfopen(overt2File, "rb");

// final overt file - after data is hidden
```

```
            status = rtf_insertion_decode();
            break;

    case WAV_CREATE_ENCODE:
            // wav creation algorithm
            covertStream = myfopen(covertFile, "rb");

// covert file - data to be hidden
            // no overt file needed
            overt2Stream = myfopen(overt2File, "wb");

// final overt file - after data is hidden
            status = wav_creation_encode();
            break;

    case WAV_CREATE_DECODE:
            // wav creation algorithm
            covert2Stream = myfopen(covert2File, "wb");

// final covert file - after data is decoded
            overt2Stream = myfopen(overt2File, "rb");

// final overt file - after data is hidden
            status = wav_creation_decode();
            break;

    case WAV_TWIDLE_ENCODE:
            // wav twidle algorithm
            covertStream = myfopen(covertFile, "rb");

// covert file - data to be hidden
            overtStream = myfopen(overtFile, "rb");

// overt file - place to hide data
            overt2Stream = myfopen(overt2File, "wb");

// final overt file - after data is hidden
            status = wav_twidle_encode();
            break;

    case WAV_TWIDLE_DECODE:
            // wav twidle algorithm
            covert2Stream = myfopen(covert2File, "wb");

// final covert file - after data is decoded
            overt2Stream = myfopen(overt2File, "rb");

// final overt file - after data is hidden
            status = wav_twidle_decode();
            break;

    case WAR_CREATE_ENCODE:
```

```
                    // wav creation algorithm
                    covertStream = myfopen(covertFile, "rb");

    // covert file - data to be hidden
                    // no overt file needed
                    overt2Stream = myfopen(overt2File, "wb");

    // final overt file - after data is hidden
                    status = war_creation_encode();
                    break;

              case WAR_CREATE_DECODE:
                    // wav creation algorithm
                    covert2Stream = myfopen(covert2File, "wb");

    // final covert file - after data is decoded
                    overt2Stream = myfopen(overt2File, "rb");

    // final overt file - after data is hidden
                    status = war_creation_decode();
                    break;

              case DOC_STUFFER_ENCODE:
                    // exe stuffing algorithm
                    covertStream = myfopen(covertFile, "rb");

    // covert file - data to be hidden
                    overtStream = myfopen(overtFile, "rb");

    // overt file - place to hide data
                    overt2Stream = myfopen(overt2File, "wb");

    // final overt file - after data is hidden
                    status = doc_stuffer_encode();
                    break;

              case DOC_STUFFER_DECODE:
                    // exe stuffing algorithm
                    covert2Stream = myfopen(covert2File, "wb");

    // final covert file - after data is decoded
                    overt2Stream = myfopen(overt2File, "rb");

    // final overt file - after data is hidden
                    status = doc_stuffer_decode();
                    break;

              case HTTP_WS_VARY_ENCODE:
                    // Store covert file as spaces and tabs in an html file
                    covertStream = myfopen(covertFile, "rb");

    // covert file - data to be hidden
```

```
            overtStream = myfopen(overtFile, "rb");

// overt file - place to hide data
            overt2Stream = myfopen(overt2File, "wb");

// final overt file - after data is hidden
            status = http_ws_vary_encode();
            break;

        case HTTP_WS_VARY_DECODE:
            // Store covert file as spaces and tabs in an html file
            covert2Stream = myfopen(covert2File, "wb");

// final covert file - after data is decoded
            overt2Stream = myfopen(overt2File, "rb");

// final overt file - after data is hidden
            status = http_ws_vary_decode();
            break;

        case WAV_SINE_CREATE_ENCODE:
            // wav creation algorithm
            covertStream = myfopen(covertFile, "rb");

// covert file - data to be hidden
            // no overt file needed
            overt2Stream = myfopen(overt2File, "wb");

// final overt file - after data is hidden
            status = wav_sine_creation_encode();
            break;

        case WAV_SINE_CREATE_DECODE:
            // wav creation algorithm
            covert2Stream = myfopen(covert2File, "wb");

// final covert file - after data is decoded
            overt2Stream = myfopen(overt2File, "rb");

// final overt file - after data is hidden
            status = wav_sine_creation_decode();
            break;
        default:
            printf("Error - No Stego routine identified!\n");
            myUsage();
            break;
    }

    if( covertStream ) {
        fflush( covertStream );
        fclose( covertStream );
    }
```

```
        if( covert2Stream ) {
            fflush( covert2Stream );
            fclose( covert2Stream );
        }
        if( overtStream ) {
            fflush( overtStream );
            fclose( overtStream );
        }
        if( overt2Stream ) {
            fflush( overt2Stream );
            fclose( overt2Stream );
        }
        if( bitStream ) {
            fflush( bitStream );
            fclose( bitStream );
        }
        if( logStream ) {
            fflush( logStream );
            fclose( logStream );
        }

        return 1;                                    // success
    } //main()
```

RTF_Insertion

This algorithm puts the covert data in a field that is nonprintable. A nonprint-able field is not "seen" when the RTF document is viewed or loaded into a word processing application, such as Word. Additionally, the new field is at the end of the overt RTF file, which also ensures that it will not be "seen" when the RTF file is viewed. Because RTF is an ASCII text file, the covert data is writ-ten in ASCII hex format in the RTF overt2 file.

```
/**************************************************
 * rtf_insertion.c
 *
 * Place data into an RTF file.  The RTF should
 * still operate normally - the insertion will
 * not show in the document.
 *
 * Code Designed and Written by Eric Cole and Jim Conley
 **************************************************
 */



//############## Load Headers ###################

#include "stegoGlobal.h"                // everyone adds
```

```
#include "rtf_insertion.h"          // define RTF_MARKER



// Prototypes
unsigned __int32 count_covert(void);
int copyRemainingOvert(void);
char xtoc(char *hex);
void ctox(char ch, char *hex);



//############ rtf_insertion_encode ##########
int rtf_insertion_encode(void) {
    int done;
    int lineCnt;
    int read_cnt;
    unsigned __int32 covert_siz;
    unsigned char ch;
    char hex[3];                                   // FF format
    char covert_siz_str[6];                        // siz in string
    char marker[RTF_MARKER_SIZ+1];
    char hdr[RTF_HDR_SIZ+1];
    char end[RTF_END_SIZ+1];

    // Initialize variables...
    lineCnt = 0;
    strcpy(hdr, RTF_HDR);
    strcpy(marker, RTF_MARKER);
    strcpy(end, RTF_END);

    // Copy all of overt file to overt2...
    copyRemainingOvert();

    // Put RTF header and marker in overt2...
    fwrite( hdr, sizeof(char), RTF_HDR_SIZ,
                    overt2Stream );
    fwrite( marker, sizeof(char), RTF_MARKER_SIZ,
                    overt2Stream );

    // Get size of covert file and rewind...
    covert_siz = count_covert();
    if(covert_siz > MAX_RTF_COVERT) {
        printf("Error - Covert file too large!\n");
        printf("Limit file to %d bytes.\n", MAX_RTF_COVERT);
        exit(0);
    } //if

    // Put convert file size in overt2 file...
    sprintf(covert_siz_str, "%5d", covert_siz);
    fwrite( covert_siz_str, sizeof(char), 5, overt2Stream );

    // Read a covert char and put in overt2 file,
    // until covert file exhausted
```

```
            done = FALSE;
        while(done == FALSE) {
            read_cnt = fread( &ch, sizeof(char), 1, covertStream );
            if(read_cnt > 0) {
                // Convert char to hex string...
                ctox(ch, hex);
                fwrite( hex, sizeof(char), 2, overt2Stream );
                // Every 40 hex writes, put a newline
                if(lineCnt >= 40) {
                    ch = '\n';
                    fwrite( &ch, sizeof(char), 1, overt2Stream );
                    lineCnt = 0;
                } else {
                    lineCnt++;
                } //if
            } else {
                done = TRUE;
            } //if
        } //while

        // Put RTF end in overt2...
        fwrite( end, sizeof(char), RTF_END_SIZ, overt2Stream );

        return SUCCESS;
} //rtf_insertion_encode();


//############ rtf_insertion_decode ##########
int rtf_insertion_decode(void) {
    int i;
    int done;
    int lineCnt;
    int read_cnt;
    __int32 covert_siz;
    unsigned char ch;
    char hex[4];                                // 2 char hex
    char covert_siz_str[6];                      // siz in string
    char marker[RTF_MARKER_SIZ+1];
    char match[RTF_MARKER_SIZ+1];

    // Initialize variables...
    lineCnt = 0;
    strcpy(marker, RTF_MARKER);

    // Search overt file until marker found...
    fread( match, sizeof(char), RTF_MARKER_SIZ-1, overt2Stream );

    done = FALSE;
    while(done == FALSE) {
        read_cnt = fread( &ch, sizeof(char), 1, overt2Stream );
        if(read_cnt > 0) {
            match[RTF_MARKER_SIZ-1] = ch;
            match[RTF_MARKER_SIZ] = 0;               // null terminate
```

```
                    if(strcmp(match, marker) == 0) {
                        done = TRUE;
                    } else {
                        for(i=0; i<(RTF_MARKER_SIZ-1); i++) {
                            match[i] = match[i+1];
                        } //for
                    } //if
                } else {
                    printf("Error, overt2 file missing marker\n");
                    exit(0);
                } //if
        } //while

        // Read 5 characters to find the size of the
        // covert file....
        fread( covert_siz_str, sizeof(char), 5, overt2Stream );
        covert_siz = atoi(covert_siz_str);
        if(covert_siz > MAX_RTF_COVERT) {
            printf("Error, in covert data size.\n");
            printf("Limit data to %d bytes.\n", MAX_RTF_COVERT);
            exit(0);
        } //if


        // Read covert_siz 2-character hex from
        // overt2 and put
        // them into the covert2 file,
        for(i=0; i<covert_siz; i++) {
            read_cnt = fread( hex, sizeof(char), 2, overt2Stream );

            if(read_cnt > 0) {
                ch = xtoc(hex);
                fwrite( &ch, sizeof(char), 1, covert2Stream );

                // Grab a newline every 40 hex reads...
                if(lineCnt >= 40) {
                read_cnt = fread( &ch, sizeof(char), 1, overt2Stream );
                    if(ch != '\n') {
                        printf("Error, new line missing!\n");
                        exit(0);
                    } //if
                    lineCnt = 0;
                } else {;
                    lineCnt++;
                } //if
            } else {
                printf("Error, overt2 file too small\n");
                exit(0);
            } //if
        } //for

        return SUCCESS;
} //rtf_insertion_decode();
```

War

This algorithm uses the covert data to determine what cards are dealt and played. Normally, cards are dealt randomly. The first card is a random choice of 1–52. In this algorithm, the choice between 1–52 is made depending on the bits in the covert file. Each bit determines whether the upper or lower part of an organized deck is chosen. Each successive bit chooses half again, until only one card remains, the card that is dealt. This method of cutting the deck into successive halves is used in order to maximize the bits that can encode a dealing of the cards. The next card is dealt with the deck ranging 1–51, the first card being removed from the ordered deck.

Normally in a card game of War each player plays a card, and the highest-value card wins the hand. Each player would have some strategy as to why he or she plays a certain card. In this algorithm, the playing of the cards is also controlled by the bits in the covert file. The choice of card is similar to dealing, except that you start with 1–13 cards instead of 1–52.

Decoding is done in a reverse fashion. For a given card, the decode algorithm decides if the card would be in the upper or lower half of the ordered deck.

```
/***************************************************
 * war_creation.c
 *
 * Use covert data to create a WAR file
 * that simulates the game War.
 *
 * Code Designed and Written by Eric Cole and Jim Conley
 ***************************************************
 */


//############# Load Headers ###################

#include "stegoGlobal.h"           // everyone adds
#include "war_creation.h"          // define WAR_MARKER


// Prototypes
unsigned __int32 count_covert(void);
void int32_to_hex(unsigned __int32 val, char *hex);
unsigned __int32 covertFile2BitFile(unsigned __int32);
unsigned __int32 bits2card(int siz, int *deckIn, int *pcard);
unsigned __int32 cardFaces2bits(char *cf,      int deckInSiz, int *deckIn);
int cf2index(char *acf, int siz, int *a_deck);
unsigned __int32 index2bits(int index, int siz);
void removeCard(int index, int siz, int *a_deck);
int cf2card(char *acf);
```

```
    void bitFile2covertFile(void);


char player[4][6] = {"North","East","South","West"};
char cardFace[52][4] = {
                                              "1s","Kh","1d","Kc",
                                              "2s","Qh","2d","Qc",
                                              "3s","Jh","3d","Jc",
                                              "4s","Th","4d","Tc",
                                              "5s","9h","5d","9c",
                                              "6s","8h","6d","8c",
                                              "7s","7h","7d","7c",
                                              "8s","6h","8d","6c",
                                              "9s","5h","9d","5c",
                                              "Ts","4h","Td","4c",
                                              "Js","3h","Jd","3c",
                                              "Qs","2h","Qd","2c",
                                              "Ks","1h","Kd","1c"
                                              };
int deck[52] = {
                                               0,  49,    2,  51,
                                               4,  45,    6,  47,
                                               8,  41,   10,  43,
                                              12,  37,   14,  39,
                                              16,  33,   18,  35,
                                              20,  29,   22,  31,
                                              24,  25,   26,  27,
                                              28,  21,   30,  23,
                                              32,  17,   34,  19,
                                              36,  13,   38,  15,
                                              40,   9,   42,  11,
                                              44,   5,   46,   7,
                                              48,   1,   50,   3 };



//############# war_creation_encode ##########
int war_creation_encode(void) {
     int i, t, p, pp;
     int card;                              // card # 1-13/52
     int hiTrick;
     int trickWinner, hiPlayer;
     int trickStarter;
     int gameScore[4];                  // player's score
     unsigned __int32 covert_siz, bitCnt;
     int chDeck[52];                 // changing deck
     int hand[4][13];                // shrinking hand

     // Initialize variables...
     dealCnt = 0;                       // count deals
     bitCnt = 0;                    // count hidden bits
     trickStarter = 0;              // player to start first

     // Get size of covert file and rewind file...
```

```
      covert_siz = count_covert();
      if(covert_siz > MAX_WAR_COVERT) {
          printf("Error - Covert file too large!\n");
          printf("Limit file to %d bytes.\n", MAX_WAR_COVERT);
          exit(0);
      } //if

      // Populate bit file, put size in first...
      covertFile2BitFile(covert_siz);

      // Put war game info into overt2...
      bitCnt = 0;
      for(i=0; i<4; i++) {
          gameScore[i] = 0;
      } //for
      while(bitCnt <= (covert_siz*8+32)) {

          // Reset Changing Deck...
          for(i=0; i<52; i++) {
              chDeck[i] = deck[(i+dealCnt)%52];
          } //for i

          // Deal the cards...
          for(p=0; p<4; p++) {
              for(t=0; t<13; t++) {
                  bitCnt += bits2card(52-(p*13+t), chDeck, &card);
                  hand[p][t] = card;
              } //for t
          } //for p

          // Write out the deal...
          fprintf(overt2Stream,"\n\nNew Deal\n");
          for(p=0; p<4; p++) {
              fprintf(overt2Stream,"%-5s ",player[p]);
              for(t=0; t<13; t++) {
                  fprintf(overt2Stream,"%s ",
                                  cardFace[(hand[p][t]+dealCnt)%52]);
              } //for t
              fprintf(overt2Stream,"\n");
          } //for p
          fprintf(overt2Stream,"\n");

          // Play each trick...
          for(t=0; t<13; t++) {
              hiTrick = 0;
              hiPlayer = 0;
//              nextStarter = trickStarter;
              trickStarter += (trickStarter+1)%4;

              // Loop thru players...
              for(p=0; p<4; p++) {
                  pp = (trickWinner+p) % 4;
                  // Get card from a set of cards (hand)
```

```
                        bitCnt += bits2card(13-t, hand[pp], &card);


                        // Write each play...
        fprintf(overt2Stream,"%-5s %s  ", player[pp], cardFace[(card+dealCnt)%52]);
                        // Determine trick winner...

                        if(card > hiTrick) {
                            hiTrick = card;
                            hiPlayer = pp;
                        } //if card
//                          nextStarter += (nextStarter+1)%4;
                    } //for p

                    trickWinner = hiPlayer;

                    // Write trick score...
                    fprintf(overt2Stream,"Trick Winner: %s\n",
                                        player[trickWinner]);
                    gameScore[trickWinner]++;
                } //for hand play

                // Print deal score...
                fprintf(overt2Stream,"\nScoring:  ");
                for(p=0; p<4; p++) {
                    fprintf(overt2Stream,"%s:%d  ",player[p], gameScore[p]);
                } //for p
                fprintf(overt2Stream,"\n");

                dealCnt += 3;
            } //while

        return SUCCESS;
    } //war_creation_encode();




//############# war_creation_decode ##########
int war_creation_decode(void) {
    int c, p, pp, t;
    int siz;
    int lead;                               // 0, 1, 2, or 3
    int index;
    int chDeck[52];                             // changes as cards used
    int hand[4][13];                        // shrinking hand
    unsigned __int32 bitCnt;
    char cf[13][3];                             // cardFaces read
    char tmp[10][20];                       // read but not used
    char leadPlayer[10];                        // N, E, S, or W

    // Initialize variables...
```

```
        dealCnt = 0;
        bitCnt = 0;

        fscanf(overt2Stream, "\n");
        while(!feof(overt2Stream)) {
            for(c=0; c<52; c++) {
                chDeck[c] = deck[(c+dealCnt)%52];
            } //for c

            // Read a deal...
            fscanf(overt2Stream, "\nNew Deal\n");
            for(p=0; p<4; p++) {
                // Scan deal lines...
fscanf(overt2Stream, "%s %s %s %s %s %s %s %s %s %s %s %s %s %s", &tmp,
&cf[0], &cf[1], &cf[2], &cf[3], &cf[4],
                &cf[5], &cf[6], &cf[7], &cf[8], &cf[9],
                &cf[10], &cf[11], &cf[12]);

                    // Convert card faces to bits...
                    for(t=0; t<13; t++) {
                        siz = 52-(p*13+t);

                        // Get the cards' index into the deck
                        index = cf2index(cf[t], siz, chDeck);

                        // Populate hand...
                        hand[p][t] = cf2card(cf[t]);

                        // Special case when siz == 1, just
                        // ignore the last card, no bits there...
                        // Determine bits to get to index
                        // Bits are written to overt2Stream...
                        bitCnt += index2bits(index, siz);

                        // Remove card from chDeck...
                        removeCard(index, siz, chDeck);
                    } //for t
            } //for p

            // Read tricks as they are played...
            for(t=0; t<13; t++) {
                // Scan trick lines...
                fscanf(overt2Stream, "%s %s %s %s %s %s %s %s %s %s %s ",
                    &leadPlayer, &cf[0], &tmp[1], &cf[1],
                    &tmp[2], &cf[2], &tmp[3], &cf[3],
                    &tmp[4], &tmp[5], &tmp[6]);

                if(strcmp(leadPlayer, "North") == 0) {
                    lead = 0;
                } else if(strcmp(leadPlayer, "East") == 0) {
                    lead = 1;
                } else if(strcmp(leadPlayer, "South") == 0) {
                    lead = 2;
```

```
                } else if(strcmp(leadPlayer, "West") == 0) {
                    lead = 3;
                }else {
                    printf("Error, bad overt2 at leadPlayer\n");
                    exit(0);
                } //if

                // Convert card faces to bits...
                for(pp=lead; pp<(4+lead); pp++) {
                    p = pp%4;

                    // Get the cards' index into the deck
                    index = cf2index(cf[pp-lead], 13-t, hand[p]);


                    // Determine bits to get to index
                    // Bits are written to overt2Stream...
                    bitCnt += index2bits(index, 13-t);

                    // Remove card from hand[][]...
                    removeCard(index, 13-t, hand[p]);
                } //for p
            } //for t

            // Read scoring line...
            fscanf(overt2Stream, "%s %s %s %s %s",
                &tmp[0], &tmp[1], &tmp[2], &tmp[3],     &tmp[4]);

            // Read a NEWLINE to check for EOF...
            fscanf(overt2Stream, "\n");

            dealCnt += 3;

        } //while

        // Write bitFile to covert2...
        bitFile2covertFile();

        return SUCCESS;
} //war_creation_decode();




//############# removeCard ##########
void removeCard(int index, int siz, int *a_deck) {
        int d;

        // Find card face in deckIn...
        for(d=index; d<siz-1; d++) {
            a_deck[d] = a_deck[d+1];
```

```
      } //for d
   } //removeCard()




//############# cf2index ##########
// Match a card in 'cardfaces'.
// Return index,
//
int cf2index(char *acf, int siz, int *a_deck) {
      int d;
      int card;
      int index;

      index = -1;

      // Find card in card faces...
      for(d=0; d<52; d++) {
          if(strcmp(acf, cardFace[(d+dealCnt)%52]) == 0) {
              card = d;
              break;
          } //if
      } //for d

      // Use card to find index into a deck...
      for(d=0; d<siz; d++) {
          if(card == a_deck[d]) {
              index = d;
              break;
          } //if
      } //for d

      if(index == -1) {
          printf("Error, index not found for %s\n", acf);
          exit(0);
      } //if

      return index;
   } //cf2index()




//############# cf2card ##########
// Match a card in 'card faces'.
// Return 'card',
//
int cf2card(char *acf) {
      int d;
```

```
    int card;

    card = -1;

    // Find card in card faces...
    for(d=0; d<52; d++) {
        if(strcmp(acf, cardFace[(d+dealCnt)%52]) == 0) {
            card = d;
            break;
        } //if
    } //for d

    if(card == -1) {
        printf("Error, card not found\n");
        exit(0);
    } //if

    return card;
} //cf2card()




//############# index2bits ##########
// Find an index position by going hi or lo,
// write out high '1' and
// lower '0' each step of the way.
//
// When decoding, mid GOES HI
//
unsigned __int32 index2bits(int index, int siz) {
    int lo, hi, mid;
    unsigned __int32 bitCnt;
    char bit;

    bitCnt = 0;
    lo = 0;
    hi = siz-1;

    while(hi != lo) {
        mid = (int)((hi-lo)/2.0 + lo + 0.5);      // mid=hi

        if(index >= mid) {                        //mid=i
            // Hi
            bit = '1';
            hi = hi;
            lo = mid;                    // mid=hi
        } else {
            // Lo
            bit = '0';
            hi = mid-1;
            lo = lo;                     // mid=hi
```

```
            } //if
            fprintf(bitStream, "%c", bit);
            bitCnt++;
        } //while

    return bitCnt;
} //index2bits()
```

```
//############# bits2card ##########
// Find a card in deck, depending on bits in bit
// file.
//    siz is cards to choose from
//    deck is array of cards
//    pcard is to return card found
//
// Each bit from bit file choose half of the deck,
// either low or hi.  If deck is an odd size, then
// the middle card GOES HI (note: in the decode
// algorithm, this mid card will have to go HI).
unsigned __int32 bits2card(int sizIn, int *deckIn,
                                                    int *pcard) {
    int i, a;
    int hi, lo, mid;
    int read_cnt;
    unsigned __int32 bitCnt;
    char bit;
//    char chDeck[52];

    // Initialize...
    if(sizIn > 52) {
        printf("Error, 'siz' too large\n");
        exit(0);
    } //if

    lo = 0;
    hi = sizIn-1;

    // Choose a card by cutting deck in half
    // repeatedly, depending on whether bit is hi '1'
    // or low '0'.
    bitCnt = 0;
    while(hi != lo) {
        read_cnt = fread( &bit, sizeof(char), 1, bitStream );
        if(read_cnt == 1) {
            bitCnt += read_cnt;
        } else {
            // choose a random bit
            bit = (hi & 0x01? '1': '0');
```

```
        } //if

        // Check for Hi/Low...
        mid = (int)((hi-lo)/2.0 + lo +0.5);              // mid=hi
        if(bit == '1') {
            // Hi, so choose Hi half...
            hi = hi;
            lo = mid;                    // mid=hi
        } else {
            // Low, so choose low half...
            hi = mid-1;              // mid=hi, so don't use it
            lo = lo;
        } //if
    } //while

    // Only one card left in deck...
    *pcard = deckIn[lo];                  // lo should == hi

    // Return deckIn without found card...
    a = 0;
    for(i=0; i<sizIn; i++) {
        if(deckIn[i] == *pcard) {
            a = 1;
        } //if
        deckIn[i] = deckIn[i+a];
    } //for

    return bitCnt;
} //bits2card();
```

Wav_Creation

This algorithm places the covert file in the data portion of a WAV file. The WAV header is generic and meaningless, and it needs to be altered only for the size of the covert data. All of the data portion of the WAV file, the portion normally holding a waveform, will be raw covert data. Because the raw covert data does not resemble a waveform, the result is a WAV file that plays a loud screeching sound. Of course, different covert files will produce different sounds, but none are expected to be intelligible.

```
/***************************************************
 * wav_creation.c
 *
 * Use covert data to create a WAV file.
 *
 * Code Designed and Written by Eric Cole and Jim Conley
 ***************************************************
```

```
    */


//############## Load Headers ###################

#include "stegoGlobal.h"           // everyone adds
#include "wav_creation.h"          // define WAV_MARKER



// Prototypes
unsigned __int32 count_covert(void);          // file.c
void int32_to_hex(unsigned __int32 val,
                                                  char     ⊃

*hex); //file.c

//############# wav_creation_encode ##########
int wav_creation_encode(void) {
    int done;
    int read_cnt;
    unsigned __int32 covert_siz, total_length;
    char tmp[250];
    unsigned char ch;

    // Initialize variables...

    // Get size of covert file and rewind...
    covert_siz = count_covert();
    if(covert_siz > MAX_WAVC_COVERT) {
        printf("Error - Covert file too large!\n");
        printf("Limit file to %d bytes.\n", MAX_WAVC_COVERT);
        exit(0);
    } //if

    // Put Riff chunk in overt2...
    strcpy(tmp, "RIFF");
    fwrite( tmp, sizeof(char), strlen(tmp), overt2Stream );

    // Put total length in overt2...
    // Total length is as follows:
    //    4          remainder of Riff chunk
    //    24         Format chunk
    //    8          beginning of Data chunk
    //    <?>        data which is covert_siz
    total_length = covert_siz + 36;
    fwrite( &total_length, sizeof(__int32), 1, overt2Stream );

    // Put remainder of Riff chunk in overt2...
    strcpy(tmp, "WAVE");
    fwrite( tmp, sizeof(char), strlen(tmp),
```

```
                              overt2Stream );

        // Put Format chunk in overt2...
        PUT8(0x66);     PUT8(0x6D);                 // 1-2
        PUT8(0x74);     PUT8(0x20);
        PUT8(0x10);     PUT8(0x00);
        PUT8(0x00);     PUT8(0x00);
        PUT8(0x01);     PUT8(0x00);
        PUT8(0x01);     PUT8(0x00);

        PUT8(0x44);     PUT8(0xAC);
        PUT8(0x00);     PUT8(0x00);
        PUT8(0x88);     PUT8(0x58);
        PUT8(0x01);     PUT8(0x00);
        PUT8(0x02);     PUT8(0x00);
        PUT8(0x10);     PUT8(0x00);

        // Put Data chunk in overt2...
        strcpy(tmp, "data");
        fwrite( tmp, sizeof(char), strlen(tmp), overt2Stream );

        // Put the size of the covert data in overt2...
        fwrite( &covert_siz, sizeof(__int32), 1, overt2Stream );


        // Read a covert char and put in overt2 file,
        // until covert file exhausted
        done = FALSE;
        while(done == FALSE) {
            read_cnt = fread( &ch, sizeof(char), 1, covertStream );
            if(read_cnt > 0) {
                fwrite( &ch, sizeof(char), 1, overt2Stream );
            } else {
                done = TRUE;
            } //if
        } //while

        return SUCCESS;
} //wav_creation_encode();




//############# wav_creation_decode ##########
int wav_creation_decode(void) {
    int read_cnt;
    unsigned __int32 i;
    unsigned __int32 mask = 1;
    unsigned __int32 covert_siz = 0;
```

```
    unsigned char ch, charr[50];

    // Initialize variables...

    // Read 36 characters in overt2.  This will
    // bypass the Riff and Format chunks...
    read_cnt = fread( charr, sizeof(char), 36, overt2Stream );
    if(read_cnt < 36) {
        printf("Error - Bad Riff and Format chunks!\n");
        exit(0);
    } //if

    // Read "data" in overt2...
    read_cnt = fread( charr, sizeof(char), 4, overt2Stream );
    if(read_cnt < 4) {
        printf("Error - Missing 'data' in WAV file!\n");
        exit(0);
    } //if
    charr[4] = 0;                          // null terminate
    if(!strcmp(charr, "data") == 0) {
        printf("Error - Bad 'data' in WAV file!\n");
        printf("Found %s instead of 'data'\n", charr);
        exit(0);
    } //if

    // Read data size in overt2...
    // A value of 0x11223344 will be stored as :
    //    22 11 44 33
    read_cnt = fread( charr, sizeof(char), 4, overt2Stream );
    if(read_cnt < 4) {
        printf("Error - Invalid WAV file!\n");
        exit(0);
    } //if
    covert_siz =  charr[0]
                            + charr[1]*256
                            + charr[2]*256*256
                            + charr[3]*256*256*256 ;

    // Read overt2 until all data is found....
    for(i=0; i<covert_siz; i++) {
        read_cnt = fread( &ch, sizeof(char), 1, overt2Stream );

        if(read_cnt < 1) {
            printf("Error - Overt2 file too small!\n");
            exit(0);
        } //if
        fwrite( &ch, sizeof(char), 1, covert2Stream );
    } //for

    return SUCCESS;
} //wav_creation_decode();
```

Wav_Sine

In this algorithm, a sine wave makes up the data portion of the WAV file's waveform. This algorithm puts the covert data in a portion of a sine wave. Either one-half, one-quarter, or one-eighth of the waveform is inserted with covert data. The fraction depends on the "-v 2|4|8" option on the command line.

```
/***************************************************
 * wav_sine_creation_encode.c
 *
 * Use covert data to create a WAV file using a sine wave.
 *
 *
 * Code Designed and Written by Eric Cole and Jim Conley
 ***************************************************
 */


//############# Load Headers ###################

#include "stegoGlobal.h"          // everyone adds
#include "wav_creation.h"         // define WAV_MARKER



// Prototypes
unsigned __int32 count_covert(void);
void int32_to_hex(unsigned __int32 val, char *hex);

//############# wav_sine_creation_encode ##########
int wav_sine_creation_encode(void) {
     int read_cnt;
     unsigned __int32 threshold;
     unsigned __int32 cwritten;
     unsigned __int32 covert_siz, total_length;
     char tmp[250];
     unsigned char ch;

     // Initialize variables...
     if(! (vary == 2 || vary == 4 || vary == 8)) {
          printf("Error - vary not valid!\n");
          printf("Values are 2, 4,or 8\n");
          printf("Set with -v <2, 4, or 8>\n");
          exit(0);
     } //if
     threshold = 128 / vary;

     // Get size of covert file and rewind...
     covert_siz = count_covert() * vary;
     if(covert_siz > MAX_WAVC_COVERT) {
```

```
        printf("Error - Covert file too large!\n");
        printf("Limit file to %d bytes.\n", MAX_WAVC_COVERT);
        exit(0);
} //if


// Put Riff chunk in overt2...
strcpy(tmp, "RIFF");
fwrite( tmp, sizeof(char), strlen(tmp), overt2Stream );

// Put total length in overt2...
// Total length is as follows:
//    4          remainder of Riff chunk
//    24         Format chunk
//    8          beginning of Data chunk
//    <?>        data which is covert_siz
total_length = covert_siz + 36;
fwrite( &total_length, sizeof(__int32), 1,
                overt2Stream );

// Put remainder of Riff chunk in overt2...
strcpy(tmp, "WAVE");
fwrite( tmp, sizeof(char), strlen(tmp),
                overt2Stream );

// Put Format Chunk in overt2...
PUT8(0x66);     PUT8(0x6D);                 // 1-2
PUT8(0x74);     PUT8(0x20);
PUT8(0x10);     PUT8(0x00);
PUT8(0x00);     PUT8(0x00);
PUT8(0x01);     PUT8(0x00);
PUT8(0x01);     PUT8(0x00);


PUT8(0x44);     PUT8(0xAC);
PUT8(0x00);     PUT8(0x00);
PUT8(0x88);     PUT8(0x58);
PUT8(0x01);     PUT8(0x00);
PUT8(0x02);     PUT8(0x00);
PUT8(0x10);     PUT8(0x00);


// Put Data chunk in overt2...
strcpy(tmp, "data");
fwrite( tmp, sizeof(char), strlen(tmp), overt2Stream );

// Put the size of the covert data in overt2...
fwrite( &covert_siz, sizeof(__int32), 1, overt2Stream );


// Read a covert char and put in overt2 file,
// until covert file exhausted
for(cwritten=0; cwritten<covert_siz; cwritten++) {
    if((cwritten%128) < threshold) {
        ch = (char)(cwritten%255);
```

```
        } else {
            read_cnt = fread( &ch, sizeof(char), 1, covertStream );
            if(read_cnt < 1) {
                printf("Error - data in covert file!\n");
                exit(0);
            } //if
        } //if

        fwrite( &ch, sizeof(char), 1, overt2Stream );
    } //for

    return SUCCESS;
} //wav_sine_creation_encode();




//############# wav_sine_creation_decode ##########
int wav_sine_creation_decode(void) {
    int read_cnt;
    unsigned __int32 threshold;
    unsigned __int32 cwritten;
    unsigned __int32 mask = 1;
    unsigned __int32 covert_siz = 0;
    unsigned char ch, charr[50];

    // Initialize variables...
    if(! (vary == 2 || vary == 4 || vary == 8)) {
        printf("Error - vary not valid!\n");
        printf("Values are 2, 4,or 8\n");
        printf("Set with -v <2, 4, or 8>\n");
        exit(0);
    } //if
    threshold = 128 / vary;

    // Read 36 characters in overt2.  This will
    // bypass the Riff and Format chunks...
    read_cnt = fread( charr, sizeof(char), 36, overt2Stream );
    if(read_cnt < 36) {
        printf("Error - Bad Riff and Format chunks!\n");
        exit(0);
    } //if

    // Read "data" in overt2...
    read_cnt = fread( charr, sizeof(char), 4, overt2Stream );
    if(read_cnt < 4) {
        printf("Error - Missing 'data' in WAV file!\n");
        exit(0);
    } //if
    charr[4] = 0;                           // null terminate
    if(!strcmp(charr, "data") == 0) {
```

```
            printf("Error - Bad 'data' in WAV file!\n");
            printf("Found %s instead of 'data'\n", charr);
            exit(0);
    } //if

    // Read data size in overt2...
    // A value of 0x11223344 will be stored as :
    //    22 11 44 33
    read_cnt = fread( charr, sizeof(char), 4, overt2Stream );
    if(read_cnt < 4) {
        printf("Error - Invalid WAV file!\n");
        exit(0);
    } //if
    covert_siz =  charr[0]
                                + charr[1]*256
                                + charr[2]*256*256
                                + charr[3]*256*256*256 ;

    // Read overt2 until all data is found....
    for(cwritten=0; cwritten<covert_siz; cwritten++) {
        read_cnt = fread( &ch, sizeof(char), 1, overt2Stream );

        if(read_cnt < 1) {
            printf("Error - Overt2 file too small!\n");
            exit(0);
        } //if

        if(! ((cwritten%128) < threshold)) {
            fwrite( &ch, sizeof(char), 1, covert2Stream );
        } //if
    } //for

    return SUCCESS;
} //wav_sine_creation_decode();
```

Wav_Twidle

This algorithm adjusts the parity of the characters in the waveform to match the bits in the covert file. On average, the parity of the overt file's data character will match the bit in the covert file 50 percent of the time. In these cases, the overt data does not have to be altered. In other cases, the overt data character is altered by adding one to the least significant bit. In this way, the WAV waveform is altered as little as possible. The effect is that the listener cannot distinguish the overt2 file from the overt file.

```
/***************************************************
 * wav_twidle.c
 *
```

```
     * Use covert data to change (twidle) values in
     * a WAV file.
     *
     *
     * Code Designed and Written by Eric Cole and Jim Conley
     ****************************************************
     */



//############# Load Headers ###################

#include "stegoGlobal.h"          // everyone adds
#include "wav_twidle.h"           // define WAV_MARKER



// Prototypes
unsigned __int32 count_covert(void);
int copyRemainingOvert(void);

//############# wav_twidle_encode #########
int wav_twidle_encode(void) {
int cnt=0;
     int i;
     int done;
     unsigned __int32 mask=1;
     int read_cnt;
     unsigned __int32 covert_siz;
     char charr[50];
     unsigned char ch;
     unsigned char och;

     // Initialize variables...

     // Get size of covert file and rewind...
     covert_siz = count_covert();
     if(covert_siz > MAX_WAVT_COVERT) {
         printf("Error - Covert file too large!\n");
         printf("Limit file to %d bytes.\n", MAX_WAVT_COVERT);
         exit(0);
     } //if

     // Read 36 characters in overt.  This will
     // bypass the Riff and Format chunks.
     // Copy these chunks to overt2...
     read_cnt = fread( charr, sizeof(char), 36, overtStream );
     if(read_cnt < 36) {
         printf("Error - Invalid WAV file!\n");
         exit(0);
     } //if
     // copy to overt2...
     fwrite( charr, sizeof(char), 36, overt2Stream );

     // Read "data" in overt and copy to overt2...
```

```
    read_cnt = fread( charr, sizeof(char), 4, overtStream );
    if(read_cnt < 4) {
        printf("Error - Invalid WAV file!");
        exit(0);
    } //if
    charr[4] = 0;                                    // null terminate
    if(!strcmp(charr, "data") == 0) {
        printf("Error - Invalid WAV file!\n");
        exit(0);
    } //if
    // copy to overt2...
    fwrite( charr, sizeof(char), 4, overt2Stream );

    // Read data size in overt and copy to overt2...
    read_cnt = fread( charr, sizeof(char), 4, overtStream );

    if(read_cnt < 4) {
        printf("Error - Invalid WAV file!\n");
        exit(0);
    } //if
    // copy to overt2...
    fwrite( charr, sizeof(char), 4, overt2Stream );

    // Put the size of the covert data into the
    // overt2 file, one bit at a time.   Covert_siz
    // is 32 bits.
    for(i=0; i<32; i++) {
        read_cnt = fread( &och, sizeof(char), 1, overtStream );
        if(read_cnt < 1) {
            printf("Error - WAV file too small!\n");
            exit(0);
        } //if

        if((covert_siz & (mask<<i)) && !(och & 0x01)) {
            och += (och != 0xFF? 1: -1);
        } else if(!(covert_siz & (mask<<i)) && (och & 0x01)) {
            och += (och != 0xFF? 1: -1);
        } //if

        fwrite( &och, sizeof(char), 1, overt2Stream );
    } //for


    // Read one char in the covert file and adjust
    // 8 characters in overt2 file.
    // Do this until the covert file is exhausted.
    done = FALSE;
    while(done == FALSE) {
        read_cnt = fread( &ch, sizeof(char), 1, covertStream );

//if(cnt<24) {      fprintf(logStream, "\n encode: ");       fflush
  (logStream);} //if logStream

        if(read_cnt < 1) {
```

```
                    done = TRUE;
            } //if


        for(i=0; i<8; i++) {
            read_cnt = fread( &och, sizeof(char), 1, overtStream );
            if(read_cnt < 1) {
                printf("Error - WAV file too small!\n");
                exit(0);
            } //if

            if((ch & (mask<<i)) && !(och & 0x01)) {
                och += (och != 0xFF? 1: -1);
            } else if(!(ch & (mask<<i)) && (och & 0x01)) {
                och += (och != 0xFF? 1: -1);
            } //if

            fwrite( &och, sizeof(char), 1, overt2Stream );

//if(cnt<24) {    cnt++;     fprintf(logStream, "%d ",(ch & (mask<<i)
 ?1:0));      fprintf(logStream, "%s",(i==3?" - ":""));      fflush(logStream);}
//if logStream

        } //for
    } //while

    // Copy remainder of overt file to overt2...
    copyRemainingOvert();

    return SUCCESS;
} //wav_twidle_encode();




//############# wav_twidle_decode ##########
int wav_twidle_decode(void) {
    int i;
    int read_cnt;
    unsigned __int32 a;
    unsigned __int32 mask = 1;
    unsigned __int32 covert_siz = 0;
    unsigned char cmask = 1;
    unsigned char ch, och, charr[50];

    // Initialize variables...

    // Read 36 characters in overt2.  This will
    // bypass the Riff and Format chunks...
    read_cnt = fread( charr, sizeof(char), 36, overt2Stream );
    if(read_cnt < 36) {
```

```
            printf("Error - Invalid WAV file!\n");
            exit(0);
    } //if

    // Read "data" in overt2...
    read_cnt = fread( charr, sizeof(char), 4, overt2Stream );
    if(read_cnt < 4) {
            printf("Error - Invalid WAV file!");
            exit(0);
    } //if
    charr[4] = 0;
    if(!strcmp(charr, "data") == 0) {
            printf("Error - Invalid WAV file!\n");
            exit(0);
    } //if

    // Read data size in overt2...
    read_cnt = fread( charr, sizeof(char), 4, overt2Stream );
    if(read_cnt < 4) {
            printf("Error - Invalid WAV file!\n");
            exit(0);
    } //if


    // Read 32 overt2 characters to find the size
    // of the covert file....
    for(i=0; i<32; i++) {
            read_cnt = fread( &och, sizeof(char), 1, overt2Stream );

            if(read_cnt < 1) {
                printf("Error - Overt2 file too small!\n");
                exit(0);
            } //if

            if(och & 0x01) {
                covert_siz = (covert_siz | (mask<<i));
            } //if
    } //for


    // Read 8 overt2 characters to produce 1 covert
    // character, until covert_siz.chars found...
    for(a=0; a<covert_siz; a++) {
            ch = 0;

//if(cnt<24) {    fprintf(logStream, "\n decode: ");    fflush
  (logStream);} //if logStream

            for(i=0; i<8; i++) {
                fread( &och, sizeof(char), 1, overt2Stream );
                if(read_cnt < 1) {
```

```
                    printf("Error - WAV file too small!\n");
                    exit(0);
              } //if
              if(och & 0x01) {
                    ch = (ch | (cmask<<i));
              } //if


         } //for

         fwrite( &ch, sizeof(char), 1, covert2Stream );
      } //for

   return SUCCESS;
} //wav_twidle_decode();
```

Chapter 8

In Chapter 8 I talked about ways to detect both crypto and stego. The programs that were referenced in the chapter are shown here.

Cryptofind

This program will go through a file and look for random bytes or a flat histogram. If the program finds such a file, it will then look at the header to see if it is enrypted or compressed, or if it is an image file by looking at the headers.

```
/*
Program that will scan files and detect encrypted files.
The program will also detect compressed files and certain types of images.
*/


#include <stdio.h>
#include <stdlib.h>
#include <string.h>
#include <io.h>
#include <math.h>
#include <dos.h>

#define  NC 7


/* Prototypes */
long  TestDir(char *thisDir, long *counts, char** output, long flag);
long  TestFile(char *fname, char **out, long *counts, long flag);
int   CheckType(FILE *strm);
```

```
void  Usage();


/*
KEY - shows which type files are kept in what part of the array
output[2] - apparently encrypted files
output[3] - small files (under 512 bytes)
output[4] - compressed files
output[5] - image files that look uniform
output[6] - warnings

KEY - shows mapping for numfiles
numfiles[0] is for total number of files
numfiles[1] is for total number of directories
*/




/* Main program */

void main(int argc, char* argv[]) {
  int  i;
  long counts[NC], flag = 0;
  char *output[NC];

  for(i=0; i<NC; i++) {
    counts[i]    = 0;
    output[i]    = malloc(1024);
    if(!output[i]) {
      printf("Error: Out of memory \n");
      exit(1);
    }
    output[i][0] = 0;
  }

  if(argc < 2) {
    Usage();    exit(1);
  } else {
    for(i=1; i<argc-1; i++) {
      if(argv[i][0] == '-') {
      switch(argv[i][1]) {
        case 'r':   /* recursive subdirectories */
          flag += 1;
          break;
        case 'v':   /* verbose output */
          flag += 2;
          break;
        case 'd':   /* debug */
          flag += 4;
          break;

        case 's':   /* small files */
```

```
              flag += 16;
              break;
            default:
              printf("Unknown switch  %s\n", argv[i]);
              Usage(); exit(1);
        }
        } else {
        Usage();    exit(1);
        }
    }

    if(argv[argc-1][0] == '-') {
      Usage();    exit(1);
    }


    TestDir(argv[argc-1], counts, output, flag);

    printf("\nTested %5d files in %4d directories\n",
        counts[0], counts[1]);
    printf("  Encrypted files:    %5d\n", counts[2]);
    printf("  Small files:        %5d\n", counts[3]);
    printf("  Compressed files:   %5d\n", counts[4]);
    printf("  Image files:        %5d\n", counts[5]);
    printf("  Warnings:           %5d\n", counts[6]);
  }

  for(i=0; i<NC; i++) { free(output[i]); }
}




long TestDir(char *thisDir, long *counts, char ** output, long flag) {
  struct _finddata_t fileinfo;
  int    i, len;
  long   done, result;
  long   verbose, recurse, debug;
  char   path[255];
  long   numfiles[NC];

  recurse = flag & 1;
  verbose = flag & 2;
  debug   = flag & 4;

  for(i=0; i<NC; i++) { numfiles[i] = 0; }
  numfiles[1] = 1;

  len = strlen(thisDir);
  if((thisDir[len-1] != ':') &&
     (thisDir[len-1] != '\\')) {
    strcat(thisDir, "\\");
  }
  strcpy(path, thisDir);
```

```
    strcat(path,"*.*");
    result =_findfirst(path, &fileinfo);
    done = (result == -1);

    while (!done) {
      strcpy(path, thisDir);
      strcat(path, fileinfo.name);
      if(fileinfo.attrib & 16) {
        /* directory */
        if(strcmp(fileinfo.name, ".") &&
        strcmp(fileinfo.name, "..")) {
       strcat(path,"\\");
       if(recurse) {
         TestDir(path, numfiles, output, flag);
       }
        } else { /* skip . and .. */ }
      } else {
        TestFile(path, output, numfiles, flag);
      }
      done = _findnext (result, &fileinfo);
    }
    for(i=0; i<NC; i++) {counts[i] += numfiles[i]; }
    return(numfiles[0]);
}



long TestFile(char *fname, char **out, long *counts, long flag) {
  int   i, ftype;
  long  fsize, read, bins[256];
  long  verbose, debug, showsmall;
  long  count, sum;
  float avg, chi2, zval, tempf;
  unsigned char buffer[1024];
  FILE *fin;

  counts[0]++;
  out[2][1] = 0;

  verbose  = flag & 2;
  debug    = flag & 4;
  showsmall = flag & 16;

  fin = fopen(fname, "rb");
  if(!fin) {
    printf("Unable to open file %s\n", fname);
    counts[6]++;
    return(-1);
  }

  fseek(fin, 0L, SEEK_END);
  fsize = ftell(fin);
```

```
  if(fsize<512) {
    counts[3]++;
    if(debug) { printf("%s  small\n", fname);}
    if(showsmall) {
      printf("%s file  Too small! size=%d\n",
          fname, fsize);
    }
    fclose(fin);
    return(-2);
  }

  /* collect data for chi squared */
  memset(bins, 0, 256*sizeof(long));
  count = 0;
  sum = 0;
  rewind(fin);
  read = fread(buffer, 1, 1024, fin);
  while(read) {
    for(i=0; i<read; i++) {
      bins[buffer[i]]++;
    }
    read = fread(buffer, 1, 1024, fin);
  }

  for(i=0; i<256; i++) {
    if(bins[i]>2) { count++; sum += bins[i]; }
  }

  if(count < 3) {
    /* too few values used to be useful */
    fclose(fin);
    return(0);
  }

  avg = (float) sum / (float) count;
  chi2 = (float) 0.0;

  for(i=0; i<256; i++) {
    if(bins[i]>2) {
      tempf = bins[i] - avg;
      chi2 += tempf*tempf/avg;
    }
  }

  /* df = count-1 */
  /* 2*count-5  = 2*df-3 */
  zval = (float) (sqrt(2.0*chi2) - sqrt(2.0*count - 5.0));

  if(zval<10.0) {
    ftype = CheckType(fin);
    counts[ftype]++;
    if(ftype == 2) {
      printf("%s may contain encrypted data.", fname);
```

```
      if(verbose) {printf("  -  %g\n", zval);}
      else {printf("\n");}
      fflush(stdout);
    }
  }

  if(debug) {
    printf("%s    %d %g\n", fname, fsize, zval);
  }

  fclose(fin);
  return(0);
}




int CheckType(FILE *fin) {

  int i;
  unsigned long  magic4, magic2;
  unsigned char buffer[1024], m2buff[4];

  /* load header data */
  fseek(fin, 0L, 0);
  i = fread(buffer, 1, 1024, fin);
  if(i == 0) {
    printf("Error\n");
    return(6);
  }
  memcpy(&magic4, buffer, 4);
  memset(m2buff, 0, 4);
  memcpy(m2buff, buffer, 2);
  memcpy(&magic2, m2buff, 4);


  /* Test image formats */
  if(buffer[0] == 0xA) { return(5); }       /* PCX */
  if(magic4 == 987654321L) { return(5); }  /* DCX */
  if((magic4 == 2771273L) || (magic4 == 2772301L)) {
    return(5);  }                            /* TIF */
  if(!strncmp((char *)buffer, "GIF87a", 6)) {
    return(5); }                  /* GIF87a */
  if(!strncmp((char *)buffer, "GIF89a", 6)) {
    return(5); }                          /* GIF89a */
  if((magic4 == 3774863615L)
     && !strncmp((char*)(buffer+6), "JFIF", 5)) {
    return(5); }                      /* jpeg (JFIF) */
  if(!strncmp((char *)buffer, "BM", 2)) { return(5); }  /* BMP */
  if(!strncmp((char *)buffer, ".snd", 4)) {
    return(5); }  /* au sound file */

  /* Test compressed formats */
```

```
    if(magic2 == 35615L) { return(4); }      /* gzip */
    if(magic4 == 67324752L)  { return(4); }  /* pkzip */
    if((buffer[0] == 26) && (buffer[1] < 10)) {
      return(4); }                           /* arc */

    /* Else - default - possible encrypted */
    return(2);
}



void Usage() {
  printf("Usage: find -r -s [path]\n");
  printf("   -r means recursive subdirectories\n");
  printf("   -s means show files too small to be tested\n");
}
```

File Group Stat

This program collects statistics on a group of files.

```
/* This program collects group statistics */
/* on a group of files                  */

#include <stdio.h>
#include <stdlib.h>
#include <string.h>
#include <memory.h>
#include <math.h>

/** Declarations **/
typedef struct _StatDat {
  int    size;
  double avg, var, skew, kurt, avg_dev;
  int    diff_vals;
} StatDat;



/** Prototypes **/
int FileStats(char *fn, StatDat *stats );



void main(int argc, char* argv[]) {
    int  test;
    char fn[128];
    StatDat stats;

    strcpy(fn, argv[1]);
```

```
        test = FileStats(fn, &stats);
        if(test == 0) {
            printf("%s   %d\n", fn, stats.size);
            printf("   %.3f   %.3f   %.3f   %.3f   %.3f   %d\n",
                    stats.avg, stats.var, stats.skew,
                    stats.kurt, stats.avg_dev, stats.diff_vals);
        } else {
            printf("Stats returned error code %d\n", test);
        }
}




/* Computes statistics on a single file     */
/* Takes filename and a StatDat structure    */
/* as arguments. Fills in the StatDat data */
/* Returns an error code - 0 for success      */

int FileStats(char *fn, StatDat *stats ) {
        /* local declarations */
        int     i, got, vals[256];
        FILE    *Fin;
        double d_temp, d_temp2, correct;
        unsigned char buffer[1024];


        /* Initialization */
        Fin = fopen(fn, "rb");
        if(!Fin) {
            printf("Unable to open input file %s\n", fn);
            return(1);
        }
        d_temp = 0.0;
        stats->avg_dev = 0.0;
        stats->var = 0.0;
        stats->skew = 0.0;
        stats->kurt = 0.0;
        stats->diff_vals = 0;
        memset(vals, 0, 256*sizeof(int));

        /* loop through file */
        got = fread(buffer, 1, 1024, Fin);
        while(got) {
            for(i=0; i<got; i++) {
                d_temp += (double) buffer[i];
                vals[buffer[i]] ++;
                printf("%d  ", buffer[i]);
            }
            printf("\n");
            got = fread(buffer, 1, 1024, Fin);
        }

        stats->size = ftell(Fin);
```

```
        stats->avg = d_temp*1.0/stats->size;

        /* Two pass higher moments a la Numerical recipes */
        fseek(Fin, 0, 0);
        got = fread(buffer, 1, 1024, Fin);
        correct = 0.0;
        while(got) {
            for(i=0; i<got; i++) {
                d_temp = buffer[i] - stats->avg;
                stats->avg_dev += fabs(d_temp);
                correct += d_temp;
                d_temp2 = d_temp * d_temp;
                stats->var += d_temp2;
                stats->skew += d_temp2 * d_temp;
                stats->kurt += d_temp2 * d_temp2;
            }
            got = fread(buffer, 1, 1024, Fin);
        }
        stats->avg_dev /= stats->size;
        stats->var = (stats->var - correct*correct/stats->size)
            /(stats->size - 1);
        if(stats->var > 0.0) {
            stats->skew /= stats->size *
                stats->var * sqrt(stats->var);
            stats->kurt /= stats->size*stats->var*stats->var;
            stats->kurt -= 3.0;
        } else {
            stats->skew = 0.0;
            stats->kurt = 0.0;
        }

        /* other */
        for(i=0; i<256; i++) {
            if(vals[i]) {
                stats->diff_vals++;
            }
        }

        fclose(Fin);
        return(0);
}
```

Filestat

This program computes basic statistics against a single file.

```
/* This program computes basic statistics */
/* on a single file==                     */

#include <stdio.h>
#include <stdlib.h>
```

```
#include <string.h>
#include <memory.h>
#include <math.h>


/** Declarations **/
typedef struct _StatDat {
  int     size;
  double avg, var, skew, kurt, avg_dev, prev, self;
  int     diff_vals;
} StatDat;


/** Prototypes **/
int FileStats(char *fn, StatDat *stats );



/*          Main program              */
void main(int argc, char* argv[]) {
    int   test;
    char fn[128];
    StatDat stats;

    strcpy(fn, argv[1]);
    test = FileStats(fn, &stats);
    if(test == 0) {
        printf(" %.3f  %.3f  %.3f  %.3f  %.3f %.4f %.4f  %d\n",
                stats.avg, stats.var, stats.skew,
                stats.kurt, stats.avg_dev,
                stats.prev, stats.self, stats.diff_vals);
    } else {
        printf("Stats returned error code %d\n", test);
    }
}




/**********************************************/
/* Computes statistics on a single file     */
/* Takes filename and a StatDat structure    */
/* as arguments. Fills in the StatDat data */
/* Returns an error code - 0 for success     */
int FileStats(char *fn, StatDat *stats ) {
    /* local declarations */
    int     i, got, vals[256];
    int     ParCnt, parity[2], SelfCnt;
    FILE    *Fin;
    double d_temp, d_temp2, correct;
    unsigned char buffer[1024];


    /* Initialization */
```

```
Fin = fopen(fn, "rb");
if(!Fin) {
  printf("Unable to open input file %s\n", fn);
  return(1);
}
d_temp = 0.0;
stats->avg_dev = 0.0;
stats->var = 0.0;
stats->skew = 0.0;
stats->kurt = 0.0;
stats->diff_vals = 0;
memset(vals,   0, 256*sizeof(int));
memset(parity, 0,   2*sizeof(int));
ParCnt = SelfCnt = 0;

/* loop through file */
got = fread(buffer, 1, 1024, Fin);
while(got) {
  for(i=0; i<got; i++) {
    d_temp += (double) buffer[i];
    vals[buffer[i]] ++;
    parity[0] = buffer[i] % 2;
    if(parity[0] == parity[1]) { ParCnt++; }
     if(parity[0] == (buffer[i]/128)) { SelfCnt++; }
    parity[1] = parity[0];
  }
  got = fread(buffer, 1, 1024, Fin);
}

stats->size = ftell(Fin);
stats->avg  = d_temp*1.0/stats->size;
stats->prev = ParCnt*1.0/stats->size;
stats->self = SelfCnt*1.0/stats->size;

/* Two pass higher moments a la Numerical recipes */
fseek(Fin, 0, 0);
got = fread(buffer, 1, 1024, Fin);
correct = 0.0;
while(got) {
    for(i=0; i<got; i++) {
        d_temp = buffer[i] - stats->avg;
        stats->avg_dev += fabs(d_temp);
        correct += d_temp;
        d_temp2 = d_temp * d_temp;
        stats->var += d_temp2;
        stats->skew += d_temp2 * d_temp;
        stats->kurt += d_temp2 * d_temp2;
    }
    got = fread(buffer, 1, 1024, Fin);
}
stats->avg_dev /= stats->size;
stats->var = (stats->var - correct*correct/stats->size)
```

```
            /(stats->size - 1);
    if(stats->var > 0.0) {
        stats->skew /= stats->size *
            stats->var * sqrt(stats->var);
        stats->kurt /= stats->size*stats->var*stats->var;
        stats->kurt -= 3.0;
    } else {
        stats->skew = 0.0;
        stats->kurt = 0.0;
    }

    /* other */
    for(i=0; i<256; i++) {
        if(vals[i]) {
            stats->diff_vals++;
        }
    }

    fclose(Fin);
    return(0);
}
```

SDetect

By examining the color table and looking for near duplicates, this program can determine whether data has been hidden in .bmp files.

```
/* This is a program that reads the header and color table from a .bmp file */
/* to see if data has been hidden with STools.                          */
/* It does this by looking for duplications in the color table */

#include <stdio.h>
#include <stdlib.h>
#include <string.h>
#include <memory.h>

typedef struct _bmp_header {
  char ID[2];
  int  size;
  char res1[2], res2[2];
  int  offset;
} bmp_header;

typedef struct _bmp_info {
  int  size, width, height;
  int  planes, BitsPerPixel;
  int  compress, BMsize;
  int  Hres, Vres;
  int  ColorsUsed, ColorsImportant;
```

```
} bmp_info;


/* Prototypes */
void load_bmp_header(FILE *BMP, bmp_header *BH);
void load_bmp_info(FILE *BMP, bmp_info *BI);

void main(int argc, char* argv[]) {
  int  i, j, i1;
  int  Dflag, Cflag, BMPsize, num_colors, dup_color;
  FILE *BMPin;
  unsigned char color_map[1024];
  bmp_header BMPHead;
  bmp_info   BMPInfo;

  /*  Initialization */
  Dflag = 0;
  Cflag = 0;

  if(argc < 2) {
    fprintf(stderr, "ERROR: No bmp file\n");
    fprintf(stderr, "Usage: SDetect [-d -c] bmp_file\n");
    fprintf(stderr, " -d gives file details\n  -c prints out color map\n");
    exit(1);
  }

  /* Look for command-line flags */
  for(i=1; i<(argc-1); i++) {
    if(argv[i][0] == '-') {
      switch (argv[i][1]) {
       case 'h':
      printf("Usage: SDetect [-d -c] bmp_file\n");
      printf(" -d gives file details\n  -c prints out color map\n");
      exit(1);
      break;
       case 'c':
      Cflag = 1;
      break;
       case 'd':
      Dflag = 1;
      break;
       default:
      printf("Error: Unknown switch %s\n", argv[i]);
      printf("Usage: SDetect [-d -c] bmp_file\n");
      printf(" -d gives file details\n  -c prints out color map\n");
      exit(1);
      break;
       }
     }
   }

  BMPin = fopen(argv[argc-1], "rb");
  if(BMPin == 0) {
```

```
     fprintf(stderr, "**Error** Unable to open input file %s\n",
         argv[argc-1]);
    exit(1);
}
fseek(BMPin, 0, 2);
BMPsize = ftell(BMPin);
fseek(BMPin, 0, 0);

load_bmp_header(BMPin, &BMPHead);
load_bmp_info(BMPin, &BMPInfo);

/* Calculate number of colors in palette */
num_colors = (BMPHead.offset - 14 - BMPInfo.size)/4;

fread(color_map, 1, BMPInfo.ColorsUsed*4, BMPin);

/* Find duplicate colors */
dup_color = 0;
for(i=0; i<BMPInfo.ColorsUsed; i++) {
    for(j=0; j<BMPInfo.ColorsUsed; j++) {
        i1 = abs(color_map[4*i] - color_map[4*j]) +
            abs(color_map[4*i+1] - color_map[4*j+1]) +
            abs(color_map[4*i+2] - color_map[4*j+2]);
        if((i1<4) && (i != j)) { dup_color++; }
    }
}


if(Cflag) {
  /* print out color map */
  printf("Color Map:\n");
  for(i=0; i<BMPInfo.ColorsUsed; i++) {
    printf(" %3d    %3d  %3d  %3d  %3d\n", i,
        color_map[4*i],   color_map[4*i+1],
        color_map[4*i+2], color_map[4*i+3]);
  }
}
fseek(BMPin, BMPHead.offset, 0);

printf("File Name:     %s\n", argv[argc-1]);
if(Dflag) {
  printf("Width:         %d   Height:        %d\n",
      BMPInfo.width, BMPInfo.height);
  printf("BitsPerPixel: %d    NumBitPlanes: %d\n",
      BMPInfo.BitsPerPixel, BMPInfo.planes);
  printf("Compression:   %d\n", BMPInfo.compress);
  printf("ColorsUsed:    %d   ColorsImportant: %d\n\n",
      BMPInfo.ColorsUsed, BMPInfo.ColorsImportant);

printf("actual size:   %d  Reported: %d\n",
    BMPsize, BMPHead.size);
printf("Duplicate colors: %d\n", dup_color);
printf("File header:   Bytes   0 - 13\n");
```

```
    printf("Bitmap header: Bytes  14 - %3d\n", 13+BMPInfo.size);
    printf("Color map:     Bytes %3d - %3d\n",
        14+BMPInfo.size, 13+BMPInfo.size+4*BMPInfo.ColorsUsed);
    printf("Image data:    Bytes %3d - %3d\n\n", BMPHead.offset,
        BMPHead.offset-1+
        (BMPInfo.width*BMPInfo.height*BMPInfo.BitsPerPixel+7)/8);
    }
    if (dup_color < 100) printf("Data has NOT been hidden in this file with
STools");
    if (dup_color >= 100)printf("*** Data HAS BEEN HIDDEN in this file with
STools ***");
    printf ("\n\n");



    fclose(BMPin);
}


void load_bmp_header(FILE *BMP, bmp_header *BH) {
    unsigned char buffer[16];

    memset(BH, 0, sizeof(bmp_header));
    fread(buffer, 1, 14, BMP);

    memcpy(BH->ID, buffer, 2);
    if((BH->ID[0] != 'B') || (BH->ID[1] != 'M')) {
        printf("Error: Bad file ID - not a BMP file!\n");
        exit(1);
    }
    memcpy(&(BH->size), buffer+2, 4);
    memcpy(BH->res1, buffer+6, 2);
    memcpy(BH->res2, buffer+8, 2);
    memcpy(&(BH->offset), buffer+10, 4);
}



void load_bmp_info(FILE *BMP, bmp_info *BI) {
    unsigned char buffer[112];

    memset(BI, 0, sizeof(bmp_info));
    fread(buffer, 1, 108, BMP);

    memcpy(&(BI->size), buffer, 4);
    if((BI->size != 40) && (BI->size != 108)) {
        printf("BitmapInfo header size is %d - cannot handle this format\n",
BI->size);
        exit(1);
    }
    /* Reset position to beginning of color table */
```

```
if(BI->size == 40) { fseek(BMP, -68, 1); }

memcpy(&(BI->width),  buffer+4, 4);
memcpy(&(BI->height), buffer+8, 4);
BI->planes      = buffer[12]+256*buffer[13];
BI->BitsPerPixel = buffer[14]+256*buffer[15];

memcpy(&(BI->compress), buffer+16, 4);
memcpy(&(BI->BMsize),   buffer+20, 4);
memcpy(&(BI->Hres),     buffer+24, 4);
memcpy(&(BI->Vres),     buffer+28, 4);
memcpy(&(BI->ColorsUsed), buffer+32, 4);
memcpy(&(BI->ColorsImportant), buffer+36, 4);

if(BI->ColorsUsed == 0) {
  BI->ColorsUsed = 1<< BI->BitsPerPixel;
}


}
```

What's on the CD-ROM

This appendix provides you with information on the contents of the CD that accompanies this book. For the latest and greatest information, please refer to the ReadMe file located at the root of the CD. Here is what you will find:

- System Requirements
- Using the CD with Windows and Linux
- What's on the CD
- Troubleshooting

System Requirements

Make sure that your computer meets the minimum system requirements listed in this section. If your computer doesn't match up to most of these requirements, you may have a problem using the contents of the CD.

For Windows 9*x*, Windows 2000, Windows NT4 (with SP 4 or later), Windows Me, or Windows XP:

- PC with a Pentium processor running at 120 Mhz or faster
- At least 32 MB of total RAM installed on your computer; for best performance, we recommend at least 64 MB

- Ethernet network interface card (NIC) or modem with a speed of at least 28,800 bps

- A CD-ROM drive

For Linux:

- PC with a Pentium processor running at 90 Mhz or faster

- At least 32 MB of total RAM installed on your computer; for best performance, we recommend at least 64 MB

- Ethernet network interface card (NIC) or modem with a speed of at least 28,800 bps

- A CD-ROM drive

Using the CD with Windows

To install the items from the CD to your hard drive, follow these steps:

1. Insert the CD into your computer's CD-ROM drive.

2. A window appears with the following options: Install, Browse, eBook, Links and Exit.

    Install: Gives you the option to install the supplied software and/or the author-created samples on the CD-ROM.

    Explore: Enables you to view the contents of the CD-ROM in its directory structure.

    Images: Includes graphic images from the book.

    Exit: Closes the autorun window.

If you do not have autorun enabled, or if the autorun window does not appear, follow these steps to access the CD:

1. Click Start > Run.

2. In the dialog box that appears, type *d:*\setup.exe, where *d* is the letter of your CD-ROM drive. This brings up the autorun window described in the preceding set of steps.

3. Choose the Install, Browse, Images, or Exit option from the menu. (See Step 2 in the preceding list for a description of these options.)

Using the CD with Linux

To install the items from the CD to your hard drive, follow these steps:

1. Log in as root.

2. Insert the CD into your computer's CD-ROM drive.

3. If your computer has Auto-Mount enabled, wait for the CD to mount. Otherwise, follow these steps:

   a. Command line instructions:

   At the command prompt type:

   ```
   mount /dev/cdrom /mnt/cdrom
   ```

   (This mounts the *cdrom* device to the mnt/cdrom directory. If your device has a different name, change *cdrom* to that device name—for instance, *cdrom1*)

   b. Graphical: Right-click the CD-ROM icon on the desktop and choose Mount CD-ROM. This mounts your CD-ROM.

4. Browse the CD and follow the individual installation instructions for the products listed below.

5. To remove the CD from your CD-ROM drive, follow these steps:

   a. Command line instructions:

   At the command prompt type:

   ```
   umount /mnt/cdrom
   ```

   b. Graphical: Right-click the CD-ROM icon on the desktop and choose UMount CD-ROM. This mounts your CD-ROM.

What's on the CD

The following sections provide a summary of the software and other materials you'll find on the CD.

Author-Created Materials

All author-created material from the book, including code listings and samples, are on the CD in the folder named Author.

The code included here is described in detail in Appendix A.

Applications

The following applications are on the CD:

ADOBE ACROBAT READER

Acrobat Reader is document reader software you can use to display the e-book version of this book.

AUDIOMARK

AudioMark (from alpha tech, ltd) is Windows-based shareware for creating watermarks in digital audio files. This is a commercially available software product; go to www.alphatecltd.com/ to learn how to purchase it.

CAMERASHY

CameraShy is included here as a demo version of a Windows-based program from Source Forge (http://sourceforge.net/projects/camerashy/). Use this single program to both hide data within a file and send the image.

CAMOUFLAGE

Camouflage is a freeware, Windows-based program that enables you to scramble files then hide them at the end of a file of virtually any format. From Camouflage Software, www.camouflagesoftware.co.uk/

COVERT TCP

Covert tcp is a Linux program that uses IP and TCP headers to hide information in network traffic. Covert tcp was written by Craig Rowland and can be downloaded from www.packetstormsecurity.com.

DPT32.EXE

DPT.32.exe is a freeware product with both strong encryption and the ability to hide data in BMP files. You can download this Windows 95/NT program from www.xs4all.nl/~bernard/home_e.html.

DATA STASH

Data Stash is a Windows-based shareware program that hides data in BMP and database format files. Download Data Stash at http://hosted.barrysworld.net/minimice/Body/Programs/ds_info.html.

DRIVECRYPT

Drivecrypt converts regular text into a play. You can then convert the play back into regular text. Windows-based freeware is available from SecurStar GmbH in English or German. (www.scramdisk.clara.net/play/playmaker.html).

EIKONAMARK

EIKONAMARK from Alpha Tec, Ltd. (www.alphatecltd.com/) is a commercially available Windows-based program used for creating and detecting digital watermarks.

GIFSHUFFLE

Gifshuffle is a command line Windows program that hides GIF images by re-sorting the color table for an image file. Gifshuffle is a freeware program from Matthew Kwan (www.darkside.com /au/gifshuffle).

GIOVANNI

Giovanni from Blue Spike (www.bluespike.com/giovanni.html) is a commercial digital watermarking program geared toward e-commerce.

HIDE IN PICTURE

Hide in Picture from Davi Tassinari de Figueiredo (www.brasil.terravista .pt/Jenipabu/2571/e_hip.htm) is available for DOS/Windows. With this freeware program you hide files in BMP files with password protection.

IN THE PICTURE

In the Picture is a Windows 95 program that embeds data in BMP files. You can also encrypt data with this drag-and-drop interface. In the Picture is a freeware program from Intar (www.intar.com/ITP /itpinfo.htm).

INVISIBLE SECRETS

Invisible Secrets: A trial version of this Windows-based program from NeoByte Solutions is included on this CD. Use this single program to both hide data within a file and send the image.

JP HIDE AND SEEK

JP Hide and Seek is a freeware program from Allan Latham. A bare bones product, but it allows you to hide files in JPEGs and make the hidden data very hard to detect. Download the Linux program at http://linux01.gwdg.de/~alatham/stego.html.

STEGDETECT

Stegdetect from Niels Provos detects hidden data in JPEG files. This is freeware available from Outguess (www.outguess.org/).

STEGHIDE

Steghide by Stefan Hetzl (www.steganos.com) is a command line shareware program for hiding data in BMP, WAV, and AU files using blowfish encryption.

VIDEOMARK

VIDEOMARK, a commercial product for Windows from Alpha Tec, Ltd. (www.alphatecltd.com/), is used to embed digital watermarks on digital video.

VOLMARK

VOLMARK a commercial product for Windows from Alpha Tec, Ltd. (www.alphatecltd.com/) is used to embed digital watermarks on 3D images.

XSTEG

XSteg from Niels Provos (www.outguess.org/) is a freeware stego program.

Shareware programs are fully functional, trial versions of copyrighted programs. If you like particular programs, register with their authors for a nominal fee and receive licenses, enhanced versions, and technical support.

Freeware programs are copyrighted games, applications, and utilities that are free for personal use. Unlike shareware, these programs do not require a fee or provide technical support. *GNU software* is governed by its own license, which is included inside the folder of the GNU product. See the GNU license for more details.

Trial, demo, or evaluation versions are usually limited either by time or functionality (such as being unable to save projects). Some trial versions are very sensitive to system date changes. If you alter your computer's date, the programs will "time out" and will no longer be functional.

Troubleshooting

If you have difficulty installing or using any of the materials on the companion CD, try the following solutions:

- **Turn off any anti-virus software that you may have running.** Installers sometimes mimic virus activity and can make your computer incorrectly believe that it is being infected by a virus. (Be sure to turn the anti-virus software back on later.)

- **Close all running programs.** The more programs you're running, the less memory is available to other programs. Installers also typically update files and programs; if you keep other programs running, installation may not work properly.

- **Reference the ReadMe:** Please refer to the ReadMe file located at the root of the CD-ROM for the latest product information at the time of publication.

If you still have trouble with the CD, please call the Customer Care phone number: (800) 762-2974. Outside the United States, call 1 (317) 572-3994. You can also contact Customer Service by e-mail at techsupdum@wiley.com. Wiley Publishing, Inc. will provide technical support only for installation and other general quality control items; for technical support on the applications themselves, consult the program's vendor or author.

Index

Wiley Publishing, Inc.
End-User License Agreement

READ THIS. You should carefully read these terms and conditions before opening the software packet(s) included with this book "Book". This is a license agreement "Agreement" between you and Wiley Publishing, Inc. "WPI". By opening the accompanying software packet(s), you acknowledge that you have read and accept the following terms and conditions. If you do not agree and do not want to be bound by such terms and conditions, promptly return the Book and the unopened software packet(s) to the place you obtained them for a full refund.

1. **License Grant.** WPI grants to you (either an individual or entity) a nonexclusive license to use one copy of the enclosed software program(s) (collectively, the "Software" solely for your own personal or business purposes on a single computer (whether a standard computer or a workstation component of a multi-user network). The Software is in use on a computer when it is loaded into temporary memory (RAM) or installed into permanent memory (hard disk, CD-ROM, or other storage device). WPI reserves all rights not expressly granted herein.

2. **Ownership.** WPI is the owner of all right, title, and interest, including copyright, in and to the compilation of the Software recorded on the disk(s) or CD-ROM "Software Media". Copyright to the individual programs recorded on the Software Media is owned by the author or other authorized copyright owner of each program. Ownership of the Software and all proprietary rights relating thereto remain with WPI and its licensers.

3. **Restrictions On Use and Transfer.**

   (a) You may only (i) make one copy of the Software for backup or archival purposes, or (ii) transfer the Software to a single hard disk, provided that you keep the original for backup or archival purposes. You may not (i) rent or lease the Software, (ii) copy or reproduce the Software through a LAN or other network system or through any computer subscriber system or bulletin- board system, or (iii) modify, adapt, or create derivative works based on the Software.

   (b) You may not reverse engineer, decompile, or disassemble the Software. You may transfer the Software and user documentation on a permanent basis, provided that the transferee agrees to accept the terms and conditions of this Agreement and you retain no copies. If the Software is an update or has been updated, any transfer must include the most recent update and all prior versions.

4. **Restrictions on Use of Individual Programs.** You must follow the individual requirements and restrictions detailed for each individual program in the About the CD-ROM appendix of this Book. These limitations are also contained in the individual license agreements recorded on the Software Media. These limitations may include a requirement that after using the program for a specified period of time, the user must pay a registration fee or discontinue use. By opening the Software packet(s), you will be agreeing to abide by the licenses and restrictions for these individual programs that are detailed in the About the CD-ROM appendix and on the Software Media. None of the material on this Software Media or listed in this Book may ever be redistributed, in original or modified form, for commercial purposes.

5. **Limited Warranty.**

   (a) WPI warrants that the Software and Software Media are free from defects in materials and workmanship under normal use for a period of sixty (60) days from the date of purchase of this Book. If WPI receives notification within the warranty period of defects in materials or workmanship, WPI will replace the defective Software Media.

(b) WPI AND THE AUTHOR OF THE BOOK DISCLAIM ALL OTHER WARRANTIES, EXPRESS OR IMPLIED, INCLUDING WITHOUT LIMITATION IMPLIED WARRANTIES OF MERCHANTABILITY AND FITNESS FOR A PARTICULAR PURPOSE, WITH RESPECT TO THE SOFTWARE, THE PROGRAMS, THE SOURCE CODE CONTAINED THEREIN, AND/OR THE TECHNIQUES DESCRIBED IN THIS BOOK. WPI DOES NOT WARRANT THAT THE FUNCTIONS CONTAINED IN THE SOFTWARE WILL MEET YOUR REQUIREMENTS OR THAT THE OPERATION OF THE SOFTWARE WILL BE ERROR FREE.

(c) This limited warranty gives you specific legal rights, and you may have other rights that vary from jurisdiction to jurisdiction.

6. **Remedies.**

   (a) WPI's entire liability and your exclusive remedy for defects in materials and workmanship shall be limited to replacement of the Software Media, which may be returned to WPI with a copy of your receipt at the following address: Software Media Fulfillment Department, Attn.: Hiding in Plain Sight: Steganography and the Art of Covert Communication, Wiley Publishing, Inc., 10475 Crosspoint Blvd., Indianapolis, IN 46256, or call 1-800-762-2974. Please allow four to six weeks for delivery. This Limited Warranty is void if failure of the Software Media has resulted from accident, abuse, or misapplication. Any replacement Software Media will be warranted for the remainder of the original warranty period or thirty (30) days, whichever is longer.

   (b) In no event shall WPI or the author be liable for any damages whatsoever (including without limitation damages for loss of business profits, business interruption, loss of business information, or any other pecuniary loss) arising from the use of or inability to use the Book or the Software, even if WPI has been advised of the possibility of such damages.

   (c) Because some jurisdictions do not allow the exclusion or limitation of liability for consequential or incidental damages, the above limitation or exclusion may not apply to you.

7. **U.S. Government Restricted Rights.** Use, duplication, or disclosure of the Software for or on behalf of the United States of America, its agencies and/or instrumentalities "U.S. Government" is subject to restrictions as stated in paragraph (c)(1)(ii) of the Rights in Technical Data and Computer Software clause of DFARS 252.227-7013, or subparagraphs (c) (1) and (2) of the Commercial Computer Software - Restricted Rights clause at FAR 52.227-19, and in similar clauses in the NASA FAR supplement, as applicable.

8. **General.** This Agreement constitutes the entire understanding of the parties and revokes and supersedes all prior agreements, oral or written, between them and may not be modified or amended except in a writing signed by both parties hereto that specifically refers to this Agreement. This Agreement shall take precedence over any other documents that may be in conflict herewith. If any one or more provisions contained in this Agreement are held by any court or tribunal to be invalid, illegal, or otherwise unenforceable, each and every other provision shall remain in full force and effect.

GNU General Public License

Version 2, June 1991
Copyright © 1989, 1991 Free Software Foundation, Inc.
59 Temple Place - Suite 330, Boston, MA 02111-1307, USA

Preamble

The licenses for most software are designed to take away your freedom to share and change it. By contrast, the GNU General Public License is intended to guarantee your freedom to share and change free software—to make sure the software is free for all its users. This General Public License applies to most of the Free Software Foundation's software and to any other program whose authors commit to using it. (Some other Free Software Foundation software is covered by the GNU Library General Public License instead.) You can apply it to your programs, too.

When we speak of free software, we are referring to freedom, not price. Our General Public Licenses are designed to make sure that you have the freedom to distribute copies of free software (and charge for this service if you wish), that you receive source code or can get it if you want it, that you can change the software or use pieces of it in new free programs; and that you know you can do these things.

To protect your rights, we need to make restrictions that forbid anyone to deny you these rights or to ask you to surrender the rights. These restrictions translate to certain responsibilities for you if you distribute copies of the software, or if you modify it.

For example, if you distribute copies of such a program, whether gratis or for a fee, you must give the recipients all the rights that you have. You must make sure that they, too, receive or can get the source code. And you must show them these terms so they know their rights.

We protect your rights with two steps: (1) copyright the software, and (2) offer you this license which gives you legal permission to copy, distribute and/or modify the software.

Also, for each author's protection and ours, we want to make certain that everyone understands that there is no warranty for this free software. If the software is modified by someone else and passed on, we want its recipients to know that what they have is not the original, so that any problems introduced by others will not reflect on the original authors' reputations.

Finally, any free program is threatened constantly by software patents. We wish to avoid the danger that redistributors of a free program will individually obtain patent licenses, in effect making the program proprietary. To prevent this, we have made it clear that any patent must be licensed for everyone's free use or not licensed at all.

The precise terms and conditions for copying, distribution and modification follow.

Terms and Conditions for Copying, Distribution and Modification

0. This License applies to any program or other work which contains a notice placed by the copyright holder saying it may be distributed under the terms of this General Public License. The "Program", below, refers to any such program or work, and a "work based on the Program" means either the Program or any derivative work under copyright law: that is to say, a work containing the Program or a portion of it, either verbatim or with modifications and/or translated into another language. (Hereinafter, translation is included without limitation in the term "modification".) Each licensee is addressed as "you".

Activities other than copying, distribution and modification are not covered by this License; they are outside its scope. The act of running the Program is not restricted, and the output from the Program is covered only if its contents constitute a work based on the Program (independent of having been made by running the Program). Whether that is true depends on what the Program does.

1. You may copy and distribute verbatim copies of the Program's source code as you receive it, in any medium, provided that you conspicuously and appropriately publish on each copy an appropriate copyright notice and disclaimer of warranty; keep intact all the notices that refer to this License and to the absence of any warranty; and give any other recipients of the Program a copy of this License along with the Program.

   You may charge a fee for the physical act of transferring a copy, and you may at your option offer warranty protection in exchange for a fee.

2. You may modify your copy or copies of the Program or any portion of it, thus forming a work based on the Program, and copy and distribute such modifications or work under the terms of Section 1 above, provided that you also meet all of these conditions:

   a) You must cause the modified files to carry prominent notices stating that you changed the files and the date of any change.

   b) You must cause any work that you distribute or publish, that in whole or in part contains or is derived from the Program or any part thereof, to be licensed as a whole at no charge to all third parties under the terms of this License.

   c) If the modified program normally reads commands interactively when run, you must cause it, when started running for such interactive use in the most ordinary way, to print or display an announcement including an appropriate copyright notice and a notice that there is no warranty (or else, saying that you provide a warranty) and that users may redistribute the program under these conditions, and telling the user how to view a copy of this License. (Exception: if the Program itself is interactive but does not normally print such an announcement, your work based on the Program is not required to print an announcement.)

   These requirements apply to the modified work as a whole. If identifiable sections of that work are not derived from the Program, and can be reasonably considered independent and separate works in themselves, then this License, and its terms, do not apply to those sections when you distribute them as separate works. But when you distribute the same sections as part of a whole which is a work based on the Program, the distribution of the whole must be on the terms of this License, whose permissions for other licensees extend to the entire whole, and thus to each and every part regardless of who wrote it.

   Thus, it is not the intent of this section to claim rights or contest your rights to work written entirely by you; rather, the intent is to exercise the right to control the distribution of derivative or collective works based on the Program.

   In addition, mere aggregation of another work not based on the Program with the Program (or with a work based on the Program) on a volume of a storage or distribution medium does not bring the other work under the scope of this License.

3. You may copy and distribute the Program (or a work based on it, under Section 2) in object code or executable form under the terms of Sections 1 and 2 above provided that you also do one of the following:

   a) Accompany it with the complete corresponding machine-readable source code, which must be distributed under the terms of Sections 1 and 2 above on a medium customarily used for software interchange; or,

   b) Accompany it with a written offer, valid for at least three years, to give any third party, for a charge no more than your cost of physically performing source distribution, a complete machine-readable copy of the corresponding source code, to be distributed under the terms of Sections 1 and 2 above on a medium customarily used for software interchange; or,

c) Accompany it with the information you received as to the offer to distribute corresponding source code. (This alternative is allowed only for noncommercial distribution and only if you received the program in object code or executable form with such an offer, in accord with Subsection b above.)

The source code for a work means the preferred form of the work for making modifications to it. For an executable work, complete source code means all the source code for all modules it contains, plus any associated interface definition files, plus the scripts used to control compilation and installation of the executable. However, as a special exception, the source code distributed need not include anything that is normally distributed (in either source or binary form) with the major components (compiler, kernel, and so on) of the operating system on which the executable runs, unless that component itself accompanies the executable.

If distribution of executable or object code is made by offering access to copy from a designated place, then offering equivalent access to copy the source code from the same place counts as distribution of the source code, even though third parties are not compelled to copy the source along with the object code.

4. You may not copy, modify, sublicense, or distribute the Program except as expressly provided under this License. Any attempt otherwise to copy, modify, sublicense or distribute the Program is void, and will automatically terminate your rights under this License. However, parties who have received copies, or rights, from you under this License will not have their licenses terminated so long as such parties remain in full compliance.

5. You are not required to accept this License, since you have not signed it. However, nothing else grants you permission to modify or distribute the Program or its derivative works. These actions are prohibited by law if you do not accept this License. Therefore, by modifying or distributing the Program (or any work based on the Program), you indicate your acceptance of this License to do so, and all its terms and conditions for copying, distributing or modifying the Program or works based on it.

6. Each time you redistribute the Program (or any work based on the Program), the recipient automatically receives a license from the original licensor to copy, distribute or modify the Program subject to these terms and conditions. You may not impose any further restrictions on the recipients' exercise of the rights granted herein. You are not responsible for enforcing compliance by third parties to this License.

7. If, as a consequence of a court judgment or allegation of patent infringement or for any other reason (not limited to patent issues), conditions are imposed on you (whether by court order, agreement or otherwise) that contradict the conditions of this License, they do not excuse you from the conditions of this License. If you cannot distribute so as to satisfy simultaneously your obligations under this License and any other pertinent obligations, then as a consequence you may not distribute the Program at all. For example, if a patent license would not permit royalty-free redistribution of the Program by all those who receive copies directly or indirectly through you, then the only way you could satisfy both it and this License would be to refrain entirely from distribution of the Program.

If any portion of this section is held invalid or unenforceable under any particular circumstance, the balance of the section is intended to apply and the section as a whole is intended to apply in other circumstances.

It is not the purpose of this section to induce you to infringe any patents or other property right claims or to contest validity of any such claims; this section has the sole purpose of protecting the integrity of the free software distribution system, which is implemented by public license practices. Many people have made generous contributions to the wide range of software distributed through that system in reliance on consistent application of that system; it is up to the author/donor to decide if he or she is willing to distribute software through any other system and a licensee cannot impose that choice.

This section is intended to make thoroughly clear what is believed to be a consequence of the rest of this License.

8. If the distribution and/or use of the Program is restricted in certain countries either by patents or by copyrighted interfaces, the original copyright holder who places the Program under this License may add an explicit geographical distribution limitation excluding those countries, so that distribution is permitted only in or among countries not thus excluded. In such case, this License incorporates the limitation as if written in the body of this License.

9. The Free Software Foundation may publish revised and/or new versions of the General Public License from time to time. Such new versions will be similar in spirit to the present version, but may differ in detail to address new problems or concerns.

   Each version is given a distinguishing version number. If the Program specifies a version number of this License which applies to it and "any later version", you have the option of following the terms and conditions either of that version or of any later version published by the Free Software Foundation. If the Program does not specify a version number of this License, you may choose any version ever published by the Free Software Foundation.

10. If you wish to incorporate parts of the Program into other free programs whose distribution conditions are different, write to the author to ask for permission. For software which is copyrighted by the Free Software Foundation, write to the Free Software Foundation; we sometimes make exceptions for this. Our decision will be guided by the two goals of preserving the free status of all derivatives of our free software and of promoting the sharing and reuse of software generally.

No Warranty

11. BECAUSE THE PROGRAM IS LICENSED FREE OF CHARGE, THERE IS NO WARRANTY FOR THE PROGRAM, TO THE EXTENT PERMITTED BY APPLICABLE LAW. EXCEPT WHEN OTHERWISE STATED IN WRITING THE COPYRIGHT HOLDERS AND/OR OTHER PARTIES PROVIDE THE PROGRAM "AS IS" WITHOUT WARRANTY OF ANY KIND, EITHER EXPRESSED OR IMPLIED, INCLUDING, BUT NOT LIMITED TO, THE IMPLIED WARRANTIES OF MERCHANTABILITY AND FITNESS FOR A PARTICULAR PURPOSE. THE ENTIRE RISK AS TO THE QUALITY AND PERFORMANCE OF THE PROGRAM IS WITH YOU. SHOULD THE PROGRAM PROVE DEFECTIVE, YOU ASSUME THE COST OF ALL NECESSARY SERVICING, REPAIR OR CORRECTION.

12. IN NO EVENT UNLESS REQUIRED BY APPLICABLE LAW OR AGREED TO IN WRITING WILL ANY COPYRIGHT HOLDER, OR ANY OTHER PARTY WHO MAY MODIFY AND/OR REDISTRIBUTE THE PROGRAM AS PERMITTED ABOVE, BE LIABLE TO YOU FOR DAMAGES, INCLUDING ANY GENERAL, SPECIAL, INCIDENTAL OR CONSEQUENTIAL DAMAGES ARISING OUT OF THE USE OR INABILITY TO USE THE PROGRAM (INCLUDING BUT NOT LIMITED TO LOSS OF DATA OR DATA BEING RENDERED INACCURATE OR LOSSES SUSTAINED BY YOU OR THIRD PARTIES OR A FAILURE OF THE PROGRAM TO OPERATE WITH ANY OTHER PROGRAMS), EVEN IF SUCH HOLDER OR OTHER PARTY HAS BEEN ADVISED OF THE POSSIBILITY OF SUCH DAMAGES.

End of Terms and Conditions